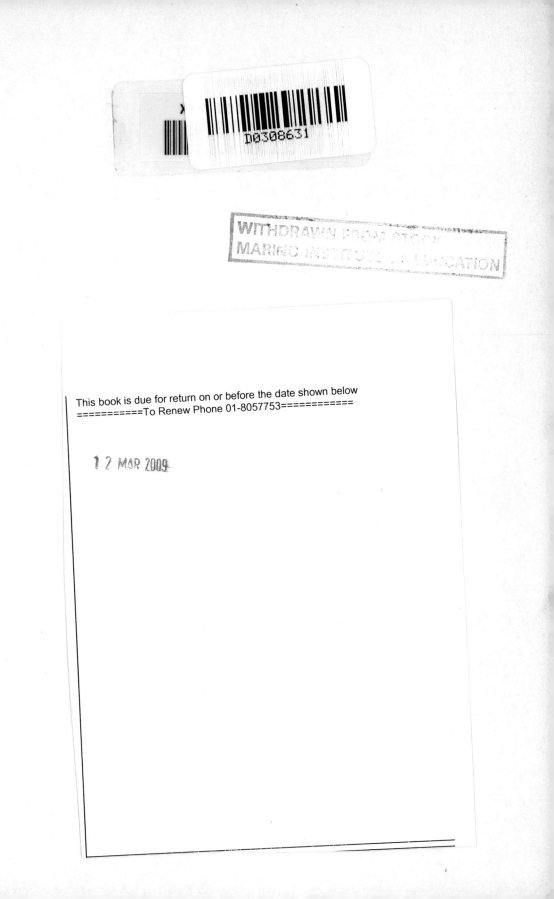

LIFELINES

LETTERS FROM FAMOUS PEOPLE ABOUT THEIR FAVOURITE POEM

Compiled by
Joann Bradish
Jacki Erskine
Carolyn Gibson
Steven Given
Julie Grantham
Paula Griffin
Nicola Hughes
Jonathan Logue
Collette Lucy
Duncan Lyster
Joy Marshall
Alice McEleney

Edited by Niall MacMonagle

Foreword by Seamus Heaney

Town House, Dublin

First published in individual volumes
in 1985, 1988, 1990 and 1992 by
The Underground Press Ltd
Wesley College, Dublin 16

This edition published by
Town House and Country House
42 Morehampton Road
Donnybrook
Dublin 4

Reprinted: October 1992,
           November 1992.

British Library Cataloguing in Publication Data available

ISBN: 0-948524-46-4 (pbk)
        0-948524-53-7 (hbk)

Text and cover design: Bill Murphy
Printed in Ireland by Colour Books

For the children of the Third World

'Children in famine . . . and the whole world
of loneliness, poverty, and pain make a
mockery of what human life should be.'

Bertrand Russell

CONTENTS

Foreword   xi
Preface   xiii

LIFELINES I

                                          page
Eavan Boland   3
Garrett FitzGerald   3
Treasa Davison   4
Bob Gallico   5
Julie O'Callaghan   6
Ulick O'Connor   7
George O Simms   8
Eileen Dunne   8
Jimmy Magee   10
Augustine Martin   11
Andrew Motion   12
Geraldine Plunkett   13
Pauline Bewick   14
Hugh Leonard   15
Bunny Carr   16
Flo McSweeney   17
Margaret MacCurtain   19
Barry Lang   20
Brendan Kennelly   20
Hilary Orpen   21
Isabel Healy   23
Bernard MacLaverty   24
Myles Dungan   25
Emer O'Kelly   28
Benedict Kiely   29
John Banville   31
Iris Murdoch   32
Tom Hickey   34
Emmet Bergin   36
Maureen Potter   36
Mary McEvoy   37

John Kavanagh   39
Gerrit van Gelderen   40
Theodora FitzGibbon   43
Alan Dukes   45
Noelle Campbell-Sharp   46
Ollie Campbell   47
Liam Ó Murchú   49
Margaret Drabble   49
T P Flanagan   50
Tomás Ó Fiaich   51
Helen Lucy Burke   53
Cyril Cusack   56
Derek Davis   59
Seán Lucy   60
Don Cockburn   63
Mick Lally   64
Tony O'Malley   68
Brian Farrell   70
Seamus Heaney   71
Nell McCafferty   72

LIFELINES II

                                          page
Frank McGuinness   77
Eithne Hand   77
Gay Byrne   78
Michael Holroyd   79
Fleur Adcock   80
Sara Berkeley   81
Victor Griffin   82
David Norris   84
Kathy Prendergast   85
Robert Ballagh   86
John Montague   87
Laurie Lee   88
Dennis O'Driscoll   89
Desmond Fennell   90

Maria Doyle	91	Mike Murphy	143
Paul Durcan	92	Nuala Ní Dhomhnaill	144
Ita Daly	94	Kenneth Blackmore	147
Jennifer Johnston	95	Joe Lynch	149
Alan Stanford	96		
Derek Mahon	98		
Kathleen Watkins	102	*LIFELINES III*	
Mary Leland	103		*page*
Maxi	105	Antony Sher	153
Rónán Johnston	106	Patrick Graham	153
Margaret Heckler	108	Mary FitzGerald	154
Fintan O'Toole	109	Larry Gogan	155
Marian Richardson	112	Rita Ann Higgins	156
Richard Kearney	113	Margaret Atwood	157
Mary Mooney	114	Ken Bourke	158
Maeve Binchy	114	Alicia Boyle	159
Thelma Mansfield	116	Rosaleen Linehan	160
Máire Mhac an tSaoi	117	Tom McCaughren	161
Jeffrey Archer	118	Thomas McCarthy	162
T A Finlay	119	Medbh McGuckian	162
John Gielgud	121	Jeremy Irons	163
Anne Doyle	122	Desmond Hogan	164
Tom Murphy	123	Alice Taylor	165
Eiléan Ní Chuilleaneáin	124	Elizabeth Cope	166
Kevin Myers	125	Brian Moore	167
Niall McCarthy	127	A S Byatt	167
John B Keane	128	David Owen	169
Mary Lavin	130	James Plunkett	170
Sr Stanislaus Kennedy	131	Adam Clayton	172
Doireann Ní Bhriain	132	Fiona Shaw	172
Padraic White	133	Mary Banotti	174
Maria Simonds-Gooding	135	Ian McKellen	176
Ellen Gilchrist	136	Kingsley Amis	178
Sue Miller	137	Amy Clampitt	180
Richard Branson	138	Camille Souter	181
Pat Kenny	139	Alice Maher	182
Judi Dench	140	Andy O'Mahony	183
Clare Boylan	141	David Lodge	184
Chaim Herzog	142	Séamus Brennan	186

Charles J Haughey	187	Ferdia MacAnna	230
Thomas Kinsella	187	Simon Armitage	231
Deirdre Purcell	191	Theo Dorgan	232
Francis Stuart	192	Joseph O'Connor	233
Macdara Woods	193	William Crozier	234
Bryan MacMahon	194	Darina Allen	236
Patricia Hurl	196	Anne Fine	236
Eilís O'Connell	197	Patricia Scanlan	238
Michael Viney	198	Glenda Jackson	239
Greg Delanty	198	Christy Moore	239
William Trevor	200	Christopher Ricks	240
Barbara Bush	204	Julian Barnes	242
Helen Vendler	206	Kenneth Branagh	243
Michael O'Loughlin	208	Mary Harney	244
Niamh Cusack	210	Sean McMahon	245
John Bayley	211	Thomas Docherty	247
Brian Lenihan	212	Anthony Cronin	248
Sue Townsend	213	Michael Longley	249
Mother Teresa	214	Amelia Stein	250
Peter Fallon	215	Richard Murphy	252
		Conor Cruise O'Brien	254
		Wendy Cope	260

LIFELINES IV

		Joan McBreen	261
	page	Alan Hollinghurst	262
Anthony Clare	219	Martin Amis	264
Dorothy Cross	219	Paula Meehan	265
Anna Scher	220	Martin Waddell	268
Micheal O'Siadhail	221	Michele Souter	269
Sebastian Barry	221	Felim Egan	270
Robin Eames	222	Ben Elton	271
Lynn Barber	223	Michael McGlynn	272
Shane Connaughton	224	Mary O'Donnell	273
Doris Lessing	225	Neil Rudenstine	275
Noël Browne	225	Vivienne Roche	277
Jilly Cooper	226	Seamus Deane	278
Ailbhe Smyth	227	James Simmons	280
V S Pritchett	228	Galway Kinnell	282
Mary Beckett	229	Lauris Edmond	283
Louis Le Brocquy	230	Joseph O'Neill	285

David Leavitt	287
Hugo Hamilton	287
Declan Kiberd	290
Sue Lawley	294
Michael Blumenthal	297
Cahal Daly	301
Gerald Barry	302
Sharon Olds	302
Patricia Donlon	305
Miroslav Holub	306

| *Notes on the contributors* | 309 |

| *Index of poets and* *their works* | 322 |

| *Index of first lines* | 331 |

| *Acknowledgements* | 337 |

FOREWORD

Towards the end of Ford Madox Ford's sequence of First World War novels, *Parade's End*, there is a scene where the protagonist, Tietjens, is preparing the soldiers under his command to sustain a barrage from the German artillery. His mind is vividly alert to the trench activity and the shelling which surround him, but it is equally receptive to memories and associations swimming in pell-mell from other, remoter strata of his consciousness. He remembers, for example, a gunner telling him that it had probably cost the two armies a total of three million pounds sterling to reduce a twenty-acre field between the lines to a pulverized nowhere; and this memory has itself been prompted by an earlier, random image of 'the quiet thing', the heavy-leaved, timbered hedge-rows around the parsonage at Bemerton, outside Salisbury, where the poet George Herbert had lived two centuries earlier. Inevitably, the sweetness and fortitude of Herbert's poetry come to mind then also, so that Tietjens's sense of value in the face of danger is both clarified and verified by the fleeting recollection of a couple of his favourite lines.

Jon Stallworthy directed my attention to this passage of Ford's after he had heard me refer to a similar moment in the life of George Seferis, when Seferis came to a realization (recorded in his *Journals*) that the work of his fellow Greek poet, Constantine Cavafy, was 'strong enough to help'. And it seems relevant to cite both occasions here again, in the foreword to a book which testifies in its own uninsistent fashion to the ways in which individuals still continue to recognize that some part of the meaning of their lives is lodged in the words and cadences of cherished passages of verse.

Meaning and value, of course, do not always entail a lofty note and an earnest message: it has been said, for example, that it would be worth a poet's while to spend a lifetime at work in order to leave behind one limerick that might distract somebody walking the last few yards to the electric chair. Certainly the pages that follow reveal that people of great talents and responsibilities do not repose their imaginative trust only in the sonorities of the Bible or the canonical voice of Shakespeare; they also turn to less solemn achievements, such as Lewis Carroll's nonsense verse, or the devastatingly light touch of Stevie Smith, or the merry logic of the early Irish 'The Scholar and his Pet Cat' — chosen respectively by Amy Clampitt, Glenda Jackson and the late Cardinal Tomás Ó Fiaich.

Other choices, of course, were made because the contributor possessed a definite sense of the figure he or she must cut in the public eye: when Michael Holroyd selected 'Biography' by D. J. Enright, and Jeffrey Archer called for Kipling, and Sister Stanislaus picked 'Street Corner Christ', they did so in the knowledge that their poem would be read in the light of their known professions and commitments. And the same kind of compatibility operates in the case of critics like Helen Vendler and Christopher Ricks, whose choice of Stevens and Tennyson complements what we know about their literary preferences from other quarters. But when Conor Cruise O'Brien chose Milton's 'Ode on the Morning of Christ's Nativity' and Chaim Herzog picked 'The Lake Isle of Innisfree', they were declaring obliquely that as private persons they live within a field of cultural force which may be at some odds with the general perception of them as public figures.

Writers, on the other hand, live precisely at the intersection of the public and the private, and it is interesting to see how their choices indulge or deflect our natural wish to establish connections between the style of what they write and what they read. Almost every selection by a poet here is corroborative of some aspect of his or her own published work, and there is a corresponding aptness to the choices made by many of the prose writers: that V. S. Pritchett should go for Clough, Jennifer Johnston for Holub, Ben Kiely for Robinson and John Banville for Celan, makes sense immediately, but there's surely just a little bit of decoy activity going on when the realistic Drabble goes for the prophetic Blake and the comedian Lodge promotes the tragedian Yeats. (Yeats, incidentally, is chosen nineteen times — proof, if it were needed, that metrical force and direct utterance remain potent factors in establishing a poem's claim upon the affections.)

This anthology was a magnificent idea from the start. The initial dedication of the pupils and their teacher at Wesley College (and, in particular, of the student compilers of Lifelines) was admirable; and the end result is a book in which poems re-enter the world refreshed rather than jaded by their long confinement inside people's heads, a book that is surprisingly various and compulsively readable. It is, after all, greatly heartening to discover that the poems of Keats and Yeats are stored like imaginative fossil fuel in the minds of the President of Harvard and the President of the State of Israel respectively; and to be provided with such credible evidence that poetry does indeed survive, as W. H. Auden said it would, 'a way of happening, a mouth.'

                                                                Seamus Heaney

PREFACE

The *Lifelines* project was set in motion in the spring of 1985 when Steven Given, Collette Lucy and Joy Marshall, three Fifth Year students from this school, wanted to do something to help the people suffering from famine in Ethiopia. They wrote to famous people and asked them to name a favourite poem. The replies were compiled and *Lifelines* was born. The book, which was cheaply produced, was a sell-out and all profits were sent to help those in the Developing World. In 1988 Julie Grantham, Jonathan Logue and Duncan Lyster compiled *Lifelines II*, and in 1990 Joann Bradish, Jacki Erskine and Carolyn Gibson compiled *Lifelines III*.

Earlier this year we published *Lifelines IV* and we are delighted that all four are now being published in a *Collected* edition. The previous *Lifelines* were produced here in school in a stencil and staple format. The book you are now holding is a much more sophisticated and beautiful production intended for a wider readership but royalties from the *Collected* edition will also be sent to the Third World.

We wrote to everyone that we (and our friends!) could think of and we are very grateful to those who replied. We would also like to thank Seamus Heaney for his kindness in writing the Foreword and Niall MacMonagle, our English teacher, who oversaw the project.

We hope that you enjoy the collection. There is a wonderful selection of poetry here: the higgledy-piggledy arrangement emphasises the richness and the variety of the poems themselves. You are supporting a very good cause if you buy this book and perhaps your knowledge of poetry will be widened. Ours certainly was.

Paula Griffin
Nicola Hughes
Alice McEleney

Wesley College
Dublin

LIFELINES I

EAVAN BOLAND   1

Upon Julia's Clothes

Whenas in silks my Julia goes,
Then, then, methinks, how sweetly flows
That liquefaction of her clothes.

Next, when I cast mine eyes, and see
That brave vibration, each way free,
O, how that glittering taketh me!

Robert Herrick (1591–1674)

*This is written by Robert Herrick who died fourteen years after the
Restoration in 1660. He has come to be known as a Caroline poet but
I think the title is misleading. He is a late, upbeat and maverick
Elizabethan. This is certainly one of my favourite poems. For a piece
supposedly written by a court poet it practises remarkable thrift. I
like the miserly economy of language played off against the
wonderful, prosperous image of the woman in silks.*

With best wishes for the project,
Eavan Boland

GARRET FITZGERALD   2

Oifig an Taoisigh
(Office of the Taoiseach)
22 April 1985

Dear Collette,
*Many thanks for your letter. I must admit I find your plan to raise
money for the Third World very original, as this is the first occasion
on which I have been asked for my favourite poem.*
*I have, from time to time, come across a poem I have enjoyed reading,
but quite frankly, on considering your letter, I found it difficult to
pinpoint any one particular poem. However, I am particularly fond of
the enclosed extract from* The Book of Ecclesiastes, *the words of
which I find thought-provoking and profound, and like to reflect on
in the rare moments when I can tear myself away from the hurly-
burly of political life. I hope this will be of assistance to you.*
Wishing you, Joy and Steven every success with the undertaking.

Yours sincerely,
Garret FitzGerald

extract from *The Book of Ecclesiastes*

All things have their season, and in their times
  all things pass under heaven.
A time to be born and a time to die.
A time to plant, and a time to pluck up that which is planted.
A time to kill, and a time to heal.
A time to destroy, and a time to build.
A time to weep, and a time to laugh.
A time to mourn, and a time to dance.
A time to scatter stones, and a time to gather.
A time to embrace, and a time to be far from embraces.
A time to get, and a time to lose,
A time to keep, and a time to cast away.
A time to rend, and a time to sew.
A time to keep silence, and a time to speak.
A time of love and a time of hatred.
A time of war, and a time of peace.
What hath man more of his labour?

TREASA DAVISON   3

RTE
18 April 1985

Dear all of you!
As requested I enclose a poem. Sort of reason is . . .
I remember when I was quite little, twirling around and around on
the footpath beside the sea in Salthill in Galway . . . show off that I
was! I twirled around and around and twirled right off the path, and
down down to the rocks below. I remember so well, looking up to my
mother, and saying 'Am I dead Am I dead?' I think somehow this has
something to do with the reason that I've always loved this little-
known poem by John Millington Synge.
The best of luck with your project and I hope it makes lots of money.

Yours sincerely,
Treasa Davison

Patch-Shaneen

Shaneen and Maurya Prendergast
Lived west in Carnareagh,
And they'd a cur-dog, a cabbage plot,
A goat, and cock of hay.

He was five foot one or two,
Herself was four foot ten,
And he went travelling asking meal
Above through Caragh Glen.

She'd pick her bag of carrageen
Or perries through the surf,
Or loan an ass of Foxy Jim
To fetch her creel of turf.

Till on one windy Samhain night,
When there's stir among the dead,
He found her perished, stiff and stark,
Beside him in the bed.

And now when Shaneen travels far
From Droum to Ballyhyre,
The women lay him sacks of straw,
Beside the seed of fire.

And when the grey cocks crow and flap
And winds are in the sky,
'Oh, Maurya, Maurya, are you dead?'
You'll hear Patch-Shaneen cry.

John Millington Synge (1871–1909)

BOB GALLICO   4

Treasure Island

Comes little lady, a book in hand,
A light in her eyes that I understand,
And her cheeks aglow from the faery breeze
That sweeps across the uncharted seas.
She gives me the book, and her word of praise
A ton of critical thought outweighs.
'I've finished it, daddie!' — a sigh thereat.
'Are there any more books in the world like that?'

No, little lady. I grieve to say
That of all the books in the world today
There's not another that's quite the same
As this magic book with the magic name.
Volumes there be that are pure delight,
Ancient and yellowed or new and bright;
But — little and thin, or big and fat —
There are no more books in the world like that.

And what, little lady, would I not give
For the wonderful world in which you live!
What have I garnered one-half as true
As the tales Titania whispers you?
Ah, late we learn that the only truth
Was that which we found in the Book of Youth.
Profitless others, and stale, and flat; —
There are no other books in the world like that.

Bert Leston Taylor

*The poem was written by my grandfather for and about my mother.
She used to read it to me when I was a nipper and it has remained a
favourite all my life — it's as fresh today as when written in 1913. It
was published in a collection of his work, entitled* Motley Measures,
in 1927.

With kind regards,
Bob Gallico

JULIE O'CALLAGHAN   5

The Alligator Girls
Remembering John Crowe Ransom

Are you to tell me where my soul is cast
Or in an alligator or a god.

Or would you like to bring the girls at ransom
Over to have a picnic beside the sweet
Clear water. This is the very day for it.
Bring your apricot brandy over. Tell the girls
The mill is off and to come on over
And we'll all put our toes in the sweet river.

An afternoon by the river with two sisters
Is something special. We shouted Gator Gator
And out came May and Bonnie lifting their skirts
Prancing with mock terror out of the shallows
To lovingly berate us. That was when
I worked in America as a young man.

I am told the river had alligators in it.
May and Bonnie are grown up and dead.
But we had some great fun, didn't we?

W S Graham (1918–1986)

*This poem is almost too sad for me to even read. It is also funny and I
can imagine W S Graham standing in some remote American river,*

yelling 'Gator, Gator' at two local girls in his Scottish accent. But then, as I'm chuckling to myself, I go on to the last three lines and my smile evaporates. W S Graham is a genius at saying devastating things in a simple way.
I hope your Poetry anthology sells well!

Sincerely,
Julie O'Callaghan

ULICK O'CONNOR   6

26 April 1985

Dear Students,
I have no favourite poem but I have a number of favourite poems. One is 'Leda and the Swan' by William Butler Yeats whose last house in Ireland was quite near you in Rathfarnham.
The reason I like this poem is that it combines a magnificent gift for poetic language with a very modern form. We see Leda, a beautiful girl walking on the banks of a river when she is suddenly ambushed by the god, Zeus, in the form of a swan. According to the belief of the ancient Greeks, this event resulted in the birth of Helen of Troy which is the explanation of the lines:

> A shudder in the loins engenders there
> The broken wall, the burning roof and tower
> And Agamemnon dead.

You will, no doubt, know one of the causes of the Trojan war centred around Helen of Troy. It might interest you to know that this is a favourite poem of John Mortimer, QC, the well-known English playwright.

Yours sincerely,
Ulick O'Connor

Leda and the Swan

A sudden blow: the great wings beating still
Above the staggering girl, her thighs caressed
By the dark webs, her nape caught in his bill,
He holds her helpless breast upon his breast.

How can those terrified vague fingers push
The feathered glory from her loosening thighs?
And how can body, laid in that white rush,
But feel the strange heart beating where it lies?

A shudder in the loins engenders there
The broken wall, the burning roof and tower
And Agamemnon dead.
                              Being so caught up,
So mastered by the brute blood of the air,
Did she put on his knowledge with his power
Before the indifferent beak could let her drop?

W B Yeats (1865–1939)

GEORGE O SIMMS   7

23 April 1985

Dear friends,
Thank you for your letter telling me of your plan to help the needy in
the Third World — a very good cause and I wish you all success.
You ask for a poem and I send you the text of one which I learned by
heart before I was in my 'teens and have not forgotten. For me, it
provides an atmosphere in which I first encountered ancient Greek as
a language and a civilisation. There is a warmth about the nostalgia
but a vision comes through of things which cannot be destroyed:

They told me, Heraclitus, they told me you were dead,
They brought me bitter news to hear and bitter tears to shed,
I wept as I remember'd how often you and I
Had tired the sun with talking and sent him down the sky.
And now that thou art lying, my dear old Carian guest,
A handful of grey ashes, long, long ago at rest,
Still are thy pleasant voices, thy nightingales, awake;
For Death, he taketh all away, but them he cannot take.

William (Johnson) Cory (1823–1892)

Kind wishes,
George O Simms

EILEEN DUNNE   8

RTE Newsroom
15 April 1985

Please find enclosed two pieces — at least one of which I hope you'll
find suitable.
'Desiderata' isn't really a poem — I know, but it's a piece that
means a lot to me. Like most teenagers in the seventies, I had a poster

of it on my wall, and then of course there was the record — a firm favourite. I went to Manor House school in Raheny, and when I was leaving in 1975 we had a graduation Mass. 'Desiderata' was on the back page of the missalettes we got that day, and I have always thought that it was excellent advice, for the nuns to send us out into the world with.

As for Prévert — well this little poem epitomises for me the power and simplicity of the French language, especially when it comes to romance and the like.

So I hope this is all of some use to you. Good luck with your project and do send me a copy of the book when it comes out, (I'll pay for it of course!).

Yours sincerely,
Eileen Dunne

Paris at Night

Trois allumettes une à une allumées dans la nuit
    La première pour voir ton visage tout entier
        La seconde pour voir tes yeux
        La dernière pour voir ta bouche
Et l'obscurité tout entière pour me rappeler tout cela
        En te serrant dans mes bras.

Jacques Prévert (1900–1977)

Desiderata

Go placidly amid the noise and haste and remember what peace there may be in silence. As far as possible without surrender be on good terms with all persons. Speak your truth quietly and clearly; and listen to others, even the dull and ignorant — they too have their story. Avoid loud and aggressive persons; they are vexations to the spirit. If you compare yourself with others, you may become vain and bitter; for always there will be greater and lesser persons than yourself. Enjoy your achievements as well as your plans. Keep interested in your own career, however humble — it is a real possession in the changing fortune of time. Exercise caution in your business affairs, for the world is full of trickery. But let this not blind you to what virtue there is; many persons strive for high ideals, and everywhere life is full of heroism. Be yourself, especially do not feign affection. Neither be cynical about love; for in the face of all aridity and disenchantment it is as perennial as the grass. Take kindly the counsel of the years, gracefully surrendering the things of youth. Nurture strength of spirit to shield you in sudden misfortune. But do

not distress yourself with imaginings. Many fears are born of
fatigue and loneliness. Beyond a wholesome discipline, be
gentle with yourself.

You are a child of the universe, no less than the trees and the
stars; you have a right to be here. And whether or not it is clear
to you, no doubt the universe is unfolding as it should.
Therefore be at peace with God, whatever you conceive him to
be. And whatever your labours and aspirations in the noisy
confusion of life, keep at peace with your soul. With all its
sham, drudgery and broken dreams, it is still a beautiful
world. Be careful. Strive to be happy.

JIMMY MAGEE   9

RTE Sports Dept.
17 April 1985

Dear Collette, Joy and Steven,
I would be pleased to be associated with your anthology project.
The poem of my choice is 'The Village Schoolmaster' by Oliver
Goldsmith. It is my favourite because of the lasting impression the
following lines made on my young mind, 'They gazed and gazed, and
still the wonder grew, That one small head could carry all he knew'.
How true for all teachers, whether in conventional school or in life
itself.

Yours sincerely,
Jimmy Magee

The Deserted Village — an excerpt

Beside yon straggling fence that skirts the way,
With blossomed furze unprofitably gay,
There, in his noisy mansion, skill'd to rule,
The village master taught his little school;
A man severe he was and stern to view,
I knew him well, and every truant knew;
Well had the boding tremblers learned to trace
The day's disasters in his morning face;
Full well they laugh'd with counterfeited glee,
At all his jokes, for many a joke had he;
Full well the busy whisper circling round,
Conveyed the dismal tidings when he frowned;
Yet he was kind, or if severe in aught,
The love he bore to learning was in fault;
The village all declared how much he knew;

'Twas certain he could write and cypher too;
Lands he could measure, terms and tides presage,
And even the story ran that he could gauge.
In arguing too, the parson owned his skill,
For e'en tho' vanquished, he could argue still;
While words of learned length, and thundering sound,
Amazed the gazing rustics ranged around,
And still they gazed, and still the wonder grew,
That one small head could carry all he knew.

But past is all his fame. The very spot
Where many a time he triumphed, is forgot.

Oliver Goldsmith (?1730–1774)

AUGUSTINE MARTIN   10

University College
Belfield
Dublin 4
24 April 1985

Dear Collette Lucy and friends,
Yours is a lovely idea.

The Drowning of Conaing

The shining waters rise and swell
And break across the shining strand,
And Conaing gazes at the land,
Swung high in his frail coracle.

Then she with the white hair of foam,
The blinding hair that Conaing grips,
Rises, to turn triumphant lips,
On all the gods that guard his home.

(Eighth-century Irish poem
Translation by Frank O'Connor 1903–1966)

The lines convey a sense of pity and terror, pity for the victim, terror
for man's fate — the full tragic sense. The fragility of human life is
epitomised in the young prince's death, 'swung high in his frail
coracle'. The rise and fall of the rhythm mimes the movement of
waves, enchanting and implacable. For a comparable statement about
man and the elements in Irish literature we had to wait a
millennium, for Synge's Riders to the Sea.

Good luck,
Gus Martin

ANDREW MOTION   11

1 May 1985

Dear Collette Lucy, Joy Marshall and Steven Given,
Thank you for your letter, and for inviting me to help you further
your excellent idea.
'They flee from me', by Thomas Wyatt, is a poem I admire
enormously. Although very well known, its long exposure to the
public gaze has done nothing to dim the power of its eroticism, or to
weaken the ways in which private feelings are related to public issues.
And the marvellously adroit irregularities of its metre guarantee
(among other things) that the freshness never fades from its
conversational tone.

Good wishes,
Andrew Motion

They Flee from Me

They flee from me, that sometime did me seke
With naked fote stalkyng within my chamber,
Once have I seen them gentle, tame, and meke,
That now are wild, and do not once remember
That sometyme they have put them selves in danger,
To take bread at my hand, and now they range,
Busily sekyng in continuall change.

Thanked be fortune, it hath bene otherwise
Twenty tymes better: but once especiall,
In thinne aray, after a pleasant gyse,
When her loose gowne did from her shoulders fall,
And she me caught in her armes long and small,
And therwithall, so swetely did me kysse,
And softly sayd: deare hart, how like you this?

It was no dreame: for I lay broade awakyng.
But all is turnde now through my gentlenesse,
Into a bitter fashion of forsakyng:
And I have leave to go of her goodnesse,
And she also to use newfanglenesse.
But, sins that I unkyndly so am served:
How like you this, what hath she now deserved?

Thomas Wyatt (1503–1542)

GERALDINE PLUNKETT   12

16 April 1985

Dear Collette, Joy and Steven,
Thank you for your letter. I think your idea is very good and would
be delighted to help.
The poem I have chosen is 'Edge' by Sylvia Plath who died on 11
February 1963 by her own hand. She was thirty. 'Edge' is the last
poem she ever wrote (5 February 1963) though she had written a
poem a day, sometimes two, almost every day in the months
preceding her death. I think the poem, though sad, is very peaceful.
The language is simple, the images striking. I find it very moving
perhaps because I know something of Sylvia's life and have great
sympathy with her.
Wishing you the best of luck in your venture,

Yours sincerely,
Geraldine Plunkett

Edge

The woman is perfected.
Her dead

Body wears the smile of accomplishment,
The illusion of a Greek necessity

Flows in the scrolls of her toga,
Her bare

Feet seem to be saying:
We have come so far, it is over.

Each dead child coiled, a white serpent,
One at each little

Pitcher of milk, now empty,
She has folded

Them back into her body as petals
Of a rose close when the garden

Stiffens and odours bleed
From the sweet, deep throats of the night flower.

The moon has nothing to be sad about,
Staring from her hood of bone.

She is used to this sort of thing.
Her blacks crackle and drag.

Sylvia Plath (1932–1963)

PAULINE BEWICK   13

April 1985

Dear Collette Lucy, Joy Marshall and Steven Given,
There are lots but this one by Seamus Heaney to my mind is
wonderful —

When you plunged
The light of Tuscany wavered
And swung through the pool
From top to bottom....

I love the mythological way he mixes otter and human

'You were beyond me' —

as an otter is!

Best wishes with your good venture,
Pauline (Bewick)

The Otter

When you plunged
The light of Tuscany wavered
And swung through the pool
From top to bottom.

I loved your wet head and smashing crawl,
Your fine swimmer's back and shoulders
Surfacing and surfacing again
This year and every year since.

I sat dry-throated on the warm stones.
You were beyond me.
The mellowed clarities, the grape-deep air
Thinned and disappointed.

Thank God for the slow loadening,
When I hold you now
We are close and deep
As the atmosphere on water.

My two hands are plumbed water
You are my palpable, lithe
Otter of memory
In the pool of the moment,

Turning to swim on your back
Each silent, thigh-shaking kick
Re-tilting the light,
Heaving the cool at your neck.

And suddenly you're out
Back again, intent as ever,
Heavy and frisky in your freshened pelt,
Printing the stones.

Seamus Heaney (b. 1939)

HUGH LEONARD   14

26 April 1985

Dear Anthologists,
My favourite poem is far too long to be included in an anthology, but
I'll leave it to you to choose an excerpt. It is 'The Old Vicarage,
Grantchester' by Rupert Brooke. It evokes, more than any other
poem I know, a love of place — in this case rural England — and a
longing for bygone summers. I can think of no richer imagery than

Oh! there are chestnuts, summer through
Beside the river made for you
A tunnel of green gloom, and sleep
Deeply above.

The poem becomes a litany of place names. Other villages are
dismissed with rural slanders, when compared with the perfection of
Grantchester, and finally there is that great couplet which embraces a
mood, a way of life and a perpetual summer of french windows,
lawns, fields and a solitary church tower:

Stands the Church clock at ten to three?
And is there honey still for tea?

Yours sincerely,
Hugh Leonard

from *The Old Vicarage, Grantchester*
(Café des Westens, Berlin, May 1912)

God! I will pack, and take a train,
And get me to England once again!
For England's the one land I know,
Where men with Splendid Hearts may go;
And Cambridgeshire, of all England,

The shire for Men who Understand;
And of that district I prefer
The lovely hamlet Grantchester . . . .

Ah God! to see the branches stir
Across the moon at Grantchester!
To smell the thrilling-sweet and rotten
Unforgettable, unforgotten
River-smell and hear the breeze
Sobbing in the little trees.
Say, do the elm-clumps greatly stand
Still guardians of that holy land?
The chestnut shade, in reverend dream,
The yet unacademic stream?
Is dawn a secret shy and cold
Anadyomene, silver-gold?
And sunset still a golden sea
From Haslingfield to Madingley?
And after, ere the night is born,
Do hares come out about the corn?
Oh, is the water sweet and cool,
Gentle and brown, above the pool?
And laughs the immortal river still
Under the mill, under the mill?
Say, is there Beauty yet to find?
And Certainty? and Quiet kind?
Deep meadows yet, for to forget
The lies, and truths, and pain?. . . Oh! yet
Stands the Church clock at ten to three?
And is there honey still for tea?

Rupert Brooke (1887–1915)

BUNNY CARR   15

1 May 1985

Dear Collette, Joy and Steven,
Privilege and fame? A modest thanks is the only response to such
flattery.
My bizarre choice may not suit the style and tone of the proposed
tome. If not I will be unhurt by an editorial decision not to include
my choice.
However I do sincerely applaud the initiative and the purpose.
I have chosen two. If I am cheating in doubling the number I believe
that the brevity of each justifies the licence (poetic?).
For me poetry at its best captures a truth. I only realised how true it
is after the arrival of our second baby.

It's a little known fact
   But unmistakeable,
The second baby's not so breakable.

I have no idea who wrote it but I am certain he/she had at least two
children.
My second choice is very personal. I wrote it. I was asked to write a
book about television. I saw it as an 'Instant Tree' — growing
instant experts, instant fame, instant opinions and instant change.

I carved my name upon the Instant tree
   In the garden of supercede
Now supercede marks flower and weed
   While the Instant Tree grows taller.

This temple's tower reflects a power
   The mast becomes the steeple
And light and shade are both betrayed
   By shadows.

So what's the tune, who pays the piper
   And who will be the caller
Has truth a voice in the land of choice
   Where the Instant Tree grows taller.

This was the foreword to that book.

Yours sincerely,
Bunny Carr

FLO McSWEENEY   16

15 April 1985

Dear Collette, Joy and Steven,
First I must apologise for my late reply but the letter you sent went
through about 200 departments before reaching me! Please don't
undermine the originality of your idea because although money has
been raised for the Third World through other mediums, the idea of a
compilation of poems is a great one. If you actually get everyone that
you have written to, to reply, it will be no mean achievement.
Anyway, on with the poem.
I particularly love John Cooper Clarke because he is one of the few
poets of today who will probably go down in the annals of history
alongside Yeats, Shakespeare, Eliot etc.
He writes about ordinary people, their lives and problems. In the
poem 'Valley of the Lost Women' he deals with the suburban
housewife who lives, trapped in the shadow of her circumstance.

I chose this poem because I think it applies so much to life in Ireland as a housewife, a role which so many of us play at some point in our lives. Irish women are often bred for careers and are then expected to throw them aside for marriage, children and their 'once a year, two week holiday in Benidorm'. They walk through three-colour brochures depicting palm on aqua-marine.
I am certainly not a fist flailing feminist but I feel that this poem by John Cooper Clarke captures perfectly the desolation and loneliness of a suburban housewife.
I wish you the best of luck in your venture and would love a copy of the pamphlet.

Yours
Flo McSweeney

valley of the lost women

the windows are frigidaire icebergs
frozen in prickly heat
the vanishing cream victims
are drip fed amnesia neat
where the test card melodies warm you
in powder blue pseudo bel air
germs and flies alarm you
they whisper the word expelair
the eyes of the night sub zero
peep through the windows of sleep
everyone's husband is a hero
and ghost insurance men creep
through the valley of the long-lost women
dreaming under the driers
eating sleeping and slimming
according to what is required
they walk through three-colour brochures
depicting palms on aqua marine
in the half-built hotels out of focus
they're mending the vending machines
where sixty italian love songs
are sung to a million guitars
they lick their drinks on sticks
among the men with important cigars
numb to the digital numbers
two three . . . . four five six
lost in a faraway rhumba
where the oildrums are beaten with sticks
she left her heart in frisco
she left her room in a mess
she left her hat in the disco
she never left her address
the diving board springs to assistance

throws you off from the shore
telephones ring in the distance
there are lifts getting stuck between floors
a truck turns into a cul-de-sac
springtime turns to ice
rucksacks turn into hunchbacks
musclemen turn into mice
in a painless panorama
with its perpendicular might
the women are going bananas
and disappearing from sight

John Cooper Clarke (b. 1948)

MARGARET MacCURTAIN   17

Child of Our Time (for Aengus)

Yesterday I knew no lullaby
But you have taught me overnight to order
This song, which takes from your final cry
Its tune, from your unreasoned end its reason;
Its rhythm from the discord of your murder
Its motive from the fact you cannot listen.

We who should have known how to instruct
With rhymes for your waking, rhythms for your sleep,
Names for the animals you took to bed,
Tales to distract, legends to protect,
Later an idiom for you to keep
And living, learn, must learn from you, dead.

To make our broken images rebuild
Themselves around your limbs, your broken
Image, find for your sake whose life our idle
Talk has cost, a new language. Child
Of our time, our times have robbed your cradle.
Sleep in a world your final sleep has woken.

Eavan Boland (b. 1944)

I love this poem because of its compassion and awareness of the tragedy that has overtaken the children of our time, particularly in the Third World, but also as a result of the wars, concentration camps, purges and forced settlements. Also I admire the poetry of Eavan Boland, one of the true poets in Ireland of the late twentieth century. Her voice, her insights, her lyric quality are authentic.

Margaret MacCurtain
Sister Benvenuta

BARRY LANG   18

RTE
10 April 1985

Dear Collette, Joy and Steven,
I must say your idea of compiling an anthology of poems for the
Third World is a super one, and I hope my small contribution will be
of some help. I have many favourite poets, but since you want only
one from me I thought an Irish one would be best. Percy French is a
man whose poetry I find very easy to read and this poem in particular
sums up in a few lines just what it's like to be in my shoes at the
moment, because the holiday always seems to be over:

The End of the Holiday

Fold up the box, the wind is chill,
The hills are turning grey,
Tomorrow I must pay my bill,
And speed me far away —
Back to the world again — but still
Thank God for such a day!

Percy French (1854–1920)

I know it's short but to me it says a lot and I hope it makes a lot for
you.
Lots of luck for the future,

Best wishes,
Barry Lang

BRENDAN KENNELLY   19

Department of Modern English,
Trinity College,
Dublin 2.
18 April 1985

Collette, Joy, Steven,
Thank you for writing to me. I think my favourite poem in the
English language is 'The Garden of Love' by William Blake. I like
it because it is a celebration of freedom.

Yours sincerely,
Brendan Kennelly

The Garden of Love

I went to the Garden of Love,
And saw what I never had seen:
A Chapel was built in the midst,
Where I used to play on the green.

And the gates of this Chapel were shut
And Thou shalt not. writ over the door;
So I turn'd to the Garden of Love,
That so many sweet flowers bore,

And I saw it was filled with graves,
And tomb-stones where flowers should be:
And Priests in black gowns, were walking their rounds,
And binding with briars, my joys & desires.

William Blake (1757–1827)

HILARY ORPEN   20

RTE
1 May 1985

Dear Collette Lucy, Joy Marshall, and Steven Given,
Thank you for your letter and for the compliment you pay in asking
me to contribute to your anthology.
Choosing a favourite poem is quite a difficult task. Moods and
situations change and with them the favourite poem of any particular
time. Among my favourite, however, is 'Entirely' by Louis
MacNeice. However if there was a short list I couldn't leave out 'The
Tyger' by William Blake or Emily Dickinson's very simple poem
'How Happy is the Little Stone'.
If though there's to be just one, let it be 'Entirely'. Why I'm choosing
it? Well, I think it's self evident. Down through the years, poets have
always written about the human condition. This poem by MacNeice
is bang up to date though the situation he writes about is not new.
'Entirely' is a celebration of life in all its complexity. We may try to
marshall and to order it to our own requirements but inevitably we
fail. Wisdom comes when we accept that as individuals we don't have
total control. And I'm a long way off wisdom so this poem by Louis
MacNeice will be by my bed for many years more.
Good luck with your efforts. I hope your book is very successful.

Yours sincerely,
Hilary Orpen

Entirely

If we could get the hang of it entirely
　　It would take too long;
All we know is the splash of words in passing
　　and falling twigs of song,
And when we try to eavesdrop on the great
　　Presences it is rarely
That by a stroke of luck we can appropriate
　　Even a phrase entirely.

If we could find our happiness entirely
　　In somebody else's arms
We should not fear the spears of the spring nor the city's
　　Yammering fire alarms
But, as it is, the spears each year go through
　　Our flesh and almost hourly
Bell or siren banishes the blue
　　Eyes of Love entirely.

And if the world were black or white entirely
　　And all the charts were plain
Instead of a mad weir of tigerish waters,
　　A prism of delight and pain,
We might be surer where we wished to go
　　Or again we might be merely
Bored but in brute reality there is no
　　Road that is right entirely.

Louis MacNeice (1907–1963)

How Happy is the Little Stone

How happy is the little Stone
That rambles in the Road alone,
And doesn't care about Careers
And Exigencies never fears —
Whose Coat of elemental Brown
A passing Universe put on,
And independent as the Sun
Associates or glows alone,
Fulfilling absolute Decree
In casual simplicity —

Emily Dickinson (1830–1886)

ISABEL HEALY   21

29 April 1985

Dear Collette, Joy and Steven,
Your invitation to contribute to your anthology is a delight in many
ways. Firstly I am glad to contribute to anything which makes us
think a little on those who suffer in the Third World; it is an
interesting way for you all to be introduced to poems you may not
otherwise have come across, and of course I am mighty chuffed that
you consider me 'privileged and famous'!
I enclose my favouritest* poem — 'A Drover'. I'm sorry if you were
expecting something mighty, learned, and esoteric which I had
translated myself from the Serbo-Croate, but which still contains no
words shorter than five syllables. If I'm absolutely honest, and shut
my eyes tight, it is always to the wet winding roads I return!

With best wishes to you all,
Isabel Healy

*You will not find this word in a dictionary — I have just made it
up!

'A Drover' *by Padraic Colum*
If I were kidnapped or imprisoned, I think Padraic Colum's poem,
above all others, a poem I would recite again and again to maintain
my sanity. It is my favourite poem because it is so pleasing and
evocative in its simplicity.
One could meditate on every line, and get from it landscape, geology
and a sense of place, philosophy, strength, gentleness and sensitivity
— a tingle for all senses. The musical rhythm of each short verse has
the crunch of a march, and the flow of fantasy. Anyway 'A Drover'
is about all the things I love: Independence and early mornings,
country roads and the warm smell of cows, and my relations who are
all cattlemen in Meath of the pastures.
Of all my favourites — The Old Testament, great chunks of
Wordsworth and Tennyson, Brian Patten, Yeats and the erotic
poetry of John Donne and Erica Jonge; it is to Colum I always return
for a security in being and a joy in words.

A Drover

To Meath of the pastures,
From wet hills by the sea,
Through Leitrim and Longford
Go my cattle and me.

I hear in the darkness
Their slipping and breathing.
I name them the bye-ways
They're to pass without heeding.

Then the wet, winding roads,
Brown bogs with black water;
And my thoughts on white ships
And the King o' Spain's daughter.

O farmer, strong farmer!
You can spend at the fair
But your face you must turn
To your crops and your care.

And soldiers — red soldiers!
You've seen many lands;
But you walk two by two,
And by captain's commands.

O the smell of the beasts,
The wet wind in the morn;
And the proud and hard earth
Never broken for corn;

And the crowds at the fair,
The herds loosened and blind,
Loud words and dark faces
And the wild blood behind.

(O strong men with your best
I would strive breast to breast,
I could quiet your herds
With my words, with my words.)

I will bring you, my kine,
Where there's grass to the knee;
But you'll think of scant croppings
Harsh with salt of the sea.

Padraic Colum (1881–1972)

BERNARD MacLAVERTY   22

7 May 1985

Dear Collette,
Thank you for your letter. I would be delighted to choose a poem for
your anthology.
It has to be another Ulsterman.

The Introduction

They were introduced in a grave glade
And she frightened him because she was young
And thus too late. Crawly crawly
Went the twigs above their heads and beneath
The grass beneath their feet the larvae
Split themselves laughing. Crawly crawly
Went the cloud above the treetops reaching
For a sun that lacked the nerve to set
And he frightened her because he was old
And thus too early. Crawly crawly
Went the string quartet that was tuning up
In the back of the mind. You two should have met
Long since, he said, or else not now.
The string quartet in the back of the mind
Was all tuned up with nowhere to go.
They were introduced in a green grave.

Louis MacNeice (1907–1963)

This is a favourite poem of mine, dealing as it does with missed opportunity and indecision. Above all there is the wit of MacNeice in the way he treats his subject and the total control he exerts over words. He can make the unexpected work.

Good luck with the whole enterprise.
Bernard MacLaverty

MYLES DUNGAN   23

RTE Radio 1
19 April 1985

Dear Collette, Joy and Steven,
Congratulations on having a very good idea. When the book comes out anthologists and writers of gimmick tomes the world over (given to compiling books such as Desert Island Menus/Laundry Lists/10 Best Films of the rich and famous) will grind their teeth and grunt 'why didn't I think of that?' I must get the wife to get me a new agent for Christmas.
In my youth poetry was something to be learned by heart first and appreciated afterwards. I liked most of it but then what you do at school tends to be like a poetic K-Tel compilation album (Now that's what I call Poetry — eighteenth-century). The trick was to be able to recite it at great speed last thing at night in the hope that you could steer your way slowly around the same course the following morning. Accordingly one of my favourite poems was one that went:

*'InxanadudidKublakhanastatelypleasuredomedecreewherealphthesacr
edriverranthroughcavernsmeasurelesstomandowntoasunlesssea —
(pause for breath) — a poem which I have recently discovered was
actually written by Frankie Goes to Hollywood and not Samuel
Taylor Coleridge as my teacher would have me believe.*
*Since those days of innocence my tastes have become more esoteric
and frankly quite elitist. During what I would describe as My Middle
Period I developed a taste for the obscure and extremely personal
statements of E Jarvis Thribb (17) in* Private Eye. *He belies his years
(he has, in fact, been seventeen for about twenty years). The apparent
simplicity of his verse is merely a ploy to deter those who do not have
eyes to see. Clever and sensitive people like me have the ability to
ignore the utter banality of the language, the artless blandness of the
sentiments and the pedestrian metre and go straight to the gaps
between the verses wherein lies the incandescence of the man. Thribb
is to the gap on the printed page what Pinter is to the theatrical
pause.*
*Take for example his sad little elegy to the jazz pianist Eubie Blake
who died at the age of a hundred.*

So Farewell
Then Eubie
Blake.

Noted Jazz
Pianist and
Composer.
Aged 100

Eubie
A strange name.

Keith says
That possibly
your initials
Were U B

Hence the
Name.

I wonder

*But aside from all that you want to know what my favourite poem is.
For me the best poetry is brief and incisive. Good comedy should also
be equally sharp. My problem is that I tend to like to see the two on
some sort of combination. This doesn't mean that I loathe poets who
are not a barrel of laughs. It just means that I am so crassly
Philistinitic that I tend to agree with Pope that 'true wit is nature to
advantage dressed/ what oft was thought but ne'er so well expressed'
— except that I mean wit in its more commonly accepted sense and I
see it as being heightened by humour in poetic form. Rhyme helps a
lot. One of the funniest things I've ever seen on stage in recent years*

*was an adaptation by (the poet) Derek Mahon for 'Field Day' of a
French farce which he re-titled* High Times. *It was written in rhyme
and this served to heighten the hilarity.*
*Put it down to a black sense of humour which desires to see poetry
perverted by humour for vaguely subversive purposes. Or just put it
down to idiosyncrasy but the kind of thing I like best is done by
Roger McGough. Here are two examples:*

Sad Aunt Madge

As the cold winter evenings drew near
Aunt Madge used to put extra blankets
over the furniture, to keep it warm and cosy
Mussolini was her lover, and life
was an outoffocus rosy tinted spectacle

but neurological experts
with kind blueeyes
and gentle voices
small white hands
and large Rolls Royces
said that electric shock treatment
should do the trick
it did. . . .

today after 15 years of therapeutic tears
and an awful lot of ratepayers' shillings
down the hospital meter
sad Aunt Madge
no longer tucks up the furniture
before kissing it goodnight
and admits
that her affair with Mussolini
clearly was not right
particularly in the light
of her recently announced engagement
to the late pope.

Motorway

            The politicians
(who are buying huge cars with hobnailed wheels
            the size of merry-go-rounds)
            have a new plan.
            They are going to
            put cobbles
            in our eyesockets
            and pebbles

in our navels
and fill us up
with asphalt
and lay us
side by side
so that we can take a more active part
in the road
to destruction.

I like Dylan Thomas as well. Honest I do!

Yours sincerely,
Myles Dungan

EMER O'KELLY   24

RTE
29 April 1985

Dear Mss Lucy and Marshall, and Mr Given,
I enclose my choice of poem for your planned anthology. 'Mother of
the Groom' by Seamus Heaney . . . and I wish you all the best with
your project.

Yours very sincerely,
Emer O'Kelly

Mother of the Groom

What she remembers
Is his glistening back
In the bath, his small boots
In the ring of boots at her feet.

Hands in her voided lap,
She hears a daughter welcomed.
It's as if he kicked when lifted
And slipped her soapy hold.

Once soap would ease off
The wedding ring
That's bedded forever now
In her clapping hand.

Seamus Heaney (b. 1939)

Seamus Heaney always seems to me to have incorporated every emotion there is in his poetry. He can even sing of the deepest female fears and love, an extraordinary feat in an era which sets the sexes at each others' throats. This poem, for me, shows that love is never without pain: the abandonment of care and obsesssion that the mother feels when her baby is helpless leads, inevitably, to the day when almost the only test of her love is to let go.

Emer O'Kelly
April 1985

BENEDICT KIELY   25

19 April 1985

Dear Collette, Joy and Steven,
Dylan Thomas said 'Read poetry until you find what you like and then read it again. So that you may always have a few poems in your head even when you have no book before you'. So I always have a few favourite poems, changing, going away, going away, returning. I have a few at the moment but I send you this one by E. A. R.
Why do I like it? The poem speaks for itself. Padraic Colum, who was a good friend of mine, knew Arlington well in the States and spoke a lot about him. A strange man. Good luck with your project.

Ben Kiely

Mr Flood's Party

Old Eben Flood, climbing alone one night
Over the hill between the town below
And the forsaken upland hermitage
That held as much as he should ever know
On earth again of home, paused warily.
The road was his with not a native near;
And Eben, having leisure, said aloud,
For no man else in Tilbury to hear:

'Well, Mr Flood, we have the harvest moon
Again, and we may not have many more;
The bird is on the wing, the poet says,
And you and I have said it here before.
Drink to the bird.' He raised up to the light
The jug that he had gone so far to fill,
And answered huskily: 'Well, Mr Flood,
Since you propose it, I believe I will'.

Alone, as if enduring to the end
A valiant armor of scarred hopes outworn,
He stood there in the middle of the road
Like Roland's ghost winding a silent horn.
Below him, in the town among the trees,
Where friend of other days had honored him,
A phantom salutation of the dead
Rang thinly till old Eben's eyes were dim.

Then, as a mother lays her sleeping child
Down tenderly, fearing it may awake,
He set the jug down slowly at his feet
With trembling care, knowing that most things break;
And only when assured that on firm earth
It stood, as the uncertain lives of men
Assuredly did not, he paced away,
And with his hand extended paused again:

'Well, Mr Flood, we have not met like this
In a long time; and many a change has come
To both of us, I fear, since last it was
We had a drop together. Welcome home!'
Convivially returning with himself,
Again he raised his jug up to the light;
And with an acquiescent quaver said:
'Well, Mr Flood, if you insist, I might.

'Only a very little, Mr Flood —
For auld lang syne. No more, sir; that will do.'
So, for the time, apparently it did,
And Eben evidently thought so too;
For soon amid the silver loneliness
Of night he lifted up his voice and sang,
Secure, with only two moons listening,
Until the whole harmonious landscape rang —

'For auld lang syne.' The weary throat gave out,
The last word wavered; and the song was done,
He raised again the jug regretfully
And shook his head, and was again alone.
There was not much that was ahead of him,
And there was nothing in the town below —
Where strangers would have shut the many doors
That many friends had opened long ago.

Edwin Arlington Robinson (1869–1935)

JOHN BANVILLE   26

6 May 1985

Dear Collette Lucy, Joy Marshall, Steven Given:
Thank you for your letter. I enclose the text of a poem which you
might like to use in your anthology. Celan's poetry is very difficult to
translate, so I hope you can carry the German as well as the English
translation. Even though many readers will not know German, the
look of the original is important.

I wish you the best of luck with your venture.
John Banville

Psalm

Niemand knetet uns weider aus Erde und Lehm,
niemand besprict unsern Staub.
Niemand.

Gelobt seist du, Niemand.
Dir zulieb wollen
wir blühn.
Dir
entgegen.

Ein Nichts
waren wir, sind wir, werden
wir bleiben, blühend:
die Nichts —, die
Niemandsrose.

Mit
dem Griffel seelenhell
dem Staubfaden himmelswüst,
der Krone rot
vom Purpurwort, das wir sangen
über, o über
dem Dorn.

Paul Celan (1920–1970)

There is no single poem which I would describe as my favourite.
However, here is the text of a very beautiful poem, which I think
would be particularly suitable for your anthology. It is by Paul Celan
(1920–1970), a Jewish poet who wrote in German. As a child during
World War II he was a prisoner in a Romanian Labour camp. His
parents were killed by the Nazis. Out of these terrible experiences he
created a heartbreaking poetry.

Psalm

No one moulds us again out of earth and clay,
no one conjures our dust.
No one.

Praised be your name, no one.
For your sake
we shall flower.
Towards
you.

A nothing
we were, are, shall
remain, flowering;
the nothing —, the
no one's rose.

With our pistil soul-bright
with our stamen heaven-ravaged
our corolla red
with the crimson word which we sang
over, o over
the thorn.

Paul Celan (1920–1970)
(Translated by Michael Hamburger)

IRIS MURDOCH   27

A Summer Night
(To Geoffrey Hoyland)

Out on the lawn I lie in bed,
Vega conspicuous overhead
    In the windless nights of June,
As congregated leaves complete
Their day's activity; my feet
    Point to the rising moon.

Lucky, this point in time and space
Is chosen as my working place,
    Where the sexy airs of summer,
The bathing hours and the bare arms,
The leisured drives through a land of farms
    Are good to a newcomer.

Equal with colleagues in a ring
I sit on each calm evening

Enchanted as the flowers
The opening light draws out of hiding
With all its gradual dove-like pleading,
    Its logic and its powers:

That later we, though parted then,
May still recall these evenings when
    Fear gave his watch no look;
The lion griefs loped from the shade
And on our knees their muzzles laid,
    And Death put down his book.

Now north and south and east and west
Those I love lie down to rest;
    The moon looks on them all,
The healers and the brilliant talkers
The eccentrics and the silent walkers,
    The dumpy and the tall.

She climbs the European sky,
Churches and power-stations lie
    Alike among earth's fixtures:
Into the galleries she peers
And blankly as a butcher stares
    Upon the marvellous pictures.

To gravity attentive, she
Can notice nothing here, though we
    Whom hunger does not move,
From gardens where we feel secure
Look up and with a sigh endure
    The tyrannies of love:

And, gentle, do not care to know,
Where Poland draws her eastern bow,
    What violence is done,
Nor ask what doubtful act allows
Our freedom in this English house,
    Our picnics in the sun.

Soon, soon, through dykes of our content
The crumpling flood will force a rent
    And, taller than a tree,
Hold sudden death before our eyes
Whose river dreams long hid the size
    And vigours of the sea.

But when the waters make retreat
And through the black mud first the wheat
    In shy green stalks appears,
When stranded monsters gasping lie,
And sounds of riveting terrify
    Their whorled unsubtle ears,

May these delights we dread to lose,
This privacy need no excuse
    But to that strength belong,
As through a child's rash happy cries
The drowned parental voices rise
    In unlamenting song.

After discharges of alarm
All unpredicted let them calm
    The pulse of nervous nations,
Forgive the murderer in his glass,
Tough in their patience to surpass
    The tigress her swift motions.

W H Auden (1907–1973)

This marvellously beautiful elegiac song, full of magisterial images,
expresses both fear and hope. It also conjures up, with great
tenderness and feeling, a particular occasion. This connection of vast
moral vistas with individual situations is typical poetic magic.

Iris Murdoch   22 April 1985

TOM HICKEY   28

18 April 1985

Dear Collette, Joy and Steven,
Thank you for your letter and congratulations on your splendid
work. I am delighted to help.
I have chosen a poem by Tom MacIntyre called 'The Yellow
Bittern'. I picked 'The Yellow Bittern' because to me it is essentially
a metaphor dealing with the consequences of deprivation of all kinds
and on several levels.
The imagery of the poem resonates with the isolation, loneliness and
tragedy of a being who is deprived of 'life's juices' — the spiritual,
emotional and physical 'touching' that is vital to all healthy
existence.

  'Christ's sake, if you'd only sent word,
  Tipped me the wink you were in a bind'.

I wish you all the success you deserve,
Tom Hickey

The Yellow Bittern

Sickens my gut. Yellow Bittern,
To see you stretched there,
Whipped — not by starvation
But the want of a jar;
Troy's fall was skittles to this.
You flattened on bare stones,
You harmed no one, pillaged no crop,
Your preference always — the wee drop.

Sours my spit, Yellow Bittern
Thought of you done for,
Heard your shout many's the night,
You mudlarkin' — and no want of a jar;
At that game I'll shape a coffin,
So all claim — but look at this,
A darlin' bird downed like a thistle,
Causa mortis: couldn't wet his whistle.

Sands my bones, Yellow Bittern, that's fact,
Your last earthlies under a bush,
Rats next — rats for the waking,
Pipes in their mouths, and them all smoking;
Christ's sake, if you'd only sent word,
Tipped me the wink you were in a bind,
Dunt of a crow-bar, the ice splitter-splatter,
Nothing to stop another week on the batter.

Heron, blackbird, thrush — they've had it too,
Sorry, friends, I'm occupied,
I'm blinds down for the Yellow Bittern,
A blood relation — on the mother's side;
Whole-hog merchants, we lived it up,
Carpe'd our *diem*, hung out our sign,
Collared life's bottle, disregarding the label,
Angled our elbows, met under the table

While the wife moaned with the rest,
'Give it up — you're finished — A year' —
I told her she lied,
My staple and staff was the regular jar,
Now — naked proof — this lad with a gullet
Who, forced on the dry, surely prayed for a bullet,
No, men, drink it up — and piss it down,
Worm them worms waitin' undergroun'.

From the original 'An Bunán Buí' (eighteenth century)
by Cathal Buí Mac Ghiolla Ghunna (Yellow-haired Charlie Gunn)

'My central aim has been to convey the gaiety of the (original)
poets clearly and faithfully.'

Tom MacIntyre

EMMET BERGIN   29

RTE
19 April 1985

Dear Collette, Joy and Steven,
Thanks for your letter, and good luck with your worthy venture. It is
hard to choose one's favourite poem, there are so many wonderful and
different works. It's like being asked to say which of one's children
one loves the most. I find it an impossible task.
However the piece I've chosen is from The Merchant of Venice, Act
V *scene (i).* I played Lorenzo at one time and never tired of speaking
these splendid lines:

How sweet the moonlight sleeps upon this bank!
Here will we sit, and let the sounds of music
Creep in our ears: soft stillness and the night
Become the touches of sweet harmony.
Sit, Jessica. Look how the floor of heaven
Is thick inlaid with patines of bright gold:
There's not the smallest orb which thou behold'st
But in his motion like an angel sings,
Still quiring to the young-eyed cherubins;
Such harmony is in immortal souls;
But whilst this muddy vesture of decay
Doth grossly close it in, we cannot hear it.

Theatrical legend says that during rehearsals for the original
production of The Merchant, *the actor playing Portia had not*
enough time to change from the male garb used in the court scene to
the female dress for Portia and complained of this to William S. who
sat down there and then and wrote this beautiful scene for Lorenzo
and Jessica. I have always felt that these lines are Shakespeare
speaking, not through a character, or to develop a character, but as
himself directly.

Good luck again,
Emmet Bergin

MAUREEN POTTER   30

26 April 1985

Dear Collette, Joy and Steven,
At the moment my favourite poet is John Betjeman, I change from
time to time.

In my business the tag, or last lines, of a Comedy Sketch are crucial. John Betjeman has a genius for unexpected Tags. For example, 'False Security' about the little boy at the party.

However my choice for your anthology must be 'A Subaltern's Love Song' all about Miss Joan Hunter Dunn. As I read it I can see them, I can hear, even smell, the place. With a word or a line he can capture an atmosphere, a picture, that should require a complete essay. Then in his own quirky way he includes a word like 'euonymus' which sent me, at least, off to the dictionary. Leading up to that Romantic tag it should have been a mid-summer moon, dreamy music from the band, instead it is 'Above us the intimate roof of the car'. Form V won't know anything about that but they WILL.

Sincerely,
Maureen Potter

MARY McEVOY   31

16 April 1985

Dear Collette, Joy and Steven,
I hope my reply isn't too late. My favourite poem, without a shadow of a doubt, is 'A Subaltern's Love-Song/Miss Joan Hunter Dunn' by John Betjeman. If you need a second choice I suppose it's 'The Planter's Daughter' by Austin Clarke.
Best of luck in your worthy cause and thank you for asking me to contribute.

Yours,
Mary McEvoy

A Subaltern's Love-Song

Miss J Hunter Dunn, Miss J Hunter Dunn,
Furnish'd and burnish'd by Aldershot sun,
What strenuous singles we played after tea,
We in the tournament — you against me!

Love-thirty, love-forty, oh! weakness of joy,
The speed of a swallow, the grace of a boy,
With carefullest carelessness, gaily you won,
I am weak from your loveliness, Joan Hunter Dunn.

Miss Joan Hunter Dunn, Miss Joan Hunter Dunn,
How mad I am, sad I am, glad that you won.
The warm-handled racket is back in its press,
But my shock-headed victor, she loves me no less.

Her father's euonymus shines as we walk,
And swing past the summer-house, buried in talk,
And cool the verandah that welcomes us in
To the six-o'clock news and a lime-juice and gin.

The scent of the conifers, sound of the bath,
The view from my bedroom of moss-dappled path,
As I struggle with double-end evening tie,
For we dance at the Golf Club, my victor and I.

On the floor of her bedroom lie blazer and shorts
And the cream-coloured walls are be-trophied with sports,
And westering, questioning settles the sun
On your low-leaded window, Miss Joan Hunter Dunn.

The Hillman is waiting, the light's in the hall,
The pictures of Egypt are bright on the wall,
My sweet, I am standing beside the oak stair
And there on the landing's the light on your hair.

By roads 'not adopted', by woodlanded ways,
She drove to the club in the late summer haze,
Into nine-o'clock Camberley, heavy with bells
And mushroomy, pine-woody, evergreen smells.

Miss Joan Hunter Dunn, Miss Joan Hunter Dunn,
I can hear from the car-park the dance has begun.
Oh! full Surrey twilight! importunate band!
Oh! strongly adorable tennis-girl's hand!

Around us are Rovers and Austins afar,
Above us, the intimate roof of the car,
And here on my right is the girl of my choice,
With the tilt of her nose and the chime of her voice,

And the scent of her wrap, and the words never said,
And the ominous, ominous dancing ahead.
We sat in the car park till twenty to one
And now I'm engaged to Miss Joan Hunter Dunn.

John Betjeman (1906–1984)

The Planter's Daughter

When night stirred at sea
And the fire brought a crowd in,
They say that her beauty
Was music in mouth
And few in the candlelight
Thought her too proud,
For the house of the planter
Is known by the trees.

Men that seen her
Drank deep and were silent
The women were speaking
Wherever she went —
As a bell that is rung
Or a wonder told shyly
And O she was the Sunday
In every week.

Austin Clarke (1896–1974)

JOHN KAVANAGH   32

Abbey Theatre
Dublin
27 April 1985

Dear Joy Marshall,
Thank you for your recent letter. Quite apart from my being a
devotee of Seamus Heaney's work, the reason I like 'Follower' so
much is because of its striking visual imagery in depicting a situation
with which we can all identify, knowing that one day the roles will be
reversed.
I congratulate you on a noble endeavour and wishing you all the best,

I remain,
Sincerely yours,
John Kavanagh

Follower

My father worked with a horse-plough,
His shoulders globed like a full sail strung
Between the shafts and the furrow.
The horses strained at his clicking tongue.

An expert. He would set the wing
And fit the bright steel-pointed sock.
The sod rolled over without breaking.
At the headrig, with a single pluck

Of reins, the sweating team turned round
And back into the land. His eye
Narrowed and angled at the ground,
Mapping the furrow exactly.

I stumbled in his hob-nailed wake,
Fell sometimes on the polished sod;
Sometimes he rode me on his back
Dipping and rising to his plod.

I wanted to grow up and plough,
To close one eye, stiffen my arm.
All I ever did was follow
In his broad shadow round the farm

I was a nuisance, tripping, falling,
Yapping always. But to-day
It is my father who keeps stumbling
Behind me, and will not go away.

Seamus Heaney (b. 1939)

GERRIT VAN GELDEREN   33

26 April 1985

Dear Collette, Joy and Steven,
Thank you for your letter. I am rather flattered that you should count
me among the famed and privileged but yours is quite a good idea,
though I guess that, in practical terms, pop records are earning more
for the Third World.
Anyhow, here is my favourite poem. It can't be, of course, any other
than 'The Stolen Child' by W B Yeats — especially the bit about 'for
the world's more full of weeping than you can understand'. Rather a
popular choice I'd say.

Where dips the rocky highland
Of Sleuth Wood in the lake,
There lies a leafy island
Where flapping herons wake
The drowsy water-rats;
There we've hid our faery vats,
Full of berries
And of reddest stolen cherries.
Come away, O human child!
To the waters and the wild
With a faery, hand in hand,
For the world's more full of weeping than you
    can understand.

Where the wave of moonlight glosses
The dim grey sands with light,
Far off by furthest Rosses
We foot it all the night,

Weaving olden dances,
Mingling hands and mingling glances
Till the moon has taken flight;
To and fro we leap
And chase the frothy bubbles,
While the world is full of troubles
And is anxious in its sleep.
Come away, O human child!
To the waters and the wild
With a faery, hand in hand,
For the world's more full of weeping than you
    can understand.

Where the wandering water gushes
From the hills above Glen-Car,
In pools among the rushes
That scarce could bathe a star,
We seek for slumbering trout
And whispering in their ears
Give them unquiet dreams;
Leaning softly out
From ferns that drop their tears
Over the young streams.
Come away, O human child!
To the waters and the wild
With a faery, hand in hand,
For the world's more full of weeping than you
    can understand.

Away with us he's going,
The solemn-eyed:
He'll hear no more the lowing
Of the calves on the warm hillside
Or the kettle on the hob
Sing peace into his breast,
Or see the brown mice bob
Round and round the oatmeal-chest.
For he comes, the human child,
To the waters and the wild
With a faery, hand in hand,
From a world more full of weeping than he
    can understand.

W B Yeats (1865–1939)

Now I was born and raised in Holland, so some of my earliest
favourites are in Dutch. There is one line by Roland Holst, a
contemporary of Yeats and in many respects his Dutch counterpart
— but not as great — that went: '. . .want wij zijn van de weinigen
dezer tijden die in de wind geboren werden . . . ', meaning literally

'. . . for we are among the few that were born in the wind . . . .' I did love that, though I've gone off it I suppose. At the time it appealed to me as I've always felt a bit of a nomad — that's what your man meant. It sounds better in Dutch.
Then there is a French poem which I could recite by heart by Jacques Prévert. He was very popular just after the war in Holland. He worked together with Michel Carné and made famous films such as 'Les enfants du Paradis', but that's all before your time. We loved him because his French is very simple and direct and not very high-falutin'. The poem is 'Barbara'.

Rappelle-toi Barbara
Il pleuvait sans cesse sur Brest ce jour-là
Et tu marchais souriante
Épanouie ravie ruisselante
Sous la pluie
Rappelle-toi Barbara
Il pleuvait sans cesse sur Brest
Et je t'ai croisée rue de Siam
Tu souriais
Et moi je souriais de même
Rappelle-toi Barbara
Toi que je ne connaissais pas
Toi qui ne me connaissais pas
Rappelle-toi
Rappelle-toi quand même ce jour-là
N'oublie pas

etc. He goes on to tell how he said hello and how it continued raining on all the buildings of Brest and ends asking himself what has become of Brest — which was totally destroyed during the war, and of Barbara:

Oh Barbara
Il pleut sans cesse sur Brest
Comme il pleuvait avant
Mais ce n'est plus pareil et tout est abîmé
C'est une pluie de deuil terrible et désolée
Ce n'est même plus l'orage
De fer d'acier de sang
Tout simplement des nuages
Qui crèvent comme des chiens
Des chiens qui disparaissent
Au fil de l'eau sur Brest
Et vont pourrir au loin
Au loin très loin de Brest
Dont il ne reste rien.

At the time it was recited by Yves Montand, a famous actor and singer of the day, on a record — a 78 — which got the Grand Prix du

Disque and when we played that record there wasn't a dry eye in the house. We all had come through a war and felt exactly the same way about our own Barbaras and bombed-out city.

Prévert, by the way, had many of his poems set to music and they were sung by Montand and other singers of the day. They were just as popular as Bob Dylan with a later generation. I'm afraid we knew very little about what went on in England and Ireland, poetry and music-wise.

I could quote you some more Dutch poems but that won't make much sense, so we'll leave it at that. Here's another Prévert:

La vie est brève
un peu de rêve
un peu d'amour
et puis — bonjour

Yours,
Gerrit van Gelderen

THEODORA FITZGIBBON   34

20 April 1985

Dear Collette Lucy et al,
I only just received your letter as I was away in England and only just home before setting off again next week. What an impossible thing you ask: my favourite poem! There is no such thing as far as I am concerned, I love so many and it would be very difficult to choose one.
However having said that I suppose I must perhaps put Dylan (Thomas) high on my list. One of his I am particularly fond of is 'Poem in October'.
This poem means quite a lot to me for I remember Dylan talking about it and reading some of the lines just before he finished it. I still hear that wonderfully sonorous voice filling our small sitting room with the music of his magical words.
Also we both shared a late October birthday which we sometimes spent together so it has a particular meaning. I had met him a few years earlier and by the time this poem was written we were firm friends.
Best wishes and all success to your venture,

Sincerely,
Theodora FitzGibbon

Poem in October

It was my thirtieth year to heaven
Woke to my hearing from harbour and neighbour wood
        And the mussel pooled and the heron
                Priested shore
                The morning beckon
With water praying and call of seagull and rook
And the knock of sailing boats on the net webbed wall
                Myself to set foot
                    That second
In the still sleeping town and set forth.

My birthday began with the water —
Birds and the birds of the winged trees flying my name
        Above the farms and the white horses
                And I rose
                In the rainy autumn
And walked abroad in a shower of all my days.
High tide and the heron dived when I took the road
                Over the border
                And the gates
Of the town closed as the town awoke.

A springful of larks in a rolling
Cloud and the roadside bushes brimming with whistling
        Blackbirds and the sun of October
                Summery
                On the hill's shoulder,
Here were fond climates and sweet singers suddenly
Come in the morning where I wandered and listened
                To the rain wringing
                    Wind blow cold
In the wood faraway under me.

Pale rain over the dwindling harbour
And over the sea wet church the size of a snail
        With its horns through mist and the castle
                Brown as owls
                But all the gardens
Of spring and summer were blooming in the tall tales
Beyond the border and under the lark full cloud.
                There could I marvel
                    My birthday
Away but the weather turned around.

It turned away from the blithe country
And down the other air and the blue altered sky
        Streamed again a wonder of summer
                With apples
            Pears and red currants

And I saw in the turning so clearly a child's
Forgotten mornings when he walked with his mother
        Through the parables
          Of sun light
  And the legends of the green chapels

  And the twice told fields of infancy
That his tears burned my cheeks and his heart moved in mine.
    These were the woods the river and sea
        Where a boy
      In the listening
Summertime of the dead whispered the truth of his joy
To the trees and the stones and the fish in the tide.
      And the mystery
        Sang alive
  Still in the water and singingbirds.

  And there could I marvel my birthday
Away but the weather turned around. And the true
    Joy of the long dead child sang burning
        In the sun.
    It was my thirtieth
Year to heaven stood there then in the summer noon
Though the town below lay leaved with October blood.
    O may my heart's truth
      Still be sung
  On this high hill in a year's turning.

Dylan Thomas (1914–1953)

ALAN DUKES   35

April 1985

Dear Collette, Joy and Steven,
I received your letter on 4 April last and regret the fact that it has taken me some little time to reply.
I read very little poetry, and read it in a rather unsystematic way. That being the case, I have no 'favourite' poem to which I would return very frequently. Some time ago, however, I came across 'June Thunder' by Louis MacNeice, and it made quite an impression on me. It captures for me the atmosphere and the sense of summer. The senses are filled with the richness of the surroundings, and the mind follows this richness in its own course.
Then comes the thunder storm which, after the event, seems like release. And yet there is a longing for something that will survive the cleansing of the thunder storm.

Yours sincerely,
Alan Dukes

June Thunder

The Junes were free and full, driving through tiny
Roads, the mudguards brushing the cowparsley,
Through fields of mustard and under boldly embattled
    Mays and chestnuts

Or between beeches verdurous and voluptuous
Or where broom and gorse beflagged the chalkland —
All the flare and gusto of the unenduring
    Joys of a season

Now returned but I note as more appropriate
To the maturer mood impending thunder
With an indigo sky and the garden hushed except for
    The treetops moving.

Then the curtains in my room blow suddenly inward,
The shrubbery rustles, birds fly heavily homeward,
The white flowers fade to nothing on the trees and rain comes
    Down like a dropscene.

Now there comes the catharsis, the cleansing downpour
Breaking the blossoms of our overdated fancies
Our old sentimentality and whimsicality
    Loves of the morning.

Blackness at half-past eight, the night's precursor,
Clouds like falling masonry and lightning's lavish
Annunciation, the sword of the mad archangel
    Flashed from the scabbard.

If only you would come and dare the crystal
Rampart of rain and the bottomless moat of thunder,
If only now you would come I should be happy
    Now if now only.

Louis MacNeice (1907–1963)

NOELLE CAMPBELL-SHARP   36

9 May 1985

Dear Miss Lucy,
Noelle Campbell-Sharp has asked me to write to thank you for your
letter re your anthology of poems. Noelle's favourite poem is 'As
Slow Our Ship' by Thomas Moore.

Yours sincerely,
Nell Stewart-Liberty

As Slow Our Ship

As slow our ship her foamy track
    Against the wind was cleaving,
Her trembling pennant still look'd back
    To that dear Isle 'twas leaving.
So loath we part from all we love,
    From all the links that bind us;
So turn our hearts as on we rove,
    To those we've left behind us.

When, round the bowl, of vanish'd years
    We talk, with joyous seeming, —
With smiles that might as well be tears,
    So faint, so sad their beaming;
While mem'ry brings us back again
    Each early tie that twined us,
Oh, sweet's the cup that circles then
    To those we've left behind us.

And when, in other climes, we meet
    Some isle, or vale enchanting,
Where all looks flow'ry, wild and sweet,
    And nought but love is wanting;
We think how great had been our bliss,
    If Heav'n had but assign'd us
To live and die in scenes like this,
    With some we've left behind us!

As trav'llers oft look back at eve,
    When eastward darkly going,
To gaze upon the light they leave
    Still faint behind them glowing, —
So when the close of pleasure's day
    To gloom hath near consign'd us,
We turn to catch one fading ray
    Of joy that's left behind us.

Thomas Moore (1779–1852)

OLLIE CAMPBELL   37

14 May 1985

Dear girls and Steven,
Please forgive me for not writing sooner. I am sure I am probably too late to help but if not here we go.
My favourite poem is 'Daffodils' by William Wordsworth. It is simple (like myself!) and for me is synonymous with being at peace.

It is spring-time, the sun is out though it is not too warm, pretty
girls are wearing their summer frocks for the first time AND the
rugby season is nearing its club climax! Though excitement is in the
air I feel calm and I feel good in myself and with the world. That's
what 'Daffodils' does for me.
Best of luck with the idea,

Yours,
Ollie Campbell

I wandered lonely as a cloud

I wandered lonely as a cloud
That floats on high o'er vales and hills,
When all at once I saw a crowd,
A host, of golden daffodils;
Beside the lake, beneath the trees,
Fluttering and dancing in the breeze.

Continuous as the stars that shine
And twinkle on the milky way,
They stretched in never-ending line
Along the margin of a bay:
Ten thousand saw I at a glance,
Tossing their heads in sprightly dance.

The waves beside them danced; but they
Out-did the sparkling waves in glee:
A poet could not but be gay,
In such a jocund company:
I gazed — and gazed — but little thought
What wealth the show to me had brought:

For oft, when on my couch I lie
In vacant or in pensive mood,
They flash upon that inward eye
Which is the bliss of solitude;
And then my heart with pleasure fills,
And dances with the daffodils.

William Wordsworth (1770–1850)

LIAM Ó MURCHÚ   38

Be Still as You are Beautiful

Be still as you are beautiful,
  Be silent as the rose;
Through miles of starlit countryside
  Unspoken worship flows
To find you in your loveless room
  From lonely men whom daylight gave
The blessing of your passing face
  Impenetrably grave.

A white owl in the lichened wood
  Is circling silently,
More secret and more silent yet
  Must be your love to me.
Thus, while about my dreaming head
  Your soul in ceaseless vigil goes,
Be still as you are beautiful,
  Be silent as the rose.

Patrick MacDonogh (1902–1961)

*A perfect lyric, as lovely as the best of Yeats, and with a haunting
and masterly sense of rhythm and sound.*

Le gach dea-ghuí,
Liam Ó Murchú

MARGARET DRABBLE   39

13 May 1985

Dear Collette, Joy and Steven,
Impossible to choose one *favourite but never mind, here is one of my
favourites — the three stanzas by Blake that begin:*

  Never seek to tell thy love.

*I love this poem because it is sad — I have always liked sad poems
best, I think — and because it is mysterious and yet compact and
because it catches the difficulty and fragility of love. I don't really
know what it means, but I respond to it very strongly.*
I hope this arrives in time and good luck with your anthology.

Yours sincerely,
Margaret Drabble

Never Seek to Tell Thy Love

Never seek to tell thy love
Love that never told can be;
For the gentle wind does move
Silently, invisibly.

I told my love, I told my love
I told her all my heart,
Trembling, cold, in ghastly fears —
Ah, she doth depart.

Soon as she was gone from me
A traveller came by
Silently, invisibly —
O, was no deny.

William Blake (1757–1827)

T P FLANAGAN   40

Thank you for your letter. One of my favourite poems is Seamus Heaney's 'Bogland' — from Door into the Dark. *This is not simply because he dedicated the poem to me, which naturally pleased me very much, but because he and I had been together at the poem's beginnings. Seamus and I and our families had spent Hallowe'en together in McFaddens Hotel at Gortahork in County Donegal. And he came with me when I went out sketching in the car. It was a dry luminous Autumn, and after the hot summer of that year the bogland was burnt the colour of marmalade. We all stood on the beach watching marvellous sunsets, and, in the twilight let off fireworks from the sand dunes to please our children. The poem is a celebration for me of a very happy and creative time in both our lives.*

Good luck with your project,
T P Flanagan

Bogland
for T P Flanagan

We have no praries
To slice a big sun at evening —
Everywhere the eye concedes to
Encroaching horizon,

Is wooed into the cyclops' eye
Of a tarn. Our unfenced country
Is bog that keeps crusting
Between the sights of the sun.

They've taken the skeleton
Of the Great Irish Elk
Out of the peat, set it up
An astounding crate full of air.

Butter sunk under
More than a hundred years
Was recovered salty and white.
The ground itself is kind, black butter

Melting and opening underfoot,
Missing its last definition
By millions of years.
They'll never dig coal here,

Only the waterlogged trunks
Of great firs, soft as pulp.
Our pioneers kept striking
Inwards and downwards,

Every layer they strip
Seems camped on before.
The bogholes might be Atlantic seepage.
The wet centre is bottomless.

Seamus Heaney (b. 1939)

TOMÁS Ó FIAICH   41

26 April 1985

Dear Collette, Joy and Steven,
Thank you for your letter enquiring about my favourite poem. I have
many favourite poems and the one I would mention to you is
'Pangur Bán' where an old monk in his scriptorium philosophises on
the meaning of life for himself and his pet cat 'Pangur Bán'. Every
time I read the poem I can see the two of them in my mind's eye as
each goes about his work.
I wish you every success with your project and remain,

Yours sincerely,
† Tomás Ó Fiaich
Cardinal Archbishop of Armagh

The Monk and His Pet Cat
(A marginal poem on *Codex S Pauli*, by a student of the monastery of Carinthia.)

I and my white Pangur
Each has his special art;
His mind is set on hunting mice
Mine on my special craft.

Better than fame I love to rest
With close study of my little book;
White Pangur does not envy me,
He loves to ply his childish art.

When we two are alone in our house
It is a tale without tedium;
Each of us has games never ending
Something to sharpen our wit upon.

At times by feats of valour
A mouse sticks in his net,
While in my net there drops
A loved law of obscure meaning.

His eye, this flashing full one,
He points against the fence wall
While against the fine edge of science
I point my clear but feeble eye.

He is joyous with swift jumping
When a mouse sticks in his sharp claw,
And I too am joyous when I have grasped
The elusive but well loved problem.

Though we thus play at all times
Neither hinders the other —
Each is happy with his own art,
Pursues it with delight.

He is master of the work
Which he does every day
While I am master of my work
Bringing to obscure laws clarity.

Anonymous (eighth or early ninth century)
Version based on translations by Whitley Stokes, John Strachan and Kuno Meyer.

HELEN LUCY BURKE 42

11 May 1985

Dear Collette Lucy, Joy Marshall and Steven Given,
I think your idea of a poetry collection is a delightful idea, and I wish
you every success with it.
After hemming and hawing for several days, rejecting some poems
because they were too long, others because they were too obscene —
or at least a trifle warm — and others because they were in the wrong
language (for I decided that you wanted English), after refreshing my
memory with the printed word, after all this, I say, I finally settled on
a poem by William Blake. It is called 'The Mental Traveller'.
I cannot give any coherent reason why I love it so, except that it has
the magic of incantation. The meaning changes every time I read or
recite it (for I have committed it to memory for use on long voyages).
I am certain that it is about Love and Hate and Death and Renewal
and Cruelty, and the Beauty of Wildness: the six last things.

Helen Lucy Burke

The Mental Traveller

I traveld thro' a Land of Men
A land of Men & Women too
And heard & saw such dreadful things
As cold Earth wanderers never knew

For there the Babe is born in joy
That was begotten in dire woe
Just as we Reap in joy the fruit
Which we in bitter tears did sow

And if the Babe is born a Boy
He's given to a Woman Old
Who nails him down upon a rock
Catches his shrieks in cups of gold

She binds iron thorns around his head
She pierces both his hands & feet
She cuts his heart out at his side
To make it feel both cold & heat

Her fingers number every Nerve
Just as a Miser counts his gold
She lives upon his shrieks and cries
And she grows young as he grows old

Till he becomes a bleeding youth
And she becomes a Virgin bright
Then he rends up his Manacles
And binds her down for his delight

He plants himself in all her Nerves
Just as a Husbandman his mould
And she becomes his dwelling place
And Garden fruitful seventy fold

An aged Shadow soon he fades
Wandring round an Earthly Cot
Full filled all with gems & gold
Which he by industry had got

And these are the gems of the Human Soul
The rubies & pearls of a lovesick eye
The countless gold of the akeing heart
The martyrs groan & the lovers sigh

They are his meat and they are his drink
He feeds the Beggar & the Poor
And the wayfaring Traveller
For ever open is his door

His grief is their eternal joy
They make the roofs & walls to ring
Till from the fire on the hearth
A little Female Babe does spring

And she is all of solid fire
And gems & gold that none his hand
Dares stretch to touch her Baby form
Or wrap her in his swaddling-band

But She comes to the Man she loves
If young or old or rich or poor
They soon drive out the aged Host
A Beggar at anothers door

He wanders weeping far away
Untill some other take him in
Oft blind & age-bent sore distrest
Until he can a Maiden win

And to allay his freezing Age
The Poor Man takes her in his arms
The Cottage fades before his sight
The Garden & its lovely Charms

The Guests are scattered thro' the land
For the Eye altering alters all
The Senses roll themselves in fear
And the flat Earth becomes a Ball

The Stars Sun Moon all shrink away
A desart vast without a bound
And nothing left to eat or drink
And a dark desart all around

The honey of her Infant lips
The bread & wine of her sweet smile
The wild game of her roving Eye
Does him to Infancy beguile

For as he eats & drinks he grows
Younger & younger every day
And on the desart wild they both
Wander in terror & dismay

Like the wild Stag she flees away
Her fear plants many a thicket wild
While he pursues her night & day
By various arts of Love beguild

By various arts of Love & Hate
Till the wide desart planted oer
With Labyrinths of wayward Love
Where roams the Lion Wolf & Boar

Till he becomes a wayward Babe
And she a weeping Woman Old
Then many a Lover wanders here
The Sun & Stars are nearer rolld

The trees bring forth sweet Extacy
To all who in the desart roam
Till many a City there is Built
And many a pleasant Shepherds home

But when they find the frowning Babe
Terror strikes thro the region wide
They cry the Babe the Babe is Born
and flee away on Every side

For who dare touch the frowning form
His arm is withered to its root
Lions Boars Wolves all howling flee
And every tree does shed its fruit

And none can touch that frowning form
Except it be a Woman Old
She nails him down upon the Rock
And all is done as I have told.

William Blake (1757–1827)

CYRIL CUSACK   43

Dear Collette, Joy and Steven,
Let me congratulate you on this very original and laudable effort of
yours to succour the poor people of the Third World. The effort
deserves every support.
Now, another thing, it is not clear to me whether you wish to have a
poem selected from my own two slender volumes of published poetry
or rather a poem I favour from the work of major poets. I think
probably the latter, but to choose my 'favourite poem' of the many
that appeal to me obviously presents a difficulty.
However, I think my only plan is to suggest two poems which for me
have a special appeal, one by Hopkins, the other by Kavanagh; and
one from myself.

'A Christmas Childhood' by Patrick Kavanagh
and
'Felix Randal' by Gerard Manley Hopkins

My reasons for these preferences are almost impossible to articulate
because they are scarcely rational, rather are they intuitive. I respond
to them emotionally, perhaps because I am an actor.
However, I may say that I relate to 'A Christmas Childhood'
because — vide the title — it is a pure evocation of the poet's
childhood, of a child's intake of beauty in so many forms and images,
and through the experiences and details of his country life and home
in its beginnings, a perfect recall of true innocence, spiritually
significant and sustaining into age. And, of course, it is tenderly,
exquisitely rendered in the verse.   ·
This poem I have spoken for audience on two occasions, once in the
National Concert Hall and again on Irish television, and on each
occasion I found myself or, rather should I say, lost myself in
identification with the poet as a child.
With this, as with 'Felix Randal', let it be said that identification
with the poet is the most desirable condition for the rendering of true
poetry, allowing no intrusion of 'theatricality' or pretence, or even a
priority of technical excellence. And what endears me to this
particular poem of Hopkins is the passionate, near Christlike,
compassion for 'child Felix, poor Felix Randal', the farrier. And,
however difficult, I would say, as in my experience, that the emotion
will carry the speaker, identifying with the poet, even through the
delicate intricacies of the verse. 'Felix Randal', some years ago, I was
privileged to commit to record and I treasure the compliment I had
from a fellow Jesuit of the poet-priest: that in hearing the record it
was as though for him, in some mysterious way, he were listening to
Gerard Manley Hopkins himself.

For my own poem which I enclose let it suffice that, as an actor, my preference for this over other poems I have written rests in the title.

Yours sincerely,
Cyril Cusack

A Christmas Childhood

I
One side of the potato-pits was white with frost —
How wonderful that was, how wonderful!
And when we put our ears to the paling-post
The music that came out was magical.

The light between the ricks of hay and straw
Was a hole in Heaven's gable. An apple tree
With its December-glinting fruit we saw —
O you, Eve, were the world that tempted me

To eat the knowledge that grew in clay
And death the germ within it! Now and then
I can remember something of the gay
Garden that was childhood's. Again

The tracks of cattle to a drinking-place,
A green stone lying sideways in a ditch
Or any common sight the transfigured face
Of a beauty that the world did not touch.

II
My father played the melodeon
Outside at our gate;
There were stars in the morning east
And they danced to his music.

Across the wild bogs his melodeon called
To Lennons and Callans.
As I pulled on my trousers in a hurry
I knew some strange thing had happened.

Outside the cow-house my mother
Made the music of milking;
The light of her stable-lamp was a star
And the frost of Bethlehem made it twinkle.

A water-hen screeched in the bog,
Mass-going feet
Crunched the wafer-ice on the pot holes,
Somebody wistfully twisted the bellows wheel.

My child poet picked out the letters
On the grey stone,
In silver the wonder of a Christmas townland,
The winking glitter of a frosty dawn.

Cassiopeia was over
Cassidy's hanging hill,
I looked and three whin bushes rode across
The horizon — the Three Wise Kings.

An old man passing said:
'Can't he make it talk' —
The melodeon. I hid in the doorway
And tightened the belt of my box-pleated coat.

I nicked six nicks on the door-post
With my penknife's big blade —
There was a little one for cutting tobacco.
And I was six Christmases of age.

My father played the melodeon,
My mother milked the cows,
And I had a prayer like a white rose pinned
On the Virgin Mary's blouse.

Patrick Kavanagh (1904–1967)

Felix Randal

Felix Randal the farrier, O he is dead then? my duty all ended,
Who have watched his mould of man, big-boned and hardy-
    handsome
Pining, pining, till time when reason rambled in it and some
Fatal four disorders, fleshed there, all contended?

Sickness broke him. Impatient, he cursed at first, but mended
Being annointed and all; though a heavenlier heart began some
Months earlier, since I had our sweet reprieve and ransom
Tendered to him. Ah well, God rest him all road ever he
    offended!

This seeing the sick endears them to us, us too it endears.
My tongue had taught thee comfort, touch had quenched thy
    tears,
Thy tears that touched my heart, child, Felix, poor Felix
    Randal;

How far from then forethought of, all thy more boisterous
    years,
When thou at the random grim forge, powerful amidst peers,
Didst fettle for the great grey drayhorse his bright and
    battering sandal!

Gerard Manley Hopkins (1844–1889)

Confiteor

O dear my Lord, but what a tricky
cute and cunning customer in me
you have across your counter, one
eluding true communion's equity.

That you, you Three in One and One in Three,
could fail to see through me, could be
wide open to my wide-eyed bribery
or guiltily contrive —
you, Father, Holy Spirit and the Son —
to look the other way, conniving
at the filching and the fun
of taking all for free . . . say
which of us would thus betray,
pretending Satan's not alive!

O I can fake and I can fable,
I can fiddle, fib and fumble,
glibly gamble with you, Lord
(and tell me, boys, who better able!)
provide you do not grumble
that I blunt Saint Michael's sword,
lay not all my cards upon your table,
refusing me, accusing me
that I, I only ape humility,
in pride but feigning to be humble.

I myself with guiltless smile
myself beguiling, shall I you beguile!

Cyril Cusack (b. 1910)

DEREK DAVIS   44

RTE
11 April 1985

Dear Collette and friends,
Thank you for your invitation to contribute to such a worthwhile
project. There are a number of poets whose work I have dipped into
with pleasure, but as a journalist I greatly admire the ability of the
Augustans to be both stylish and succinct. My favourite of these was
an old country Vicar called George Crabbe whose best known work is
a collection called 'The Parish Register' from which the story of
Peter Grimes is taken. My favourite Crabbe poem is 'The Death of
Widow Goe'. Any journalist who could provide such a
comprehensive character study in such a short amount of space

would be much in demand.
I remember Crabbe's work with affection because it was introduced to
me by an old school master called Fergus O'Duffy who opened the
door for many of us to an appreciation of literature.

Best wishes,
Derek Davis

from *The Parish Register*

Next died the Widow Goe, an active dame,
Famed ten miles round, and worthy all her fame;
She lost her husband when their loves were young,
But kept her farm, her credit and her tongue:
Full thirty years she ruled, with matchless skill,
With guiding judgement and resistless will;
Advice she scorned, rebellions she suppressed,
And sons and servants bow'd at her behest . . .
Thus long she reigned, admired, if not approved
Praised, if not honoured; feared, if not beloved —
When as the busy days of spring drew near . . .
Then dread o'ercame her that her days were spent.
'Bless me! I die, and not a warning given
With much to do on earth . . . .
My mind unsettled and my will unmade —
A lawyer haste, and in your way, a priest;
And let me die in one good work at least'
She spake, and trembling, dropped upon her knees,
Heaven in her eye and in her hand her keys . . . .

George Crabbe (1754–1832)

SEÁN LUCY   45

7 May 1985

Dear Collette, Joy and Steven,
I enclose a copy of a poem by an Irish poet, Patrick Galvin. Patrick
Galvin is still alive and is a member of Aosdána.
This is not my favourite poem, it is one of my favourite poems. I
don't have a favourite poem and think that if one knows a great deal
of poetry it is almost impossible to have an absolute favourite. There
are so many kinds of poetry. I therefore decided to send you a poem
which speaks to the twentieth century and to its needs and sorrows in
a way that most people can understand, and which is in its own right
a very fine piece of work.
You ask for a few lines to say why I like the poem. I like it because it

is realistic; because it says what can happen to whole groups of people, and also to the individual soul in real life and in real persecution. I like it because it is full of anger and humour which are hidden behind the official words of the regulations in a way that gives a fine tension to the poem. I like it because of its enormous mastery of rhythm, which makes it both into a plain set of rules and into a great angry invocation of how things should not be for the human spirit and for human lives.

I hope that this is of some use to you and I apologise for not getting in touch sooner. I was out of the country for a while.

Every good wish with the project,

Yours very sincerely,
Seán Lucy

Prisoners of the Tower

I can see them now
Prisoners of the tower
Their faces blind
From centuries of barbed-wire.

If you are guilty
You know you are guilty
If you are innocent
You would not be here.

You are here
Therefore . . .

When the cell door closes
Behind you
You are free.
When the cell door closes
Behind you
You are free.
When the cell door closes behind you
It will remain closed
But you are free to weep
Endlessly — without tears.

It is an offence to shed tears
In the tower
It is an offence to grow old
In the tower
It is an offence to sit
In the tower
But you may walk freely
From wall to wall
And contemplate the absence
Of bread.

Under our system of Government
A man has these rights:
You may walk freely from wall to wall
And contemplate the absence of bread.

You may hear voices.

All prisoners
Who hear voices
Will report such voices
To the Keeper of the tower.
These voices do not exist
And if they do exist
They will be shot.
The shooting of voices
Is essential
To the harmony of the tower.

All prisoners
Who fail to report the hearing of voices
Will be shot.
All prisoners
Who report the hearing of voices
Will be sent to a lunatic asylum.
Prisoners
Who are sent to a lunatic asylum
May lose the freedom of the tower
But the voices will stop.

Under our system of Government
A man has these rights:
You may lose the freedom of the tower
But you will not hear voices.

You are free to die.

All prisoners
Are entitled to death.
All prisoners
Are entitled to a speedy death.
Any prisoner
Unable to commit suicide
Will be shot.
Any prisoner
Failing to report a desire to commit suicide
Will be shot.

When a prisoner dies in his cell
His body will remain in his cell.
It is an offence to remove the dead
From their cells.

It is assumed that in due time
Nature will corrupt the flesh
But the bones, if any
Remain the sole property of the prisoner.
He may return for these bones
at any time.

Under our system of Government
The dead also have rights:
You may return for these bones
At any time.

You are free to have them.

Patrick Galvin (b. 1927)

DON COCKBURN   46

RTE

Dear Collette,
It was very kind of you to invite me to contribute to your proposed
anthology. Although I like poetry I cannot say that I have a favourite
poem. However, I'll nominate three and leave it to you to choose the
one most suitable for your anthology.
'The Drover' by Padraic Colum seems to me to bring together some
of the most vital and vibrant elements of this island of ours —
elements which must impress themselves on anybody born here.
There's the Atlantic climate:

  'Wet hills by the sea'
and
  'the wet winding roads
  Brown bogs with black water'

and Cattle — the age-old measure of Irish wealth:

  'their slipping and breathing'
and
  'O the smell of the beasts,
  The wet wind in the morn
  And the proud and hard earth'

But it's the following stanza that for me most typifies the traditional
Irish scene — 'part of what we are'.

  'And the crowds at the fair
  The herds loosened and blind
  Loud words and dark faces
  And the wild blood behind'.

I have to nominate something by Dylan Thomas because his poetry comes so close to music — my first love. I have chosen 'Fern Hill', which is full of magic and the final lines are like the ending of some great symphony.

Oh as I was young and easy in the mercy of his means,
   Time held me green and dying
  Though I sang in my chains like the sea.

The sea also comes into my third choice — a stanza by Swinburne written into one of my old notebooks. It says all I could wish to say about those early youthful swims at various points on the East coast from Bettystown down to Rosslare. Oh the magic of those mornings! As one that ere a June day rise . . .

Best of luck with the project.

Yours sincerely,
Don Cockburn

As one that ere a June day rise
Makes seaward for the dawn and tries
The water with delighted limbs
That tastes the sweet dark sea, that swims
Right eastward under strengthening skies,
And sees the gradual rippling rims
Of waves whence day breaks blossom wise
Take fire ere light peer well above
And laughs from all his heart.

Algernon Charles Swinburne (1837–1909)

MICK LALLY   47

RTE

Dear Miss Lucy et al,
Sorry for inordinate delay but I hope I'm not too late. I've been moving house and everything got mixed up and delayed.
It's a great idea and I hope it works out well and exciting for you all. Enclosed find 'Saoirse' by Seán Ó Ríordáin.
For many years, Seán Ó Ríordáin was one of our foremost poets writing in the Irish language. Many, including myself, would regard him as one of the finest poets to write in modern Ireland.
That he, and others writing in Irish, were not included in recent

anthologies of poetry in Ireland render those anthologies incomplete and not wholly representative. 'Saoirse' is typical of Ó Ríordáin's poetry. He is obsessed with questioning himself and by extension us. He is obsessed with language, creativity, and perhaps, more importantly, spirituality. He is obsessed with the Irish language and with extending the potency and the precision of the language.

Writers of plays are generally referred to as playwrights. Poets often as word-smiths; this, of course, should be wordwrights. Ó Ríordáin was a wordwright and he wrought well in a language in need of much wrighting.

Yours sincerely,
Mick Lally

Saoirse

Raghaidh mé síos i measc na ndaoine
De shiúl mo chos
Is raghaidh mé síos anocht.

Raghaidh mé síos ag lorg daoirse
Ón mbinibshaoirse
Tá ag liú anseo:

Is ceanglód an chonairt smaointe
Tá ag drannadh im thimpeall
San uaigneas:

Is loirgeod an teampall rialta
Bhíonn lán de dhaoine
Ag am fé leith:

Is loirgeod comhluadar daoine
Nár chleacht riamh saoirse,
Ná uaigneas:

Is éistfead leis na scillingsmaointe,
A malartaítear
Mar airgead:

Is bhféarfad gean mo chroí do dhaoine
Nár samhlaídh riamh leo
Ach macsmaointe.

Ó fanfad libh de ló is d'oíche,
Is beidh mé íseal,
Is beidh mé dílis,
D'bhur snabsmaointe.

Mar do chuala iad ag fás im intinn,
Ag fás gan chuimse,
Gan mheasarthacht.

Is do thugas gean mo chroí go fíochmhar
Don rud tá srianta,
Don gach macrud:

Don smacht, don reacht, don teampall daoineach,
Don bhfocal bocht coitianta
Don am fé leith:

Don ab, don chlog, don seirbhíseach
Don chomparáid fhaitíosach,
Don bheaguchtach:

Don luch, don tomhas, don dreancaid bhídeach,
Don chaibidil, don líne
Don aibítir:

Don mhórgacht imeachta is tíochta,
Don chearrbhachas istoíche,
Don bheannachtain:

Don bhfeirmeoir ag tomhas na gaoithe
Sa bhfómhar is é ag cuimhneamh
Ar pháirc eornan:

Don chomhthuiscint, don chomh-sheanchuimhne,
Do chomhiompar comhdhaoine,
Don chomh-mhacrud.

Is bheirim fuath anois is choíche
Do imeachtaí na saoirse,
Don neamhspleáchas.

Is atuirseach an intinn
A thit in iomar doimhin na saoirse,
Ní mhaireann cnoc dar chruthaigh Dia ann,
Ach cnoic theibí, sainchnoic shamhlaíochta.
Is bíonn gach cnoc díobh lán de mhianta
Ag dreapadóireacht gan chomhlíonadh,
Níl teora leis an saoirse
Ná le cnoca na samhlaíochta,
Ná níl teora leis na mianta,
Ná faoiseamh
Le fáil.

Seán Ó Ríordáin (1916–1977)

Liberty

I will go down amongst the people
on foot
and I will go down tonight.

I will go down seeking bondage
from the venom-liberty
that howls here:

And I will tie the pack of thoughts
that snarl round me
in the solitude:

And I will seek an ordered temple
where people congregate
at a set time:

And I will seek out people
who never practised liberty
or solitude:

And I will listen to the shilling-thoughts
that are exchanged
like money:

And I will give the love of my heart to people
who never imagined
other than second hand.

Oh, I will remain with you day and night,
And I will be lowly
and I will be faithful
to your stub-thoughts.

Because I heard them grow in my mind,
grow without control,
without moderation.

And I gave my heart's love fiercely
to the thing that is bridled,
to every copied thing:

To discipline, to law, to the peopled temple,
To the poor and commonplace word,
to the set time:

To the abbott, the bell, the servant,
to the hesitant comparison,
to cowardice:

To the mouse, to measurement, to the tiny flea,
to the chapter and the line
to the alphabet:

To the majesty of going and coming,
to gambling at night,
to salutations:

To the farmer measuring the wind
in the autumn as he thinks
of a field of barley:

To co-understanding, to co-tradition,
to co-behaviour of co-people,
to the co-copied thing.

And I bestow my hatred now and forever
on the doings of liberty,
on independence.

Weary is the mind
that has fallen in the deep trough of liberty,
no hill erected by God exists there,
only abstract hills, the particular hills of the imagination,
and each such hill is full of desires,
climbing, unfulfilled,
liberty is without limit,
so are the hills of the imagination,
the desires are unlimited,
and there exists
no release.

TONY O'MALLEY   48

13 May 1985

To: Collette Lucy
Joy Marshall
Steven Given
of Form V

Dear Above,
I hope you will excuse the delay in replying to your letter (may I say
I feel honoured that you asked me and I would love to help such a
good cause in any way I can). Your idea of an anthology is an
excellent one and I wish you every success.
I have many favourite poems — but for me the poetry of a modern
Irish poet stands out. He was the late Padraic Fallon (died October
1974). One of his poems I particularly like — it is called 'Book of
Job'. What can I say about this poem except that it has a profound
and powerful effect on me at each reading and it has to be read over
and over again to experience this.
I do hope I have been of some assistance and again I wish you every
success in your charitable work and in your careers when you leave
school. It is good to hear of such good endeavours in these days.

Yours sincerely,
Tony O'Malley

Book of Job

The simple thing is to die
So often and painfully that I
One day in one breath
May live the whole life of death.

The daily thing is to be
Defeated daily, that this psychology
Of victory be unlearned
And sham into shame be turned.

For this Image is not Me;
This worldling satisfied and stately, with his family
Thanksgiving, and each day success,
The world always answering yes.

In this gift of luck I have lost
The naked traffic of the ghost,
Trapped in an image I projected
Not of God but God's elected.

So the next thing is to ride
Horse and all under and be no more a pride;
No, nor an humility,
For that's pride too, on one knee.

But to be nothing till
Flesh fall off and my heartbeat sounds real;
Until my heart is heard
Stammering with excitement its one word.

Come then rags and plagues
I am honoured to lend you my legs;
Enter this suffering house
Where honours fall off, where I delouse,

And bless me no more, You
In the twittering evening: O tall fall of dew,
You fathered me so much ease
I ponder all misery now to find my peace:

I have my occupation; I will die
Into nothing after nothing, but live no lie,
Stripped to a faint shiver, waiting here
On a faint illumination in the air.

Padraic Fallon (1905–1974)

BRIAN FARRELL   49

15 May 1985

Dear Wesley Form V,
That seems the best way round the collectivity. Forgive the delay in
writing. I'm afraid mail rather piles up. Now to your project which
sounds both fun and worthwhile. Would something like the following
do:
There is no simple answer to 'what is your favourite poem?' Choose
any one and you forego so many others. I'd be tempted to say the
Shakespeare sonnet — 'Shall I compare thee to a summer's day' —
must rank high. I first read the first two lines in an article and it
haunted me until I captured the full text. Or there's

Time was away and somewhere else
And you were there and I was there
And time was away

(Don't trust me on the lines) — that sticks in my mind because on
one occasion, rather exuberantly, I met Paddy Kavanagh and said
that it must be wonderful to be able to write something like that; he
grunted and eventually said 'Yes, only I didn't do it'. Among all the
modern Irish poets there is so much richness to choose — forced to
choose just one I think I'd plump for Austin Clarke:

Men that had seen her
Drank deep and were silent,
The women were speaking
Wherever she went —

Still among the lyrics it's hard to pass Byron — 'We'll go no more a
roving . . .' That's a name that turns your mind to satire. There's
Byron's own:

(So, we'll go no more a roving
    So late into the night)
I met murder on the way
    He wore a face like Castlereagh

and the deliciously bitchy poet on verse-makers:

Some people praise the restraint you show.
I'm with them there, of course.
You use the snaffle and the bit alright
But where's the bloody horse.

And, for some reason — maybe the tum-te-tum tone — I think of something entirely different like Belloc's still splendid Don John of Austria.

But, in the end of it all, push me into some dark anthological corner and hold me up to poetic ransom and I think it would be back to Yeats. Out of all that rich, musical, magnificent cornucopia of words it's difficult to do better than a poem I first heard from Dr Roger McHugh when I was a freshman student in University College thirty-five years ago:

Memory

One had a lovely face,
And two or three had charm,
But charm and face were in vain
Because the mountain grass
Cannot but keep the form
Where the mountain hare has lain.

Good luck with the enterprise,
Best wishes,

Sincerely,
Brian Farrell

SEAMUS HEANEY   50

18 May 1985

Dear Collette Lucy,
One of my favourite poems is 'Cuchulain Comforted' by W B Yeats. Written a few days before his death, it is a mysterious and difficult poem, but one which seems to fulfil Yeats's stated ambition 'to hold in a single thought reality and justice'. It presents a confrontation between heroism and cowardice, between violence and resignation, between life and death, and communicates a deep sense of peace and understanding.

Sincerely,
Seamus Heaney

Cuchulain Comforted

A man that had six mortal wounds, a man
Violent and famous, strode among the dead;
Eyes stared out of the branches and were gone.

Then certain Shrouds that muttered head to head
Came and were gone. He leant upon a tree
As though to meditate on wounds and blood.

A Shroud that seemed to have authority
Among those bird-like things came, and let fall
A bundle of linen. Shrouds by two and three

Came creeping up because the man was still.
And thereupon the linen-carrier said:
'Your life can grow much sweeter if you will

'Obey our ancient rule and make a shroud;
Mainly because of what we only know
The rattle of those arms makes us afraid.

'We thread the needles' eyes, and all we do
All must together do.' That done, the man
Took up the nearest and began to sew.

'Now we must sing and sing the best we can,
But first you must be told our character:
Convicted cowards all, by kindred slain

'Or driven from home and left to die in fear.'
They sang, but had nor human tunes nor words,
Though all was done in common as before;

They had changed their throats and had the throats of birds.

W B Yeats (1865–1939)

NELL McCAFFERTY   51

Dear Collette, Joy and Steven,
My favourite poem is 'Hens' by Evelyn Conlon. This is my favourite
poem because it was the only thing said during the entire campaign
to amend the Constitution on abortion that ever made sense to me.

Love,
Nell (McCafferty)

Hens

Author's note: This poem was written not as a public poem but
to make myself laugh during the 'anti-amendment' anti-
woman campaign of 1984, when women became for all intents

and purposes mere production machines. You wouldn't in fact
know during that year whether we were hens, chickens, eggs,
or egg carriers. I suspect the latter. I salute the hens of the
country, including the Battery ones.

P.S. 1992. More fiascoes, even more need for small private
words to make us titter.

I'm a hen
Yes I'm a hen
Indeed I'm a hen
But there's one thing I'm not
And that's a bird.

You just watch me sometime
when danger struts into our yard, threatening my chickens or
    me,
See the hair on my hen's neck get straighter
Just see how much beadier my eyes can get
when I look danger slap in the beak.
Yes I'm a hen
Of course I'm a hen
I don't mind being a hen
I'll tell you one thing I do mind though
— these people coming in here to our yard calling me a bird.

One day — funny thing — last week
I met Bessie.
She has no chickens
And I've more chickens than I can count.
We both dropped eggs and it *was* a funny thing —
we both said
suddenly —
— as if we'd discussed it before and we hadn't
'I'm not hatching That.' Full stop.
We walked away. Just walked away and left the poor eggs
    there.
No-one noticed.

Yes we're hens
Of course we are hens
More than half of Roosterkind is hens
Proud to be hens
Hard to be hens though sometimes
Just you mind you don't call us birds.
Times are hard enough for hens now.
Myself, I don't like clucking about it too much
I only get depressed
I have enough else to depress me what with my chickens and
    all that.

I KNOW there's all those hens stuck in cages
I KNOW they're only battery hens when they've finished with
   them
I KNOW we should do something
EVERYONE who has read THAT book knows we should do
   something
But I don't really have the time.
I don't want to go on about this
I don't want to go overboard or anything
But I think that's maybe why I deserted the egg that day.
(On top of everything else
You know — all the chickens I've had have been roosters.
I mean it's no laughing matter —
36 bloody roosters.
I'll tell you someone who never wants to hear that line again
It's another lovely Cock.)

You laugh — easy for you,
I had to rear the damn things as well.
And they'll probably grow up calling me a you know what.
Here I'm away, I'm getting depressed.

I AM a hen.
Of course I'm a hen
Proud to be a hen
Please please don't call me a bird.

Evelyn Conlon (b. 1952)

LIFELINES II

FRANK McGUINNESS   52

Sonnet 109

O, never say that I was false of heart,
Though absence seemed my flame to qualify.
As easy might I from myself depart
As from my soul, which in thy breast doth lie.
That is my home of love; if I have ranged,
Like him that travels I return again,
Just to the time, not with the time exchanged,
So that myself bring water for my stain.
Never believe, though in my nature reigned
All frailties that besiege all kinds of blood,
That it could so preposterously be stained
To leave for nothing all thy sum of good;
  For nothing this wide universe I call
  Save thou, my rose; in it thou art my all.

William Shakespeare (1564–1616)

This is one of my favourite poems because it is an expression of great love and I wish someone had written it for me.

Frank McGuinness   13 January 1988

EITHNE HAND   53

RTE
19 January 1988

Dear Julie, Jonathan and Duncan,
Thanks for your letter. I hope your planned book works out well and raises heaps of money. It's very difficult to pick an all-time favourite poem but I suppose I'd have to go for Robert Frost's 'The Road Not Taken'. Reasons? — well, it just seems to pop back into my head any time I come to a crossroads — either in actuality or metaphorically. The final verse in particular sums up that dilemma of choice — who's to say that the way we choose is the right one etc.
Hope this fits the bill!

Good luck, regards,
Eithne (Hand)

The Road Not Taken

Two roads diverged in a yellow wood,
And sorry I could not travel both
And be one traveler, long I stood
And looked down one as far as I could
To where it bent in the undergrowth;

Then took the other, as just as fair,
And having perhaps the better claim,
Because it was grassy and wanted wear;
Though as for that the passing there
Had worn them really about the same,

And both that morning equally lay
In leaves no step had trodden black.
Oh, I kept the first for another day!
Yet knowing how way leads on to way,
I doubted if I should ever come back.

I shall be telling this with a sigh
Somewhere ages and ages hence:
Two roads diverged in a wood, and I —
I took the one less traveled by,
And that has made all the difference.

Robert Frost (1874–1963)

GAY BYRNE   54

RTE
19 January 1988

Dear Compilers, all,
Glad to be included in your anthology. Hope you like my choice. I
cannot say it's my favourite poem of all time, but I found my wife
Kathleen reading it recently and it tickled my heart, for three reasons:
(1) I've been insulted, abused and kicked by TV viewers and radio
listeners so often through the years, that I'm sadistically delighted
when I see someone else getting a lash — even if they're dead.
(2) I'm a firm believer in the maxim that if you're going to do
someone down, you should do a thorough job; and I think you'll agree
that AMANDA ROS does a thorough job on her hated lawyer. No
pussyfooting or skirting the issue here — she lets her readers know
precisely her opinion of the offending corpse.
(3) Anyone who has had a run-in with the legal profession in this
country will relish the poem.

Gay Byrne

Amanda Ros was born in County Down. Lived 1860–1939. She had a major grudge against people in the legal profession, for what reason I do not know.

Jamie Jarr

Here lies a blooming rascal
Once known as Jamie Jarr;
A lawyer of the lowest type,
Who loved your name to char.
Of clownish ways and manners,
He aped at speaking fine,
Which proved as awkward to him
As a drawing-room to swine.

I stood while the ground was hollowed
To admit this pile of stink;
They placed the coffin upside down
(The men upon the brink).
How the stony mould did thunder
Upon the coffin's rump,
The fainter grew the rattle
The deeper Jamie sunk.

His mouth now shut for ever,
His lying tongue now stark —
His 'paws' lie still, and never more
Can stab you in the dark.
Earth is by far the richer,
Hell — one boarder more —
Heaven rejoices to be free
From such a legal 'bore'.

Amanda Ros (1860–1939)

MICHAEL HOLROYD   55

18 January 1988

Dear Julie Grantham, Jonathan Logue and Duncan Lyster,
Thanks for your letter inviting me to choose a favourite poem and give a reason for my choice. Good luck with the book which I hope makes a lot of money for Ethiopia.

Best wishes,
Michael Holroyd

'Biography' *by D J Enright.*
I like this poem because it brings together neatly and wittily, and
with considerable feeling, the arguments against what James Joyce
called literary 'biografiends' such as myself. It's a humane and
appealing case that D J Enright pleads, and one that any biographer
should confront before deciding whether to write someone's Life. *One*
possible defence may be found in Pope's Essay on Man:

'Know then thyself, presume not God to scan;
The proper study of mankind is man.'

Biography

Rest in one piece, old fellow
May no one make his money
Out of your odd poverty

Telling what you did
When the streets stared blankly back
And the ribbon fell slack

The girls you made
(And, worse, the ones you failed to)
The addled eggs you laid

Velleities that even you
Would hardly know you felt
But all biographers do

The hopes that only God could hear
(That great non-tattler)
Since no one else was near

What of your views on women's shoes?
If you collected orange peel
What *did* you do with the juice?

Much easier than your works
To sell your quirks
So burn your letters, hers and his —
Better no Life at all than this.

D J Enright (b. 1920)

FLEUR ADCOCK   56

17 January 1988

Dear Julie, Jonathan and Duncan,
Thank you for asking me to contribute to your book in aid of the
Third World. Naturally I'm happy to do so, but I find it an extra-

ordinarily difficult task. Because I'm involved with poetry all the time I have hundreds of favourite poems, and I'm constantly adding new ones or changing my mind about old ones. I couldn't possibly settle for one. (Also some of them are far too long for your purpose.)

So what I'm sending you is a poem which has been one of my favourites for a long time: John Donne's sonnet 'Death be not proud' (not a very original choice I'm afraid). Like many people's favourites, it's one that I've known by heart since I was at school: this means that I don't need to look it up when I want to be reminded of it; it's a permanent fixture in my mind. It's the kind of poem that would be comforting in circumstances of desperation or extremity, such as in prison or during a war — or so I imagine. It was included in the second book of poetry I ever bought (at 16; the first was by T S Eliot). I'm enclosing a copy of the text in the original spelling.

And good luck with the project!

Yours sincerely,
Fleur Adcock

Death Be Not Proud

Death be not proud, though some have called thee
Mighty and dreadfull, for, thou art not soe,
For, those, whom thou think'st, thou dost overthrow,
Die not, poore death, nor yet canst thou kill mee.
From rest and sleepe, which but thy pictures bee,
Much pleasure, then from thee, much more must flow,
And soonest our best men with thee doe goe,
Rest of their bones, and soules deliverie.
Thou art slave to Fate, Chance, kings, and desperate men,
And dost with poyson, warre, and sicknesse dwell,
And poppie, or charmes can make us sleepe as well,
And better then thy stroake; why swell'st thou then?
One short sleepe past, wee wake eternally,
And death shall be no more; death, thou shalt die.

John Donne (1572–1631)

SARA BERKELEY   57

18 January 1988

Dear Julie, Jonathan and Duncan,
I was really chuffed to get your letter and would love to contribute to your book for such a great cause. It's a really simple, interesting way of making a bit of money for Ethiopia.
My favourite poem is Stevie Smith's 'Not Waving but Drowning'.

It may seem like a morbid poem but I like it because it is so matter-of-fact and simple. I think of it often when I'm waving to people and hope they don't imagine I'm drowning, and sometimes I think of it when I'm drowning and wish someone would realise I wasn't waving.

The best of luck with Lifelines!
Sara Berkeley

Not Waving But Drowning

Nobody heard him, the dead man,
But still he lay moaning:
I was much further out than you thought
And not waving but drowning.

Poor chap, he always loved larking
And now he's dead
It must have been too cold for him his heart gave way,
They said.

Oh, no no no, it was too cold always
(Still the dead one lay moaning)
I was much too far out all my life
And not waving but drowning.

Stevie Smith (1902–1971)

VICTOR GRIFFIN   58

St Patrick's Deanery
St Patrick's Close
Dublin 8
15 January 1988

Dear Julie, Jonathan and Duncan,
Thank you for your letter re poem and all good wishes to your efforts on behalf of the starving people of the world. I don't think I have a favourite poem. But to choose, rather at random, a poem which has impressed me I'd go for 'Death the Leveller' by James Shirley. It cuts us all down to size and teaches us to see things in the perspective of eternity — not to be over anxious when beset with problems, since for us all, this life's pilgrimage ends in dust and

Only the actions of the just
Smell sweet and blossom in their dust.

Another poem I like is 'Say Not the Struggle Naught Availeth' by Arthur Hugh Clough — a great tonic when all seems dark and hopeless — when all our best efforts seem to be of no avail.

All good wishes,
Victor Griffin

Dirge
from *The Contention of Ajax and Ulysses*

The glories of our blood and state,
    Are shadows, not substantial things,
There is no armour against fate,
    Death lays his icy hand on Kings,
        Sceptre and crown,
        Must tumble down,
And in the dust be equal made,
With the poor crooked sithe and spade.

Some men with swords may reap the field,
    And plant fresh laurels where they kill,
But their strong nerves at last must yield,
    They tame but one another still;
        Early or late,
        They stoop to Fate,
And must give up their murmuring breath,
When they pale Captives creep to death.

The Garlands wither on your brow,
    Then boast no more your mighty deeds,
Upon Death's purple Altar now,
    See where the Victor-victim bleeds,
        Your heads must come,
        To the cold Tomb,
Onely the actions of the just
Smell sweet, and blossom in their dust.

James Shirley (1596–1666)

Say Not the Struggle Naught Availeth

Say not, the struggle naught availeth,
The labour and the wounds are vain,
The enemy faints not, nor faileth,
And as things have been they remain.

If hopes were dupes, fears may be liars;
It may be, in yon smoke conceal'd,
Your comrades chase e'en now the fliers,
And, but for you, possess the field.

For while the tired waves, vainly breaking,
Seem here no painful inch to gain,
Far back, through creeks and inlets making,
Comes silent, flooding in, the main.

And not by eastern windows only,
When daylight comes, comes in the light;
In front the sun climbs slow, how slowly!
But westward, look, the land is bright!

Arthur Hugh Clough (1819–1861)

DAVID NORRIS   59

Seanad Éireann
Baile Átha Cliath

Dear Julie, Jonathan and Duncan,
Thank you for your letter about your project for raising money for
famine victims, about publishing a selection of poems. I am very
flattered that you consider me notorious enough for inclusion!
I have just come across a poem which has moved me greatly. This is a
poem called 'Mary' by my valued friend and colleague Brendan
Kennelly. It is based on an early 13th Century poem called 'A Poem
Addressed To The Blessed Virgin Mary' by Muirdeach Albanach Ó
Dálaigh. In his little introduction Brendan says: 'The poem attracted
me from the moment I read it because Ó Dalaigh speaks with rare
candour, freshness and emotional fullness. These are the qualities I
have tried to capture in this version.'
In my view Brendan has succeeded in capturing exactly these
qualities and makes the image of holiness both accessible and human.
It also attracted me because the Church to which I belong, the Church
of Ireland, has always been a little bit coy about the Blessed Virgin
Mary while the Roman Catholic Church has gone rather to the other
extreme. This poem makes the Virgin Mary a real and movingly
human being. I particularly like the idea that sensuality and divinity
are not necessarily opposed qualities.
I wish you every success with your venture.

Yours sincerely,
David Norris

Mary — an excerpt (from the Irish)

The three Marys took three husbands,
    Three women with luxuriant
Heavy wavy hair became slow-footed
    And pregnant

The three women had three sons,
    Three lights cutting through cloud
To illuminate dark hearts, dark places.
    The youngest of these was God.

One of the women was the mother of James,
    From the worst troubles she went free.
One was Mary the mother of John, their names
    Have not appeared in poetry.

You are Mary the Mother of God
    Nobody touches your fame;
The King of heaven, branch split in three,
    Was in your womb;
Your womb, though He rules undreamable fields, is
    His true kingdom.

Let me enter your house, your stronghold,
    My dear one, great Mary,
O yellow gold, o flourishing
    Apple tree,

O my food, clothes on my body,
    Mother, kinswoman,
Love of my dark heart, protect
    Your kinsman.

Because your Son is my kinsman
    It is right
You should protect me, man alone,
    By day and night
There where you are, here where I am
    At your gate.

Brendan Kennelly (b. 1936)

KATHY PRENDERGAST   60

18 January 1992

Dear Ms Grantham, Mr Logue and Mr Lyster,
Thank you for your letter informing me of your project and asking
*me to forward to you the title of my favourite poem. It is: '*maggie
and milly and molly and may*' by e e cummings.*
I like the whole poem because it describes what walking by the sea
means to me. But most of all I love the line 'as small as a world and
as large as alone'. It makes me think of many other things than what
it means in the poem: like how we all are as individuals.
Best wishes with the project,

Yours sincerely,
Kathy Prendergast

maggie and milly and molly and may

maggie and milly and molly and may
went down to the beach(to play one day)

and maggie discovered a shell that sang
so sweetly she couldn't remember her troubles,and

milly befriended a stranded star
whose rays five languid fingers were;

and molly was chased by a horrible thing
which raced sideways while blowing bubbles:and

may came home with a smooth round stone
as small as a world and as large as alone.

For whatever we lose(like a you or a me)
it's always ourselves we find in the sea

e e cummings (1894–1962)

ROBERT BALLAGH   61

20 January 1988

Dear Duncan, Jonathan, Julie,
To answer your letter of inquiry. A favourite poem of mine is
'Immram' by Paul Muldoon.
My reasons:
1. In my opinion, Paul Muldoon is our best contemporary poet.
2. I illustrated the Gallery Press edition of this poem.

Yours sincerely,
Robert Ballagh

Immram — an excerpt

My mother had just been fed by force,
A pint of lukewarm water through a rubber hose.
I hadn't seen her in six months or a year,
Not since my father had disappeared.
Now she'd taken an overdose
Of alcohol and barbiturates,
And this, I learned, was her third.
I was told then by a male nurse
That if I came back at the end of the week
She might be able to bring herself to speak.

Which brought me round to the Atlantic Club,
The Atlantic Club was an old grain-silo
That gave on to the wharf.
Not the kind of place you took your wife
Unless she had it in mind to strip
Or you had a mind to put her up for sale.
I knew how my father had come here by himself
And maybe thrown a little crap
And watched his check double, and treble,
With highball hard on the heels of highball.

She was wearing what looked like a dead fox
Over a low-cut sequinned gown,
And went by the name of Susan, or Suzanne.
A girl who would never pass out of fashion
So long as there's an 'if' in California . . .

Paul Muldoon (b. 1951)

JOHN MONTAGUE   62

Sailing To Byzantium

I
That is no country for old men. The young
In one another's arms, birds in the trees
—Those dying generations — at their song,
The salmon-falls, the mackerel-crowded seas,
Fish, flesh, or fowl, commend all summer long
Whatever is begotten, born, and dies.
Caught in that sensual music all neglect
Monuments of unageing intellect.

II
An aged man is but a paltry thing,
A tattered coat upon a stick, unless
Soul clap its hands and sing, and louder sing
For every tatter in its mortal dress,
Nor is there singing school but studying
Monuments of its own magnificence;
And therefore I have sailed the seas and come
To the holy city of Byzantium.

III
O sages standing in God's holy fire
As in the gold mosaic of a wall,
Come from the holy fire, perne in a gyre,
And be the singing-masters of my soul.
Consume my heart away; sick with desire

And fastened to a dying animal
It knows not what it is; and gather me
Into the artifice of eternity.

IV

Once out of nature I shall never take
My bodily form from any natural thing,
But such a form as Grecian goldsmiths make
Of hammered gold and gold enamelling
To keep a drowsy Emperor awake;
Or set upon a golden bough to sing
To lords and ladies of Byzantium
Of what is past, or passing, or to come.

W B Yeats (1865–1939)

It is hard for me to choose one *poem but if I had to it would probably
be 'Sailing to Byzantium'. I love its defiance, its clangour, and
while I have no desire to be a golden bird I recognise and enjoy the
final flourish, oratorical though it be!*

John Montague   20 January 1988

LAURIE LEE   63

20 January 1988

Dear Julie, Jonathan, Duncan,
'Stopping by Woods on a Snowy Evening' *(Robert Frost)*
For its atmosphere and rhyme-scheme, timelessly satisfying.
For its gauche imperfections —

   'Whose woods these are I think I know.
   His house is in the village, though'

Well, does he or doesn't he?
*And for the shattering repetition of the two last lines. A stumbling
accident of writing, according to Frost, as most revelations are.*

Laurie Lee

Stopping By Woods On A Snowy Evening

Whose woods these are I think I know.
His house is in the village though;
He will not see me stopping here
To watch his woods fill up with snow.

My little horse must think it queer
To stop without a farmhouse near
Between the woods and frozen lake
The darkest evening of the year.

He gives his harness bells a shake
To ask if there is some mistake.
The only other sound's the sweep
Of easy wind and downy flake.

The woods are lovely, dark, and deep,
But I have promises to keep,
And miles to go before I sleep,
And miles to go before I sleep.

Robert Frost (1874–1963)

DENNIS O'DRISCOLL   64

20 January 1988

Dear Julie, Jonathan and Duncan,
Although I read poetry as often as I'm allowed, and though I keep an
emergency supply in my head, I still have no difficulty in choosing
one poem from among the many that I admire. It is the elegy which
Chidiock Tichborne wrote for himself as he awaited execution in the
Tower of London in 1586. He was twenty-eight years of age and had
been condemned to death for his part in a plot on the Queen. His
response to his plight is a dignified one — he neither screams nor
shouts; but the cry he emits is a piercing and moving one,
nonetheless. In trying to puzzle out the riddle of his own early death,
Tichborne speaks for all those who have been condemned to
premature death, including those who starve as a result of injustice,
indifference or greed.
Thank you for allowing me to be associated with your laudable
project.

Best wishes,
Dennis O'Driscoll

Tichborne's Elegy
written with his own hand in the Tower before his execution.

My prime of youth is but a frost of cares,
My feast of joy is but a dish of pain,
My crop of corn is but a field of tares,
And all my good is but vain hope of gain;
The day is past, and yet I saw no sun,
And now I live, and now my life is done.

My tale was heard and yet it was not told,
My fruit is fall'n and yet my leaves are green,
My youth is spent and yet I am not old,
I saw the world and yet I was not seen;
My thread is cut and yet it is not spun,
And now I live, and now my life is done.

I sought my death and found it in my womb,
I looked for life and saw it was a shade,
I trod the earth and knew it was my tomb,
And now I die, and now I was but made;
My glass is full, and now my glass is run,
And now I live, and now my life is done.

Chidiock Tichborne (1558–1586)

DESMOND FENNELL   65

Finit

Le seans a chuala uathu scéala an chleamhnais
Is b'ait liom srian le héadroime na gaoithe —
Do bhís chomh hanamúil léi, chomh domheabhartha,
Chomh fiáin léi, is chomh haonraic, mar ba chuimhin liom.

Féach feasta go bhfuil dála cáich i ndán duit,
Cruatan is coitinne, séasúr go céile,
Ag éalú i ndearúd le hiompú ráithe
Gur dabht arbh ann duit riamh, ná dod leithéidse . . .

Ach go mbeidh poirt anois ná cloisfead choíche
Gan tú bheith os mo chomhair arís sa chúinne
Ag feitheamh, ceol ar láimh leat, roimh an rince
Is diamhaireacht na hoíche amuigh id shúile.

Máire Mhac an tSaoi (b. 1922)

*Hearing by chance that a man she once knew is engaged, the poet is
surprised that so sprightly and solitary a character could be
spancelled. Sad, only ordinariness awaits him now, and a gradual
drift into oblivion. But there will be tunes she will never hear without
seeing him again before her in the corner, waiting for the dance, 'the
bewitchment of the night outside' in his eyes. In this poem the
language and meaning fit so closely together, with such music of
rhythm and sound, that you almost have it off by heart at one
reading. Its stateliness and theme combined have resonances for me
that are difficult to catch hold of. One is Ronsard's 'Allons voir,*

mignonne...' And then, again, that sad second stanza is a Last Post, followed by the Reveille of the upbeat final stanza (I should know, I heard them as recently as yesterday at Seán MacBride's funeral).

Desmond Fennell   19 January 1988

P.S. Ronsard's 'Quand you serez vieille...' not 'Allons voir, mignonne...'. Sorry about that.

MARIA DOYLE   66

The Harlot's House

We caught the tread of dancing feet,
We loitered down the moonlit street,
And stopped beneath the harlot's house.

Inside, above the din and fray,
We heard the loud musicians play
The *'Treues Liebes Herz'* of Strauss.

Like strange mechanical grotesques,
Making fantastic arabesques,
The shadows raced across the blind.

We watched the ghostly dancers spin
To sound of horn and violin,
Like black leaves wheeling in the wind.

Like wire-pulled automatons,
Slim silhouetted skeletons
Went sidling through the slow quadrille.

They took each other by the hand,
And danced a stately saraband;
Their laughter echoed thin and shrill.

Sometimes a clockwork puppet pressed
A phantom lover to her breast,
Sometimes they seemed to try to sing.

Sometimes a horrible marionette
Came out, and smoked its cigarette
Upon the steps like a live thing.

Then, turning to my love, I said,
'The dead are dancing with the dead,
The dust is whirling with the dust'.

But she — she heard the violin,
And left my side and entered in:
Love passed into the house of lust.

Then suddenly the tune went false,
The dancers wearied of the waltz.
The shadows ceased to wheel and whirl.

And down the long and silent street,
The dawn with silver-sandalled feet,
Crept like a frightened girl.

Oscar Wilde (1854–1900)

Julie, Jonathan, Duncan,
This is my favourite poem. I love Wilde's poetry and writings and
have always been fascinated by his life. This particular poem is simple
but strong.

Maria Doyle   18 January 1988

PAUL DURCAN   67

19 January 1988

Dear Julie, Jonathan and Duncan,
I love good anthologies and Lifelines I *was unquestionably one of the*
best anthologies put together anywhere in recent years. I am looking
forward immensely, therefore, to Lifelines II.
I have hundreds of 'favourite poems'. Here are some titles as they
come to mind: 'To my Wife' by Knut Hamsun; 'Innocent When You
Dream' by Tom Waits; 'One Art' by Elizabeth Bishop; 'In St
Etheldreda's' by Sara Berkeley; 'Almost Communication' by Rita
Ann Higgins; 'The Dark Sobrietee' by Macdara Woods; 'White
Shirts in Childhood' by Dermot Bolger; 'Summertime in England' by
Van Morrison'; 'To Margot Heineman' by John Cornford; 'The Fall
of Rome' by W H Auden; 'The Pleasant Joys of Brotherhood' by
James Simmons; 'Sunday Morning' by Wallace Stevens; 'The Keen
Stars Were Twinkling' by Percy Shelley; 'In Parenthesis' by David
Jones; 'Voracities and Verities Sometimes are Interacting' by
Marianne Moore; 'Lisdoonvarna' by Christy Moore; 'The Bronze
Horseman' by Alexander Pushkin; 'On Raglan Road' by Patrick
Kavanagh; 'Four Quartets' by T S Eliot; 'Everness' by Jorge Luis
Borges; 'One Too Many Mornings' by Bob Dylan; 'The Collar-Bone
Of A Hare' by W B Yeats; 'The Silken Tent' by Robert Frost; 'Thirty
Bob A Week' by John Davidson; 'Of the Great and Famous Ever-to-

*be-honoured Knight, Sir Francis Drake, and of My Little-Little Self'
by Robert Hayman; 'Return Thoughts' by Anthony Cronin; '7
Middagh Street' by Paul Muldoon; 'Ireland 1944' by Francis Stuart;
'Born in the USA' by Bruce Springsteen; 'Lament for Ignacio
Sanchez Mejias' by Federico Garcia Lorca; 'Midnight Trolleybus' by
Bulat Okudjhava; 'Let's Be Sad' by Irina Ratushinskaya; 'He Among
Them Nightly Moving' by John Stephen Moriarty; 'A Bat on the
Road' by Seamus Heaney; 'Barbara' by Jacques Prévert; 'Antarctica'
by Derek Mahon; 'Intoxication' by Boris Pasternak; 'Skrymtymnym'
by Andrei Voznesensky; 'The Princess of Parallelograms' by Medbh
McGuckian; 'In the Luxembourg Gardens' by Tom McCarthy . . . .
But the poem I would like you to play for me today is* 'Shut Up, I'm
Going To Sing You A Love Song' *by Ellen Gilchrist, an American
word-magician who is the author of at least two stunning books of
stories,* Victory Over Japan *and* In The Land of Dreamy Dreams.
I hope you collect buckets of money for the people of Ethiopia.

Salut,
Paul Durcan

Shut Up, I'm Going To Sing You A Love Song
for F S K

I dream to save you
I must leap from an ocean pier
into water of uncertain depth
You flail below me in a business suit
Knowing I must jump I frown
Knowing we will drown together
Knowing the dark sea will bloom for a moment
with the red hibiscus I refuse to wear
over either ear

Sighing I dive my special Red Cross dive
straight into the sea
which is deeper than either of us dreamed
it would be
Sit still there is nothing to fear
Undo my dress I am here you are here

Ellen Gilchrist (b. 1935)
(from *The Land Surveyor's Daughter*, 1980)

ITA DALY   68

Dear Julie, Jonathan and Duncan,
Thank you for your letter and for asking me to take part in your
project.
The poem I have chosen is 'To His Coy Mistress' by Andrew
Marvell. Marvell is one of my favourites and I have chosen this poem,
because it is sensuous, witty and wise. I share its philosophy and I
admire its execution.
A comfort on dark winter nights.

Sincerely,
Ita Daly

To His Coy Mistress

Had we but World enough, and Time,
This coyness Lady were no crime.
We would sit down, and think which way
To walk, and pass our long Loves Day.
Thou by the Indian Ganges side
Should'st Rubies find: I by the Tide
of Humber would complain. I would
Love you ten years before the Flood:
And you should if you please refuse
Till the Conversion of the Jews.
My vegetable Love should grow
Vaster than Empires, and more slow.
An hundred years should go to praise
Thine Eyes, and on thy Forehead Gaze.
Two hundred to adore each Breast:
But thirty thousand to the rest.
An Age at least to every part,
And the last Age should show your Heart.
For Lady you deserve this State;
Nor would I love at lower rate.
But at my back I alwaies hear
Times winged Chariot hurrying near:
And yonder all before us lye
Desarts of vast Eternity.
Thy Beauty shall no more be found;
Nor, in thy marble Vault, shall sound
My ecchoing Song; then Worms shall try
That long preserv'd Virginity:
And your quaint Honour turn to dust;

And into ashes all my Lust.
The Grave's a fine and private place,
But none I think do there embrace.
  Now therefore, while the youthful hew
Sits on thy skin like morning dew,
And while thy willing Soul transpires
At every pore with instant Fires,
Now let us sport us while we may;
And now, like am'rous birds of prey,
Rather at once our Time devour,
Than languish in his slow-chapt pow'r.
Let us roll all our Strength, and all
Our sweetness, up into one Ball:
And tear our Pleasures with rough strife,
Through the Iron gates of Life.
Thus, though we cannot make our Sun
Stand still, yet we will make him run.

Andrew Marvell (1621–1678)

JENNIFER JOHNSTON   69

20 January 1988

Dear Three,
Thank you for your letter.
I can't possibly let you have the text of my FAVOURITE poem, as I
have quite a few... and anyway I expect that lots of people will send
you the same poems over and over again. Here, however, is a short
poem that I like very much and it seems to have relevance to what
you are trying to do.
It is called 'Fairy Tale'.
It is written by a Czech poet called Miroslav Holub.
I don't know how you pronounce that, but that doesn't matter. It is
simple, truthful and sad and filled with beautiful imagination.
It has for me the innocence and simplicity of a child's painting,
bright, honest, unselfconscious, and the sad wisdom of the adult; all
wrapped up into such a few lines.
I hope you like it also.
Good luck with the project and have a happy 1988.

Yours in friendship,
Jennifer Johnston

Fairy Tale

He built himself a house,
    his foundations,
      his stones,
      his walls,
      his roof overhead,
      his chimney and smoke,
      his view from the window.

He made himself a garden,
    his fence,
    his thyme,
    his earthworm,
    his evening dew.

He cut out his bit of sky above.

And he wrapped the garden in the sky
and the house in the garden
and packed the lot in a handkerchief
and went off
lone as an arctic fox
through the cold
unending
rain
into the world.

Miroslav Holub (b. 1923)
(From the Czech, translated by George Theiner)

ALAN STANFORD   70

Gate Theatre
Dublin 1
22 January 1988

A favourite poem rather like a favourite part or play is really an impossibility as each part, play and poem provides differing opportunities for discovery and enjoyment. However if a choice must be made it would be 'Fern Hill' by Dylan Thomas for its invocation of youth, its memories of innocence and its joy in the discovery of nature. To me it is my youth and my discovery of life and remembrance of my innocence.

Alan Stanford

Fern Hill

Now as I was young and easy under the apple boughs
About the lilting house and happy as the grass was green,
    The night above the dingle starry,
      Time let me hail and climb
    Golden in the heydays of his eyes,
And honoured among wagons I was prince of the apple towns
And once below a time I lordly had the trees and leaves
      Trail with daisies and barley
    Down the rivers of the windfall light.

And as I was green and carefree, famous among the barns
About the happy yard and singing as the farm was home,
    In the sun that is young once only,
      Time let me play and be
    Golden in the mercy of his means,
And green and golden I was huntsman and herdsman, the
      calves
Sang to my horn, the foxes on the hills barked clear and cold,
      And the sabbath rang slowly
    In the pebbles of the holy streams.

All the sun long it was running, it was lovely, the hay
Fields high as the house, the tunes from the chimneys, it
          was air
    And playing, lovely and watery
      And fire green as grass.
    And nightly under the simple stars
As I rode to sleep the owls were bearing the farm away,
All the moon long I heard, blessed among stables, the night-
      jars
    Flying with the ricks, and the horses
      Flashing into the dark.

And then to awake, and the farm, like a wanderer white
With the dew, come back, the cock on his shoulder: it was all
    Shining, it was Adam and maiden,
      The sky gathered again
    And the sun grew round that very day.
So it must have been after the birth of the simple light
In the first, spinning place, the spellbound horses walking
      warm
    Out of the whinnying green stable
      On to the fields of praise.

And honoured among foxes and pheasants by the gay house
Under the new made clouds and happy as the heart was long,
    In the sun born over and over,
      I ran my heedless ways,
    My wishes raced through the house high hay

And nothing I cared, at my sky blue trades, that time allows
In all his tuneful turning so few and such morning songs
    Before the children green and golden
        Follow him out of grace,

Nothing I cared, in the lamb white days, that time would
        take me
Up to the swallow thronged loft by the shadow of my hand,
    In the moon that is always rising,
        Nor that riding to sleep
    I should hear him fly with the high fields
And wake to the farm forever fled from the childless land.
Oh as I was young and easy in the mercy of his means,
        Time held me green and dying
    Though I sang in my chains like the sea.

Dylan Thomas (1914–1953)

DEREK MAHON   71

19 January 1988

Dear Miss Grantham and friends,
I don't know if it's necessarily my favourite poem, but it's one I like
very much: 'The Moose' by Elizabeth Bishop. The title is a pun on
'The Muse', and the poem describes a bus journey at night from Nova
Scotia to Boston during which a moose appears on the road, to
everyone's delighted astonishment. It's a poem about the magical in
the ordinary, a poem about poetry itself in a sense: one of the great
underrated poems of the century. I recommend it to all those who
want to know what poetry means, and wish you well in your efforts
on behalf of the Third World.

Sincerely,
Derek Mahon

The Moose
For Grace Bulmer Bowers

From narrow provinces
of fish and bread and tea,
home of the long tides
where the bay leaves the sea
twice a day and takes
the herrings long rides,

where if the river
enters or retreats
in a wall of brown foam
depends on if it meets
the bay coming in,
the bay not at home;

where, silted red,
sometimes the sun sets
facing a red sea,
and others, veins the flats'
lavender, rich mud
in burning rivulets;

on red, gravelly roads,
down rows of sugar maples,
past clapboard farmhouses
and neat, clapboard churches,
bleached, ridged as clamshells,
past twin silver birches,

through late afternoon
a bus journeys west,
the windshield flashing pink,
pink glancing off of metal,
brushing the dented flank
of blue, beat-up enamel;

down hollows, up rises,
and waits, patient, while
a lone traveller gives
kisses and embraces
to seven relatives
and a collie supervises.

Goodbye to the elms,
To the farm, to the dog.
The bus starts. The light
grows richer; the fog,
shifting, salty, thin,
comes closing in.

Its cold, round crystals
form and slide and settle
in the white hens' feathers,
in gray glazed cabbages,
on the cabbage roses
and lupins like apostles;

the sweet peas cling
to their wet white string
on the whitewashed fences;

bumblebees creep
inside the foxgloves,
and evening commences.

One stop at Bass River.
Then the Economies —
Lower, Middle, Upper;
Five Islands, Five Houses,
where a woman shakes a tablecloth
out after supper.

A pale flickering. Gone.
The Tantramar marshes
and the smell of salt hay.
An iron bridge trembles
and a loose plank rattles
but doesn't give way.

On the left, a red light
swims through the dark:
a ship's port lantern.
Two rubber boots show,
illuminated, solemn.
A dog gives one bark.

A woman climbs in
with two market bags,
brisk, freckled, elderly.
'A grand night. Yes, sir,
all the way to Boston.'
She regards us amicably.

Moonlight as we enter
the New Brunswick woods,
hairy, scratchy, splintery;
moonlight and mist
caught in them like lamb's wool
on bushes in a pasture.

The passengers lie back.
Snores. Some long sighs.
A dreamy divagation
begins in the night,
a gentle, auditory,
slow hallucination. . .

In the creakings and noises,
an old conversation
— not concerning us,
but recognizable, somewhere,
back in the bus:
Grandparents' voices

uninterruptedly
talking, in Eternity:
names being mentioned,
things cleared up finally;
what he said, what she said,
who got pensioned;

deaths, deaths and sicknesses;
the year he remarried;
the year (something) happened.
She died in childbirth.
That was the son lost
when the schooner foundered.

He took to drink. Yes.
She went to the bad.
When Amos began to pray
even in the store and
finally the family had
to put him away.

'Yes . . .' that peculiar
affirmative. 'Yes. . .'
A sharp, indrawn breath,
half groan, half acceptance,
that means 'Life's like that.
We know *it* (also death).'

Talking the way they talked
in the old featherbed,
peacefully, on and on,
dim lamplight in the hall,
down in the kitchen, the dog
tucked in her shawl.

Now, it's all right now
even to fall asleep
just as on all those nights.
— Suddenly the bus driver
stops with a jolt,
turns off his lights.

A moose has come out of
the impenetrable wood
and stands there, looms, rather,
in the middle of the road.
It approaches; it sniffs at
the bus's hot hood.

Towering, antlerless,
high as a church,
homely as a house

(or, safe as houses).
A man's voice assures us
'Perfectly harmless . . . .'

~~Some of the passengers~~
exclaim in whispers,
childishly, softly,
'Sure are big creatures.'
'It's awful plain.'
'Look! It's a she!'

Taking her time,
she looks the bus over,
grand, otherworldly.
Why, why do we feel
(we all feel) this sweet
sensation of joy?

'Curious creatures,'
says our quiet driver,
rolling his r's.
'Look at that, would you.'
Then he shifts gears.
For a moment longer,

by craning backward,
the moose can be seen
on the moonlit macadam;
then there's a dim
smell of moose, an acrid
smell of gasoline.

Elizabeth Bishop (1911–1979)

KATHLEEN WATKINS   72

26 January 1988

'Clearances' — *a sonnet sequence
in memoriam M K H, 1911–1984
by Seamus Heaney*

*I love these lines because they are so simple and clear and one can see
vivid pictures when reading them. Most people would probably
identify with them also. To enjoy poetry, which I do very much, I
must understand it perfectly and the pictures always have to be very
clear.*

Kathleen Watkins

Sonnet 3

When all the others were away at Mass
I was all hers as we peeled potatoes.
They broke the silence, let fall one by one
Like solder weeping off the soldering iron:
Cold comforts set between us, things to share
Gleaming in a bucket of clean water.
And again let fall. Little pleasant splashes
From each other's work would bring us to our senses.

So while the parish priest at her bedside
Went hammer and tongs at the prayers for the dying
And some were responding and some crying
I remembered her head bent towards my head,
Her breath in mine, our fluent dipping knives —
Never closer the whole rest of our lives.

Seamus Heaney (b. 1939)
(From 'Clearances', an eight-sonnet sequence.)

MARY LELAND   73

25 January 1988

Dear Editors,
Forgive my delay in replying to your request for a favourite poem; it
was harder than I had expected to select just one. It seems that the
proposed title of your collection — Lifelines *— explains some part of*
the difficulty: poetry, and some prose, has provided me, as others,
with lifelines when the going got rough — or even when some other
way of describing something good or beautiful was required. And in
either of those circumstances we need more than one lifeline to help
us cling to what is important, real, and right.
My commonplace book has Pound, Vaughan, Arnold, and Housman,
Mahon and Montague among others. Yeats and Kavanagh and
Richard Murphy join Heaney, Kinsella, Jennings, and Heath-Stubbs
on my shelves. At different times, in different ways, some of the work
of all of these and of so many others has mattered, has helped or has
inspired. It would not do, perhaps, for a desert island, but of them all
I find myself still being grateful — thanks with admiration — for
Philip Larkin's: 'An Arundel Tomb'.
The last line answers an old question; the right answer, I want to
think. As for the rest, I'm happy to know that when I stand, as I do at
any opportunity, before the kind of effigies depicted in the poem and
ponder at them, and at the people they enshrine, I am simply one of a
whole community of observant wonderers.

Yours,
Mary Leland

An Arundel Tomb

Side by side, their faces blurred,
The earl and countess lie in stone,
Their proper habits vaguely shown
As jointed armour, stiffened pleat,
And that faint hint of the absurd —
The little dogs under their feet.

Such plainness of the pre-baroque
Hardly involves the eye, until
It meets his left-hand gauntlet, still
Clasped empty in the other; and
One sees, with a sharp tender shock,
His hand withdrawn, holding her hand.

They would not think to lie so long.
Such faithfulness in effigy
Was just a detail friends would see:
A sculptor's sweet commissioned grace
Thrown off in helping to prolong
The Latin names around the base.

They would not guess how early in
Their supine stationary voyage
The air would change to soundless damage,
Turn the old tenantry away;
How soon succeeding eyes begin
To look, not read, Rigidly they

Persisted, linked, through lengths and breadths
Of time. Snow fell, undated. Light
Each summer thronged the glass. A bright
Litter of birdcalls strewed the same
Bone-riddled ground. And up the paths
The endless altered people came,

Washing at their identity.
Now, helpless in the hollow of
An unarmorial age, a trough
Of smoke in slow suspended skeins
Above their scrap of history,
Only an attitude remains:

Time has transfigured them into
Untruth. The stone fidelity
They hardly meant has come to be
Their final blazon, and to prove
Our almost-instinct almost true:
What will survive of us is love.

Philip Larkin (1922–1985)

MAXI   74

RTE
25 January 1988

Dear Julie, Jonathan and Duncan,
Thank you very much for including me in your list of celebrities for
Lifelines. I am delighted to take part.
My favourite poem is 'Rita' by Pat Ingoldsby. The words burned into
my brain, the very first time I heard him recite them on television.
This year, with the news of Christopher Nolan, and the Whitbread
award, I think they have special significance.

Kind regards,
Maxi

For Rita With Love

You came home from school
on a special bus
full of people
who look like you
and love like you
and you met me
for the first time
and you loved me.
You love everybody
so much that it's not safe
to let you out alone.
Eleven years of love
and trust and time for you to learn
that you can't go on loving like this.
Unless you are stopped
you will embrace every person you see.
Normal people don't do that.
Some Normal people will hurt you
very badly because you do.

Cripples don't look nice
but you embrace them.
You kissed a wino on the bus
and he broke down and he cried
and he said 'Nobody has kissed me
for the last 30 years.
But you did.
You touched my face
with your fingers and said
'I like you'.

The world will never
be ready for you.
Your way is right
and the world will
never be ready.

We could learn everything
that we need to know
by watching you
going to your special school
in your special bus
full of people
who look like you
and love like you
and it's not safe
to let you out alone.
If you're not normal
there is very little hope
for the rest of us.

Pat Ingoldsby

RÓNÁN JOHNSTON   75

RTE
18 January 1988

Dear Julie, Jonathan, Duncan,
Enclosed is 'Up and Down the Strip' by the inimitable Pat
Ingoldsby, who by the way should be nominated for a Nobel Prize.
It's such a relief to read poetry that you can really get involved with
— terse, acute and wry. So much poetry is self-indulgent navel-
gazing — Thankfully this isn't. And Leeson Street is really like this
— a marvellous blend between poetry and stand-up comedy. It
should be on the Leaving Cert. Course.

Rónán Johnston

P.S. Pat for Archbishop.

Up and Down the Strip

It's the tingle between your legs
that takes you down to Leeson Street,
down to the The Strip
down to meet
tight jeans tight thighs
denim bottoms hopes high

standing and sitting
sipping the wine
buy you a bottle
make you mine
and the Stones
can't get no satisfaction.

Business men working late
grey haired overweight
white shirts club ties
credit cards white lies
cigar smoke bald spots
big stomachs big shots
wrinkles over rugby scars
randy thoughts company cars
and the Stones
can't get no satisfaction.

Eyes meet look away
how do you start?
what do you say?
look unmarried
like you couldn't care less
look unfrustrated
they'll never guess
pray to God that
your daughter's not here
hold in your stomach
swallow your fear
grab two glasses
bottle of wine
take a sip
make you mine
and the Stones
can't get no
satisfaction.

Jump suits open zipped
legs crossed leather hipped
tight jeans young blood
long skirts looking good
some do some don't
how can you tell
which one won't
more important
which one will
onto the dance floor
get in for the kill
dance fast dance slow
move in closer
now you know

dance fast dance slow
nuzzle the neck
here we go
will you take off
your clothes?

No! Not down here!
and not in my place
no bloody fear
you'll waken the wife
disturb the kids
we'll do it in your place
keep it all hid
and the Stones
can't get no satisfaction.

Up the steps
tired and slow
she drank your wine
she's still below
up the steps
tired and slow
the taxis are waiting
all in a row
and the Stones
can't get no satisfaction.

Pat Ingoldsby

MARGARET HECKLER   76

Embassy of the United States of America
Dublin
25 January 1988

Dear Ms Grantham,
I commend your concern and that of the other pupils from Wesley
College in Dublin for famine victims in Ethiopia and, more
importantly, your initiative to do something about it. I am happy to
help.
My favorite poem comes from one of America's most important
twentieth-century poets, Robert Frost (1874–1963) who is from my
home state of Massachusetts. In his poem 'The Road Not Taken' he
reminds us that the obvious, easy path may not be the most
rewarding. The final stanza has always been my guide:

I shall be telling this with a sigh
Somewhere ages and ages hence:

Two roads diverged in a wood, and I —
I took the one less traveled by,
And that has made all the difference.

*And it still causes me to sigh to think of that poem again, of choices I
made years ago, and to pass it on to you.
Good luck in your endeavors,*

Sincerely,
Margaret M Heckler
Ambassador

('*The Road Not Taken*' was also Eithne Hand's choice. The poem appears in full
on page 78.)

FINTAN O'TOOLE   77

26 January 1988

*Dear Julie, Jonathan and Duncan,
Thanks very much for your letter and for the invitation to contribute
to the book. My sincere congratulations on your initiative and
dedication in producing a book — I have some idea of the amount of
perseverance and sheer hard labour involved. It is terrible that such
efforts should have any place in a supposedly civilised world, that
other people's lives should depend on them. But so long as they do we
are all prisoners of conscience.
I hope you like the poem I've chosen. It's by the Chilean Nobel Prize
winner Pablo Neruda, who died of a heart-attack during the savage
coup in his country in 1973. I've chosen it both because I think it's a
wonderful poem and because I think it's appropriate to the
inspiration of your book: our responsibility not to ignore the suffering
of our fellow human beings. This is what I'd like to say about it:*

*Pablo Neruda's poem is both a work of great formal beauty and a
statement of the insufficiency of beauty in an ugly world. Neruda, a
poet of the magical and the mysterious was Chile's consul in Madrid
at the time of the Spanish Civil War. There, through the friendship of
fellow-poets like Federico Garcia Lorca (the 'Federico' of the poem),
murdered by the Fascists, he discovered his responsibility to his
fellow man in the face of barbarity and atrocity. What is wonderful
about the poem, however, is that the devastation of death is set
against the vigour, colour and flow of life. The poem is tragic but also
an affirmation of the joy of living. Against the accusation that he no
longer writes 'pure poetry' Neruda puts forward both a vision of the
richness of humanity and an invocation of the terror of its*

destruction by the Fascist bombing of Madrid. I can never read it
without a mixture of horror, anger and hope.
Good luck with the entire project,

All the best,
Fintan O'Toole

I'm Explaining a Few Things

You are going to ask: and where are the lilacs?
and the poppy-petalled metaphysics?
and the rain repeatedly spattering
its words and drilling them full
of apertures and birds?

I'll tell you all the news.

I lived in a suburb,
a suburb of Madrid, with bells,
and clocks, and trees.

From there you could look out
over Castille's dry face:
a leather ocean.

      My house was called
the house of flowers, because in every cranny
geraniums burst: it was
a good-looking house
with its dogs and children.

            Remember, Raul?
Eh, Rafael?
      Federico, do you remember
From under the ground
my balconies on which
the light of June drowned flowers in your mouth?
                  Brother, my brother!
Everything
loud with big voices, the salt of merchandises,
pile-ups of palpitating bread,
the stalls of my suburb of Arguelles with its statue
like a drained inkwell in a swirl of hake:
oil flowed into spoons,
a deep baying
of feet and hands swelled in the streets,
metres, litres, the sharp
measure of life,
      stacked-up fish,
the texture of roofs with a cold sun in which
the weather vane falters,
the fine, frenzied ivory of potatoes,
wave on wave of tomatoes rolling down to the sea.

And one morning all that was burning,
one morning the bonfires
leapt out of the earth
devouring human beings —
and from then on fire,
gunpowder from then on,
and from then on blood.
Bandits with planes and moors
bandits with finger-rings and duchesses,
bandits with black friars spattering blessings
came through the sky to kill children
and the blood of children ran through the streets
without fuss, like children's blood.

Jackals that the jackals would despise,
stones that the dry thistle would bite on and spit out,
vipers that the vipers would abominate!

Face to face with you I have seen the blood
of Spain tower like a tide
to drown you in one wave
of pride and knives!

Treacherous
generals:
see my dead house,
look at broken Spain:
from every house burning metal flows
instead of flowers,
from every socket of Spain
Spain emerges
and from every dead child a rifle with eyes,
and from every crime bullets are born
which one day will find
the bull's eye of your hearts.

And you will ask: why doesn't his poetry
speak of dreams and leaves
and the great volcanoes of his native land?

Come and see the blood in the streets.
Come and see
the blood in the streets.
Come and see the blood
in the streets!

Pablo Neruda (1904–1973)
(Translated by Nathaniel Tarn)

MARIAN RICHARDSON

RTE
7 March 1988

Dear Julie, Jonathan and Duncan,
Thank you for inviting me to contribute to your anthology: I'm
honoured to be asked. It's obviously very difficult to choose one poem.
I thought of many: John Donne's 'The Good Morrow' . . . Paul
Durcan's 'At the Funeral of the Marriage', Louis MacNeice's
'Sunlight on the Garden', 'Scar an Nollaig Sinn' by Liam Ó
Muirthile . . . and any of Nuala Ní Dhomhnaill's work. It is to her
writing in Irish that I always return for the light of language and
poetry.
So I hope you enjoy 'Fáilte Bhéal Na Sionna Don Iasc'. . . 'The
Shannon Estuary Welcoming the Fish'.

Marian Richardson

Fáilte Bhéal na Sionna Don Iasc

Léim an bhradáin
Sa doircheacht
Lann lom
Sciath airgid,
Mise atá fáiltiúil, líontach
Sleamhain,
Lán d'fheamnach,
Go caise ciúin
Go heireaball eascon.

Bia ar fad
Is ea an t-iasc seo
Gan puinn cnámh
Gan puinn putóg
Fiche punt teann
De mheatáin iata
Dírithe
Ar a nead sa chaonach néata.

Is seinim seoithín
Do mo leannán
Tonn ar thonn
Leathrann ar leathrann,
Mo thine ghealáin mar bhairlín thíos faoi
Mo rogha a thoghas féin ón iasacht.

Nuala Ní Dhomhnaill (b. 1952)

The Shannon Estuary Welcoming the Fish

The leap of the salmon
in darkness,
naked blade
shield of silver.
I am welcoming, full of nets,
enveighling,
slippery with seaweed,
quiet eddies
and eel-tails.

This fish
is nothing but meat
with very few bones
and very few entrails;
twenty pounds of muscle tauted,
aimed
at its nest in the mossy place.

And I will sing a lullaby
to my lover
wave on wave,
stave upon half-stave,
my phosphorescence as bed-linen under him,
my favourite, whom I, from afar have chosen.

(Translated by the author.)

RICHARD KEARNEY   79

27 January 1988

Dear Julie Grantham, Jonathan Logue, Duncan Lyster,
'Psalm' by the modern German Jewish poet, Paul Celan, is, for me, a
cry of hope from the darkest abyss. It celebrates the defiant power of
song even as one struggles through the darkest night of the soul or
the most despairing hour of history. The 'I Am' of the Bible is here
invoked in the contemporary idiom of the 'no one' — a power of love
which can become present to us even in those times it appears most
absent.

With every best wish,
Richard Kearney

('*Psalm*' was also John Banville's choice. The poem appears in full on page 32.)

MARY MOONEY   80

Dáil Éireann
Baile Átha Cliath 2
28 January 1988

Dear Julie, Jonathan and Duncan,
Thank you for your letter regarding the poem.
One of my favourite poems is 'The Stolen Child' by W B Yeats. The
reason I like it is because it's a magical poem and it reminds me of
when we were kids and were 'threatened with the fairies'. We thought
they were real people and lived amongst us. We really did. They were
good memories.
I wish you every success with your fund raising and hope you will
contact me again if you feel I can help you.

Yours sincerely,
Mary
Ald Mary Mooney TD

('The Stolen Child' was also Gerrit van Gelderen's choice. The poem appears
in full on pages 40-41.)

MAEVE BINCHY   81

1 February 1988

Dear Julie, Jonathan, Duncan,
I know Adrian Mitchell and have heard him reading his poetry from
time to time, but even though he has written poems which may have
stronger messages, poetry against war of all kinds, nothing ever
struck me as being so immediate and something that everyone could
understand as this. We have all been in a playground of some sort or
other, there has always been violence and hurt and cruelty. I saw this
as a child and as a teacher. People pick on others often without any
idea of the damage and the hurt they have caused.
But the end of the poem is very true and very full of hope. When you
are older and more or less grown up it becomes easier to take charge
of your own life and not to feel a victim of the bullies and those who
wound you with words or with war in the Killing Ground.

All the best,
Maeve Binchy

Back in the Playground Blues

I dreamed I was back in the playground, I was
    about four feet high
Yes dreamed I was back in the playground,
    standing about four feet high
Well the playground was three miles long and
    the playground was five miles wide

It was broken black tarmac with a high wire
    fence all around
Broken black dusty tarmac with a high fence
    running all around
And it had a special name to it, they called
    it The Killing Ground

Got a mother and a father, they're one
    thousand years away
The rulers of The Killing Ground are coming
    out to play
Everybody thinking: 'Who they going to play
    with today?'

    Well you get it for being Jewish
    And you get it for being black
    Get it for being chicken
    And you get it for fighting back
    You get it for being big and fat
    Get it for being small
    Oh those who get it get it and get it
    For any damn thing at all

Sometimes they take a beetle, tear off its
    six legs one by one
Beetle on its black back, rocking in the
    lunchtime sun
But a beetle can't beg for mercy, a beetle's
    not half the fun

I heard a deep voice talking, it had that
    iceberg sound,
'It prepares them for Life' — but I have
    never found
Any place in my life worse than The Killing Ground.

Adrian Mitchell (b. 1932)

THELMA MANSFIELD   82

RTE
1 February 1988

Dear Julie,
Enclosed a piece of poetry about the joys of finding a lost hawk. I'm
sure nobody else will send you anything as odd.
Hope all goes well for you,

Thelma Mansfield

The Lover Compareth Himself To The Painful Falconer

The soaring hawk from fist that flies,
  Her Falconer doth constrain
Sometime to range the ground unknown
  To find her out again:
And if by sight or sound of bell,
  His falcon he may see,
Wo ho ho, he cries with cheerful voice,
  The gladdest man is he.
By lure then in finest sort,
  He seeks to bring her in,
But if that she full gorgëd be,
  He can not so her win:
Although her becks and bending eyes,
  She many proffers makes,
Wo ho ho, he cries, away she flies,
  And so her leave she takes.
This woeful man with weary limbs
  Runs wand'ring round about:
At length by noise of chattering pies,
  His hawk again found out,
His heart was glad his eyes had seen
  His falcon swift of flight:
Wo ho ho, he cries, she empty gorged,
  Upon his lure doth light.
How glad was then the falconer there,
  No pen nor tongue can tell:
He swam in bliss that lately felt
  Like pains of cruel hell.
His hand sometime upon her train,
  Sometime upon her breast,
Wo ho ho, he cries with cheerful voice,
  His heart was now at rest.

My dear, likewise behold thy love,
  What pains he doth endure:
And now at length let pity move
  To stoop unto his lure
A hood of silk and silver bells,
  New gifts I promise thee:
Wo ho ho, I cry, I come then say,
  Make me as glad as he.

Anonymous (mid sixteenth century)

MÁIRE MHAC AN tSAOI   83

1 February 1988

Dear Julie, Jonathan and Duncan,
I applaud your initiative for the help of Ethiopia and I wish you every
success.
After a lot of thought I think the poem that I love most dearly and
that would do most to cheer me were I on a desert island or in
solitary confinement is G K Chesterton's 'Ballad of the White
Horse'. I never tire of the deep humanity of his understanding of
history nor of the superb accomplishment of the narrative verse in
which this is realised. I hope that many more people will be led to
enjoy it by reading your book.
Again, every good wish. I look forward to seeing the new Lifelines.

Yours very sincerely,
Máire Cruise O'Brien
(Máire Mhac an tSaoi)

[The Ballad of the White Horse *was first published on 31 August*
1911. It is a ballad of the reign of King Alfred, and describes that
monarch's noble exploits, his character, his struggle with the Danes,
the story of the white horse and the battle of Ethandune.
It is over one thousand lines long. We print an excerpt.]

from *The Ballad of the White Horse*

Before the gods that made the gods
    Had seen their sunrise pass,
The White Horse of the White Horse Vale
    Was cut out of the grass.

Before the gods that made the gods
    Had drunk at dawn their fill,
The White Horse of the White Horse Vale
    Was hoary on the hill.

Age beyond age on British land,
    Aeons on aeons gone,
Was peace and war in western hills,
    And the White Horse looked on.

For the White Horse knew England
    When there was none to know;
He saw the first oar break or bend,
    He saw heaven fall and the world end,
    O God, how long ago.

For the end of the world was long ago —
    And all we dwell today
As children of some second birth,
Like a strange people left on earth
    After a judgement day.

For the end of the world was long ago,
    When the ends of the world waxed free,
When Rome was sunk in a waste of slaves,
    And the sun drowned in the sea.

G K Chesterton (1874–1936)

JEFFREY ARCHER   84

25 January 1988

Dear Miss Grantham,
Many thanks for your letter.
My favourite poem is 'The Thousandth Man' by Rudyard Kipling
because it reflects my own attitude to loyalty and friendship. I am a
great admirer of Kipling because he had a great command of the
language as well as being a first class story teller.
May I wish your project every success,

Yours sincerely,
Jeffrey Archer

The Thousandth Man

One man in a thousand, Solomon says,
Will stick more close than a brother.
And it's worth while seeking him half your days
If you find him before the other.
Nine hundred and ninety-nine depend
On what the world sees in you,
But the Thousandth Man will stand your friend
With the whole round world agin you.

'Tis neither promise nor prayer nor show
Will settle the finding for 'ee.
Nine hundred and ninety-nine of 'em go
By your looks, or your acts, or your glory.
But if he finds you and you find him,
The rest of the world don't matter;
For the Thousandth Man will sink or swim
With you in any water.

You can use his purse with no more talk
Than he uses yours for his spendings,
And laugh and meet in your daily walk
As though there had been no lendings.
Nine hundred and ninety-nine of 'em call
For silver and gold in their dealings;
But the Thousandth Man he's worth 'em all,
Because you can show him your feelings.

His wrong's your wrong, and his right's your right
In season or out of season.
Stand up and back it in all men's sight —
With *that* for your only reason!
Nine hundred and ninety-nine can't bide
The shame or mocking or laughter,
But the Thousandth Man will stand by your side
To the gallows-foot — and after!

Rudyard Kipling (1865–1936)

T A FINLAY   85

An Chúirt Uachtarach
(The Supreme Court)
Baile Átha Cliath 7
(Dublin 7)
1 February 1988

Dear Julie Grantham, Jonathan Logue and Duncan Lyster,
Thank you very much for your letter concerning your project to
produce a book called Lifelines *for the purpose of raising funds for*
the Third World.
It is an excellent idea and I hope you are very successful with it.
It gives me great pleasure to take part in it and to give any assistance
I can.
The poem which I have chosen is one of which I have been very fond
*for a long time: '*The Death and Last Confession of Wandering
Peter*', written by Hilaire Belloc.*
The reason I have chosen this poem is that, firstly, I find it very

felicitously expressed and beautifully written. Secondly, and more
importantly, I have always been immensely attracted by the concept
that Peter Wanderwide would by reason of all the people he had
known, of all the places he had seen and, I rather assume, of all the
good company he had met with would find himself protected against
too harsh a judgement on the Day of Judgement.
Furthermore, it seems to me that he retained up to the end of his life
what I consider to be one of the most precious of all attributes, and
that was a sense of humour. The concept of telling the 'Blessed
doubtful things of Val d'Aran and Perigord' seems always to me to
be irresistible.
I wish you every success with your good project.

Yours sincerely,
T A Finlay
An Príomh-Bhreitheamh
(Mr Justice Thomas A Finlay
The Chief Justice)

The Death and Last Confession of Wandering Peter

When Peter Wanderwide was young
He wandered everywhere he would:
And all that he approved was sung,
And most of what he saw was good.

When Peter Wanderwide was thrown
By Death himself beyond Auxerre,
He chanted in heroic tone
To priests and people gathered there:

'If all that I have loved and seen
Be with me on the Judgment Day,
I shall be saved the crowd between
From Satan and his foul array.

'Almighty God will surely cry,
"St Michael! Who is this that stands
With Ireland in his dubious eye,
And Perigord between his hands,

' "And on his arm the stirrup-thongs,
And in his gait the narrow seas,
And in his mouth Burgundian songs,
But in his heart the Pryenees?"

'St Michael then will answer right
(And not without angelic shame),
"I seem to know his face by sight:
I cannot recollect his name . . . . ?"

'St Peter will befriend me then,
Because my name is Peter too:
"I know him for the best of men
That ever wallopped barley brew.

' "And though I did not know him well
And though his soul were clogged with sin,
I hold the keys of Heaven and Hell.
Be welcome, noble Peterkin."

'Then shall I spread my native wings
And tread secure the heavenly floor,
And tell the Blessed doubtful things
Of Val d'Aran and Perigord.'

This was the last and solemn jest
Of weary Peter Wanderwide.
He spoke it with a failing zest,
And having spoken it, he died.

Hilaire Belloc (1870–1953)

JOHN GIELGUD   86

1 February 1988

My favourite poem is 'Bredon Hill' *from A E Housman's*
Shropshire Lad, *as I spoke it for my first audition in 1921 when I
got a scholarship at my first Dramatic School, and used to recite it at
Troop Concerts during the war, and once very successfully in a
Television Talk Show in America not many years ago.*

Sincerely yours,
John Gielgud

Bredon Hill

In summertime on Bredon
    The bells they sound so clear;
Round both the shires they ring them
    In steeples far and near,
    A happy noise to hear.

Here of a Sunday morning
    My love and I would lie,
And see the coloured counties,
    And hear the larks so high
    About us in the sky.

The bells would ring to call her
    In valleys miles away:
'Come all to church, good people;
    Good people, come and pray.'
    But here my love would stay.

And I would turn and answer
    Among the springing thyme,
'Oh, peal upon our wedding,
    And we will hear the chime,
    And come to church in time.'

But when the snows at Christmas
    On Bredon top were strown,
My love rose up so early
    And stole out unbeknown
    And went to church alone.

They tolled the one bell only,
    Groom there was none to see,
The mourners followed after,
    And so to church went she,
    And would not wait for me.

The bells they sound on Bredon,
    And still the steeples hum,
'Come all to church, good people' —
    Oh, noisy bells, be dumb;
    I hear you, I will come.

A E Housman (1859–1936)

ANNE DOYLE   87

RTE
2 February 1988

Dear Duncan, Julie, Jonathan,
Very difficult to nominate an absolute favourite, but I'll go for
Patrick Kavanagh's 'Epic'.
Already I'm having second and third thoughts — so without further
ado I'll wish you well and leave you with best regards,

Anne (Doyle)

Epic

I have lived in important places, times
When great events were decided, who owned
That half a rood of rock, a no-man's land
Surrounded by our pitchfork-armed claims.
I heard the Duffys shouting 'Damn your soul'
And old McCabe stripped to the waist, seen
Step the plot defying blue cast-steel —
'Here is the march along these iron stones'.
That was the year of the Munich bother. Which
Was more important? I inclined
To lose my faith in Ballyrush and Gortin
Till Homer's ghost came whispering to my mind
He said: I made the Iliad from such
A local row. Gods make their own importance.

Patrick Kavanagh (1904–1967)

TOM MURPHY   88

7 February 1988

Dear Julie, Jonathan, Duncan,
Thank you for yours. My choice of poem is 'The Salley Gardens'. *I*
hope my comments/sentiments regarding it are worthy of your
anthology. My congratulations for your achievements at Wesley in
aid of Ethiopia and my very best wishes for Lifelines II.

Sincerely,
Tom Murphy

A favourite poem is 'The Salley Gardens' *by W B Yeats. I like the*
poem for its sheer simplicity, yet it is very profound in its expression
of an elemental distinction that exists between the male and female
attitude: the male, in ever-increasing circles, futilely chasing his tail;
the female softness — serenity — in tune with the Earth, Nature —
the Infinite? (What I am saying is a generalisation, of course).
I like to hear the poem sung — unaccompanied voice. Invariably I
think of Ibsen's Peer Gynt. *Peer Gynt going off on his strange and*
wild adventures, returning as an old man, explaining to the wife he
left behind him that the goal of all his journeying was to find himself;
her reply to the effect: how could you find yourself when you were
here with me all the time?
Ibsen, I would imagine, in Peer Gynt, *was doing a 'recast' of*
Goethe's Faust. *(A well-nigh impossible work to come to terms with.)*
One of the strongest threads through Faust *is the movement from*

Gretchen (Margaret) to Helen, to the Mater Gloriosa. The final lines in Faust:

All things corruptible
Are but a parable;
Earth's insufficiency
Here finds fulfilment;
Here the ineffable
Wins life through love;
Eternal Womanhood
Leads us above.

Tom Murphy   7 February 1988

Down by the Salley Gardens

Down by the salley gardens my love and I did meet;
She passed the salley gardens with little snow-white feet.
She bid me take love easy, as the leaves grow on the tree;
But I, being young and foolish, with her would not agree.

In a field by the river my love and I did stand,
And on my leaning shoulder she laid her snow-white hand.
She bid me take life easy, as the grass grows on the weirs;
But I was young and foolish, and now am full of tears.

W B Yeats (1865–1939)

EILÉAN NÍ CHUILLEANEÁIN   89

Trinity College
Dublin 2
3 February 1988

Dear Julie, Jonathan, Duncan,
Thank you very much for your letter. I assume that when you ask for
'a favourite poem', you mean one by someone else, not my favourite
among my own poems. I am enclosing a copy of a poem,
'Houserules', by Macdara Woods. I like it because it is about me —
perhaps that's not a good reason. I like it as well, and more seriously,
because it is about marriage in the modern world, it's both witty and
a bit frightening. A reviewer called it 'horrific but adoring'. I think
'adoring' is too strong, the poem is too astringent for that.
I hope both the poem and my reasons for liking it appeal to you.
Good luck with your book,

Yours sincerely,
Eiléan Ní Chuilleaneáin

Houserules

Hoop-la said my working wife
this woman says there were two sorts of amazons
(and she looked at me over her tee ell ess)
the ones that went in for househusbands
and the others . . . random copulators
who only hit the ground in spots

Measuring-up to my responsibilities
I called to my wife starting out for work
could you take my head in to town today please
have my hair cut and my beard trimmed
for this poetry-reading on Thursday
(I was dusting my high-heeled Spanish boots)

Gladly: she threw the talking head
in the back of the car with her lecture notes
her handbag fur coat and galley proofs
tricks of trade and mercantile accoutrements
Otrivine stuffed firmly up my nostrils
to stop catarrh and Hacks for my throat

Leaving me headless and in some straits:
considering the ways of well set-up amazons
as I fumbled helplessly around the garden
playing blind man's buff to a dancing clothesline
stubbing my pegs on air and thinking with envy
of my neighbour and his empire of cabbages.

Macdara Woods (b. 1942)

KEVIN MYERS   90

*I was brought up to believe that poetry should have rhyme, rhythm,
and resonance. One could declaim it. Good stuff with metres that
would run on the lines of de-dum, de-dum, de-dum, de-da, de-dum,
de-dum, de-dum, de-do . . . If you can't recite it t'ain't poetry.*
*As for my own choice, it is the stuff to give the troops when you're
three sheets to the wind and about to pass out. Longfellow, now, is
the sort of fellow I'm talking about. Good manly stuff with
punctuation and rhymes and pace you can beat time to.*
And it is Kipling that I choose for my contribution — 'The Gods of
the Copybook Headings' *having just about everything. All the
rhyme and the rhythm and the internal resonance that you could
want. Plus a message. Good poems should always have a message.*

Kevin Myers

The Gods of the Copybook Headings

As I pass through my incarnations in every age and race,
I make my proper prostrations to the Gods of the Market-Place.
Peering through reverent fingers I watch them flourish and fall,
And the Gods of the Copybook Headings, I notice, outlast them
   all.

We were living in trees when they met us. They showed us each
   in turn
That Water would certainly wet us, as Fire would certainly burn:
But we found them lacking in Uplift, Vision and Breadth of
   Mind,
So we left them to teach the Gorillas while we followed the
   March of Mankind.

We moved as the Spirit listed. *They* never altered their pace,
Being neither cloud nor wind-borne like the Gods of the Market
   Place;
But they always caught up with our progress, and presently
   word would come
That a tribe had been wiped off its icefield, or the lights had gone
   out in Rome.

With the Hopes that our World is built on they were utterly out
   of touch,
They denied that the Moon was Stilton; they denied she was
   even Dutch.
They denied that Wishes were Horses; they denied that a Pig
   had Wings.
So we worshipped the Gods of the Market Who promised these
   beautiful things.

When the Cambrian measures were forming, They promised
   perpetual peace.
They swore, if we gave them our weapons, that the wars of the
   tribes would cease.
But when we disarmed They sold us and delivered us bound to
   our foe,
And the Gods of the Copybook Headings said: '*Stick to the Devil
   you know.*'

On the first Feminian Sandstones we were promised the Fuller
   Life
(Which started by loving our neighbour and ended by loving his
   wife)
Till our women had no more children and the men lost reason
   and faith,
And the Gods of the Copybook Headings said: '*The Wages of Sin
   is Death.*'

In the Carboniferous Epoch we were promised abundance for
    all,
By robbing selected Peter to pay for collective Paul;
But, though we had plenty of money, there was nothing our
  · money could buy,
And the Gods of the Copybook Headings said: *'If you don't work
    you die.'*

Then the Gods of the Market tumbled, and their smooth-tongued
    wizards withdrew,
And the hearts of the meanest were humbled and began to
    believe it was true
That All is not Gold that Glitters, and Two and Two make Four —
And the Gods of the Copybook Headings limped up to explain it
    once more.

As it will be in the future, it was at the birth of Man —
There are only four things certain since Social Progress began: —
That the Dog returns to his Vomit and the Sow returns to her
    Mire,
And the burnt Fool's bandaged finger goes wabbling back to the
    Fire;

And that after this is accomplished, and the brave new world
    begins
When all men are paid for existing and no man must pay for his
    sins,
As surely as Water will wet us, as surely as Fire will burn,
The Gods of the Copybook Headings with terror and slaughter
    return!

Rudyard Kipling (1865–1936)

NIALL McCARTHY   91

An Chúirt Uachtarach
(The Supreme Court)
Baile Átha Cliath 7
(Dublin 7)
4 February 1988

Dear Julie, Jonathan and Duncan,
Thank you for your letter, you compliment me. A favourite poem is
'In Memory of Eva Gore-Booth and Con Markiewicz' by W B
Yeats. It is a poignant recall of a passing time, its later ravages, the
withering of dreams and the arrested pictures of young beauty.

Good luck,
Niall McCarthy

In Memory of Eva Gore-Booth and Con Markiewicz

The light of evening, Lissadell,
Great windows open to the south,
Two girls in silk kimonos, both
Beautiful, one a gazelle.
But a raving autumn shears
Blossom from the summer's wreath;
The older is condemned to death,
Pardoned, drags out lonely years
Conspiring among the ignorant.
I know not what the younger dreams —
Some vague Utopia — and she seems,
When withered old and skeleton-gaunt
An image of such politics.
Many a time I think to seek
One or the other out and speak
Of that old Georgian mansion, mix
Pictures of the mind, recall
That table and the talk of youth,
Two girls in silk kimonos, both
Beautiful, one a gazelle.

Dear shadows, now you know it all,
All the folly of a fight
With a common wrong or right.
The innocent and the beautiful
Have no enemy but time;
Arise and bid me strike a match
And strike another till time catch;
Should the conflagration climb,
Run till all the sages know.
We the great gazebo built,
They convicted us of guilt;
Bid me strike a match and blow.

W B Yeats (1865–1939)

JOHN B KEANE   92

9 February 1988

Dear Julie, Jonathan and Duncan,
I offer the poem 'Water' by Brendan Kennelly, professor of English
Literature in Trinity College. It is from his volume Bread *published*
by Gallery Books in 1971.
Because it is a poem which cherishes the one thing in this country we
most take for granted and extols as well the gentleness which makes it
so powerful.

John B Keane

Water

Chuckling in gutters,
Active in the corner of a field
Or barely bending the slightest flowers

Its pace is perfect.
Bridge between earth and sky,
Lucid contract

Between all things that wish to grow,
I feel it when I stand,
Uncouth watcher, flow

Through me with a shock
That makes me love
Its definition of rock

And stone, its gracious wavering
From those things
To which it pays attention.

It lives so completely it does not need
To bully what comes in its path.
The unresting colourless blood

Of creation is content to approach,
Digress, but rarely overwhelm.
Nothing has a lighter touch.

It has many voices and I
Have heard a few.
I like most what it says of recovery

And movement, the will
To continue while acknowledging the possible
Superiority of remaining still.

Disciple of its fluency, I
Follow it everywhere.
Sometimes I think the sky

Exults with it and I listen
To the heartbeat of the sea
At the centre of the stone,

Laughter down the side of a hill,
A playful rumpus at
The doorway, the freckled thrill

On the river's face; and I marvel again
At the presence that lives
Because it is gone.

Brendan Kennelly (b. 1936)

MARY LAVIN   93

9 February 1988

Dear Julie, and all you,
I am not sure if you want an attempt of my own at poetry or a poem
by a real poet. To save time I am sending an effort of my own that I
wrote long ago before the short story cast its spell over me.
I had spent far too long going over books of poetry until I realised
that trying to make a striking choice was really a subtle form of
vanity. Most of the poems that I found gave me the greatest joy and
were, oddly enough, those I had learned off by heart at school. Then
suddenly I remembered a poem I first read in UCD which had stayed
in my mind without my having consciously memorised it and I am
sending it because it pays tribute to all the great poetry and prose
that has sustained me throughout a long life, and probably had given
me the impetus to dare to try writing myself, fairly late in life.
Incidentally I have learned that the intoxication of writing comes
from straining to write as well as one can and not from success.

Good luck,
Mary Lavin

I think continually of those who were truly great.
Who, from the womb, remembered the soul's history
Through corridors of light where the hours are suns,
Endless and singing. Whose lovely ambition
Was that their lips, still touched with fire,
Should tell of the Spirit, clothed from head to foot in song.
And who hoarded from the Spring branches
The desires falling across their bodies like blossoms.

What is precious, is never to forget
The essential delight of the blood drawn from ageless springs
Breaking through rocks in worlds before our earth.
Never to deny its pleasure in the morning simple light
Nor its grave evening demand for love.
Never to allow gradually the traffic to smother
With noise and fog, the flowering of the Spirit.

Near the snow, near the sun, in the highest fields,
See how these names are fêted by the waving grass
And by the streamers of white cloud
And whispers of wind in the listening sky.
The names of those who in their lives fought for life,
Who wore at their hearts the fire's centre.
Born of the sun, they travelled a short while towards them
And left the vivid air signed with their honour.

Stephen Spender (b. 1909)

Christ If You Wanted My Shining Soul

Christ if you wanted my shining soul
That flashed its happy fins
And splashed in the silent seas of sin,
Then Christ, keenest fisherman
On the Galilean shore,
If you wanted to catch my shivering soul
Why did you let down nets that were worn,
Unravelled and floating light?
I slid along the ribbony web
In and out
And when the nets slime-wet and black
Crawled over the prow of your boat again
Empty as nets that sway all day
In an empty sea
My sly soul waited
And swam aloft
To play at leaping the ripples
And showing its silver dapples
To the silently floating fishes
On the outer-side of the wave
The little silver minnows of the moon.

Mary Lavin (b. 1912)

SR STANISLAUS KENNEDY   94

Focus Point
15 Eustace Street
Dublin 2
11 February 1988

Dear Julie, Jonathan and Duncan,
'Street Corner Christ' is a poem very close to my own heart and given the nature of your cause, I feel an appropriate contribution. I have kept my comments to the bare minimum and although my few lines do not do justice to this poem it is my heartfelt wish that in helping to raise funds for Ethiopia they may allow justice to be done elsewhere.
If there is any other way in which I can be of assistance please don't hesitate to contact me.
With kindest regards,

Yours sincerely,
Sr Stanislaus Kennedy

'Street Corner Christ' *by Patrick Kavanagh*
At first reading, the reader is struck by the simple poignancy of this
poem and touched by the sadness which tinges the poet's description of
his subject matter — 'an uncouth ballad seller with tail-matted hair'.
But to be merely touched by the images which predominate the verse
and not to recognise the harsh criticism which the poet is levelling at
society, would not do Kavanagh justice. It would be similar in fact, to
becoming 'as blind and deaf' as the 'pieties' within the poem whose
narrowness of vision prohibits them from seeing the truth.
Indeed acceptance of such criticism is integral to identifying with the
poet and to understanding and empathising with the message *of the*
poem. It was Christ, after all, who said 'whatever you do to the least of
these my brethren, you do unto me'. Surely, it follows, then, that if it
takes a little bit of poetic licence to bring these words home to us and to
help all those who seek to find their own street corner Christ in the
'rags of a beggar', then God Bless Paddy Kavanagh!

Street Corner Christ

I saw Christ today
At a street corner stand,
In the rags of a beggar he stood
He held ballads in his hand.

He was crying out: 'Two for a penny
Will anyone buy
The finest ballads ever made
From the stuff of joy?'

But the blind and deaf went past
Knowing only there
An uncouth ballad seller
With tail-matted hair.

And I whom men call fool
His ballads bought,
Found Him whom the pieties
Have vainly sought.

Patrick Kavanagh (1904–1967)

DOIREANN NÍ BHRIAIN   95

RTE
22 January 1988

Dear Julie, Jonathan and Duncan,
Thank you for inviting me to contribute to your book.
When I went to school in the 1960s, I never read any contemporary

poetry in English. I had to learn long chunks of poetry by rote and it meant nothing to me. I still remember the excitement and exhilaration I felt when, after I'd left school, I came across Seamus Heaney's work. I bought myself a hardback copy of Door Into the Dark *for my nineteenth birthday — I don't think I'd ever bought a hardback book before that and certainly never a book of poetry. 'The Forge' is from that collection. It was the first poem in English I ever learnt by heart because I wanted to!*

The Forge

All I know is a door into the dark.
Outside, old axles and iron hoops rusting;
Inside, the hammered anvil's short-pitched ring,
The unpredictable fantail of sparks
Or hiss when a new shoe toughens in water.
The anvil must be somewhere in the centre,
Horned as a unicorn, at one end square,
Set there immoveable: an altar
Where he expends himself in shape and music.
Sometimes, leather-aproned, hairs in his nose,
He leans out on the jamb, recalls a clatter
Of hoofs where traffic is flashing in rows;
Then grunts and goes in, with a slam and flick
To beat real iron out, to work the bellows.

Seamus Heaney (b. 1939)

I hope you enjoy compiling the book.
With very best wishes for the success of your project,

Doireann Ní Bhriain

PADRAIC WHITE   96

The universal greatness of Patrick Kavanagh.
I came to Dublin in 1960 to get my first job in the strange world to me of an 'office' in the big city of Dublin which was equally mysterious to me.
I was brought up in the peaceful village of Kinlough in County Leitrim and within walking distance of some beautiful countryside, lakes, rivers and ocean in Leitrim, Donegal and Sligo.
There was much talk in Dublin about Patrick Kavanagh at that time. He had come from a very rural part of Monaghan, was largely self taught, despite many vicissitudes of life was moved to write a great body of poetry and prose.

When I came to Dublin he wrote articles in newspapers for a part living, was a well known habitué of Baggot Street, its precincts and pubs. He died in 1967 at the age of sixty-two years.
I probably had a particular interest in his writing because I could identify with his rural background. With the passing of time, his true greatness becomes clearer.
I like Patrick Kavanagh's writing for two particular reasons which my choice of poems illustrate. First, he could take small rural or everyday incidents and show their universal relevance as in the poem 'Epic'.

Epic

I have lived in important places, times
When great events were decided, who owned
That half a rood of rock, a no-man's land
Surrounded by our pitchfork-armed claims.
I heard the Duffys shouting 'Damn your soul'
And old McCabe stripped to the waist, seen
Step the plot defying blue cast-steel —
'Here is the march along these iron stones'.
That was the year of the Munich bother. Which
Was more important? I inclined
To lose my faith in Ballyrush and Gortin
Till Homer's ghost came whispering to my mind
He said: I made the Iliad from such
A local row. Gods make their own importance.

Patrick Kavanagh (1904–1967)

Second, he was always true to himself and to the ultimate truth of life. This side of Kavanagh is beautifully illustrated in a poem about him entitled 'A Man I Knew — in memory of Patrick Kavanagh' by Brendan Kennelly, who comes from Kerry, is an outstanding contemporary Irish poet and lectures at Trinity College, Dublin.

Yours sincerely,
Padraic White   10 February 1988

A Man I Knew
In memory of Patrick Kavanagh

I
'I want no easy grave' he said to me,
'Where those who hated me can come and stare,
Slip down upon a servile knee,
Muttering their phoney public prayer.
In the wilds of Norfolk I'd like to lie,

No commemorative stone, no sheltering trees,
Far from the hypocrite's tongue and eye,
Safe from the praise of my enemies.'

II
A man I knew who seemed to me
The epitome of chivalry
Was constantly misunderstood.
The heart's dialogue with God
Was his life's theme and he
Explored its depths assiduously
And without rest. Therefore he spat
On every shoddy value that
Blinded men to their true destiny —
The evil power of mediocrity,
The safety of the barren pose,
All that distorted natural grace.
Which is to say, almost everything.
Once he asked a girl to sing
A medieval ballad. As her voice rang out,
She was affronted by some interfering lout.
This man I knew spat in his face
And wished him to the floor of hell.
I thought then, and still think it well
That man should wear the spittle of disgrace
For violating certain laws.
Now I recall my friend because
He lived according to his code
And in his way was true to God.
Courage he had and was content to be
Himself, whatever came his way
There is no other chivalry.

Brendan Kennelly (b. 1936)

MARIA SIMONDS-GOODING   97

10 February 1988

Dear Julie, Jonathan, and Duncan,
Thank you for your letter and for asking me to select a poem of my
choice.
I wish you success in your project,

Yours sincerely,
Maria Simonds-Gooding

from William Wordsworth's *The Prelude*

>   but that the Soul
> Remembering how she felt, but what she felt
> Remembering not, retains an obscure sense
> Of possible sublimity, whereto
> With growing faculties she doth aspire,
> With faculties still growing, feeling still
> That whatsoever point they gain, they yet
> Have something to pursue.

The reason I choose this poem, by Wordsworth, is the philosophy
behind it and this aspiration drives me, beyond and beyond.

ELLEN GILCHRIST   98

Petition

Sir, no man's enemy, forgiving all
But will its negative inversion, be prodigal:
Send to us power and light, a sovereign touch
Curing the intolerable neural itch,
The exhaustion of weaning, the liar's quinsy,
And the distortions of ingrown virginity.
Prohibit sharply the rehearsed response
And gradually correct the coward's stance;
Cover in time with beams those in retreat
That, spotted, they turn though the reverse were great;
Publish each healer that in city lives
Or country houses at the end of drives;
Harrow the house of the dead; look shining at
New styles of architecture, a change of heart.

W H Auden (1907–1973)

Over the years lines from this poem have taught me different things
at different times, and, always, as I grew older, it has reminded me to
'look shining at new styles of architecture, a change of heart'.
It has kept my heart from calcifying. The heart is very near the
thymus gland, where the t-lymphocytes and killer glands of the
immune system get their training. Very important to stay flexible in
that area.
Also, if one is going to posit and address a higher being it should
always be as sir or madam.
I loved Lifelines I *and look forward to the new one.*

All best wishes,
Ellen Gilchrist
                                                28 January 1988

SUE MILLER   99

'The Old Fools' *by Philip Larkin*
This poem seems remarkable to me in describing an alien state, in its use of language, and in its ability, finally to force the reader into crossing some boundary between himself and 'the other' — in this case the old, the disoriented.

Sue Miller   4 February 1988

The Old Fools

What do they think has happened, the old fools,
To make them like this? Do they somehow suppose
It's more grown-up when your mouth hangs open and drools,
And you keep on pissing yourself, and can't remember
Who called this morning? Or that, if they only chose,
They could alter things back to when they danced all night,
Or went to their wedding, or sloped arms some September?
Or do they fancy there's really been no change,
And they've always behaved as if they were crippled or tight,
Or sat through days of thin continuous dreaming
Watching light move? If they don't (and they can't), it's strange:
                    Why aren't they screaming?

At death, you break up: the bits that were you
Start speeding away from each other for ever
With no one to see. It's only oblivion, true:
We had it before, but then it was going to end,
And was all the time merging with a unique endeavour
To bring to bloom the million-petalled flower
Of being here. Next time you can't pretend
There'll be anything else. And these are the first signs:
Not knowing how, not hearing who, the power
Of choosing gone. Their looks show that they're for it:
Ash hair, toad hands, prune face dried into lines –
                    How can they ignore it?

Perhaps being old is having lighted rooms
Inside your head, and people in them, acting.
People you know, yet can't quite name; each looms
Like a deep loss restored, from known doors turning,
Setting down a lamp, smiling from a stair, extracting
A known book from the shelves; or sometimes only
The rooms themselves, chairs and a fire burning,
The blown bush at the window, or the sun's
Faint friendliness on the wall some lonely

Rain-ceased midsummer evening. That is where they live:
Not here and now, but where all happened once.
                    This is why they give.

An air of baffled absence, trying to be there
Yet being here. For the rooms grow farther, leaving
Incompetent cold, the constant wear and tear
Of taken breath, and then crouching below
Extinction's alp, the old fools, never perceiving
How near it is. This must be what keeps them quiet:
The peak that stays in view wherever we go
For them is rising ground. Can they never tell
What is dragging them back, and how it will end? Not at night?
Not when the strangers come? Never, throughout
The whole hideous inverted childhood? Well
                    We shall find out.

Philip Larkin (1922–1985)

RICHARD BRANSON   100

Virgin Group
London W8 7AR
19 February 1988

Dear Julie, Jonathan and Duncan,
Richard has asked me to thank you for your letter. His favourite poem
is Ted Hughes's 'An Otter'. He loves otters!
Hope you raise lots of money with your book!

Best wishes,
Clodagh Simonds
Secretary to Richard Branson

An Otter

I

    Underwater eyes, an eel's
Oil of water body, neither fish nor beast is the otter:
  Four-legged yet water-gifted, to outfish fish;
    With webbed feet and long ruddering tail
    And a round head like an old tomcat.

    Brings the legend of himself
From before wars or burials, in spite of hounds and vermin-
       poles;
  Does not take root like the badger. Wanders, cries;
    Gallops along land he no longer belongs to;
    Re-enters the water by melting.

Of neither water nor land. Seeking
Some world lost when first he dived, that he cannot come at
              since,
    Takes his changed body into the holes of lakes;
        As if blind, cleaves the stream's push till he licks
        The pebbles of the source; from sea

    To sea crosses in three nights
Like a king in hiding. Crying to the old shape of the starlit
              land,
    Over sunken farms where the bats go round,
        Without answer. Till light and birdsong come
        Walloping up roads with the milk wagon.

II
The hunt's lost him. Pads on mud,
Among sedges, nostrils a surface bead,
The otter remains, hours. The air,
Circling the globe, tainted and necessary,

Mingling tobacco-smoke, hounds and parsley,
Comes carefully to the sunk lungs.
So the self under the eye lies,
Attendant and withdrawn. The otter belongs

In double robbery and concealment —
From water that nourishes and drowns, and from land
That gave him his length and the mouth of the hound.
He keeps fat in the limpid integument

Reflections live on. The heart beats thick,
Big trout muscle out of the dead cold;
Blood is the belly of logic; he will lick
The fishbone bare. And can take stolen hold

On a bitch otter in a field full
Of nervous horses, but linger nowhere.
Yanked above hounds, reverts to nothing at all,
To this long pelt over the back of a chair.

Ted Hughes (b. 1930)

PAT KENNY   101

15 February 1988

Dear Julie, Jonathan and Duncan,
I found it quite impossible to nominate an all-time favourite. So
much depends on the mood, the weather, the circumstance. Because I
work with the spoken word all the time, I have an infatuation with its

beauty whether it's in the sonnets of Shakespeare, the lyricism of Yeats or in the words of some popular songs. However, my first realisation that poetry didn't, wasn't always about nature, life, love or despair came with the discovery of Sir John Betjeman. It also helped me to realise as a schoolboy that you didn't have to be dead to be recognised as a poetic genius. I can recommend any of his poems to your readers, but perhaps 'Business Girls' captures the world of bed-sit London, and to some extent Dublin, to perfection.

Yours sincerely,
Pat Kenny

Business Girls

From the geyser ventilators
Autumn winds are blowing down
On a thousand business women
Having baths in Camden Town.

Waste pipes chuckle into runnels
Steam's escaping here and there,
Morning trains through Camden cutting
Shake the Crescent and the Square.

Early nip of changeful Autumn,
Dahlias glimpsed through garden doors,
At the back precarious bathrooms
Jutting out from upper floors;

And behind their frail partitions
Business women lie and soak,
Seeing through the draughty skylight
Flying clouds and railway smoke.

Rest you there, poor unbelov'd ones,
Lap your loneliness in heat.
All too soon the tiny breakfast,
Trolley bus and windy street!

John Betjeman (1906–1984)

JUDI DENCH   102

16 February 1988

Dear Julie, Jonathan and Duncan,
I was so pleased to have your letter and to read about the book you are putting together. I am particularly pleased to be asked to contribute as both my parents went to Wesley College, and I have lovely memories of several visits to Dublin.

One of my favourite poems is 'Adlestrop' by Edward Thomas. I love it because of its essential Englishness and because it reminds me of the time of steam trains and that special hiss that announced their arrivals and departures. It is a very nostalgic poem about a part of England that I know well, and I hope its inclusion will introduce the poem to lots of new readers.

With best wishes,
Judi Dench

Adlestrop

Yes. I remember Adlestrop —
The name, because one afternoon
Of heat the express-train drew up there
Unwontedly. It was late June.

The steam hissed. Someone cleared his throat.
No one left and no one came
On the bare platform. What I saw
Was Adlestrop — only the name

And willows, willow-herb, and grass,
And meadowsweet, and haycocks dry,
No whit less still and lonely fair
Than the high cloudlets in the sky.

And for that minute a blackbird sang
Close by, and round him, mistier,
Farther and farther, all the birds
Of Oxfordshire and Gloucestershire.

Edward Thomas (1878–1917)

CLARE BOYLAN   103

2 March 1988

Dear Julie Grantham,
In reply to your request for a choice of poem for your anthology:
I haven't got a favourite poem but I like the work of Emily Dickinson because she uses Victorian sentiment as a vehicle for irony and at the same time touches the heart by connecting the ordinary and the domestic to the great emotions.
The simple, untitled poem below (written in 1866) sets a scene which is recognisable to everybody and heightens the poignancy by wryly imposing the platitudes of outsiders upon the bereaved, for 'The sweeping up the heart, and putting love away' is the hope of the

comforter and not the reality for anyone who has lost someone they
love.
I am sorry for the delay in replying to your request, but this is the
first clear space I have had this year. I wish you every success with
the venture.
With all good wishes,

Yours,
Clare Boylan

The Bustle in a House
The Morning after Death
Is solemnest of industries
Enacted upon Earth —

The Sweeping up the Heart
And putting Love away
We shall not want to use again
Until Eternity.

Emily Dickinson (1830–1886)

CHAIM HERZOG   104

State of Israel
Jerusalem
15 February 1988

Dear Julie, Jonathan and Duncan,
Many thanks for your letter dated January 1988. I am very happy to
help you in your efforts to raise money for famine victims in
Ethiopia. I congratulate you on the success of your efforts, following
the production of Lifelines I *and wish you every success in your*
further endeavours to help the starving people in the Third World.
It is very difficult, indeed, for me to choose a particular poem or poet.
A very deep appreciation and love of poetry was instilled in me when
I was a pupil at Wesley College. The result is that I have far too many
favourite poets and favourite poems and it is, therefore, not easy for
me to choose one. However, since I am contributing to an effort in
Ireland let me say that one of my favourite poets is W B Yeats. His
poem that has remained with me as a favourite is 'The Lake Isle of
Innisfree'. *I believe that few poems have given life to a rustic scene*
as has done this poem. Everything as it were comes to life — the
beauty of the quietness of the glade in which he will build a small
cabin, the bees, the cricket, the shimmer and glimmer of the morning
and the night and the birds. All this against the background of the
lake with the water lapping by the shores. Yeats was certainly one of

the greatest poets of our time. He succeeded in his beautiful poems to bring to life so many aspects of nature, of life and of art. All this against the background of his deep love for Ireland and its legends and his idealistic devotion to the cause of the Irish Revolution. W B Yeats is, in my mind, a poet who will survive the ages and who belongs to eternity.
With best wishes,

Yours sincerely,
Chaim Herzog

The Lake Isle of Innisfree

I will arise and go now, and go to Innisfree,
And a small cabin build there, of clay and wattles made:
Nine bean-rows will I have there, a hive for the honey-bee,
And live alone in the bee-loud glade.

And I shall have some peace there, for peace comes dropping
    slow,
Dropping from the veils of the morning to where the cricket
    sings;
There midnight's all a glimmer, and noon a purple glow,
And evening full of the linnet's wings.

I will arise and go now, for always night and day
I hear lake water lapping with low sounds by the shore;
While I stand on the roadway, or on the pavements grey,
I hear it in the deep heart's core.

W B Yeats (1865–1939)

MIKE MURPHY   105

3 March 1988

Dear Julie Grantham,
My apologies for the delay in replying to your letter — I'm afraid that it just got mislaid and I have only found it today.
My choice of poem would be 'Elegy in a Country Churchyard' by Thomas Gray because in my opinion it is one of the gentliest, most provocative poems ever written. I don't need yoga, valium, or any other relaxant. When necessary I recite the first few verses and I feel the better for it.

Kind regards,
Mike (Murphy)

from *Elegy Written in a Country Churchyard*

The curfew tolls the knell of parting day,
The lowing herd wind slowly o'er the lea,
The plowman homeward plods his weary way,
And leaves the world to darkness and to me.

Now fades the glimmering landscape on the sight,
And all the air a solemn stillness holds,
Save where the beetle wheels his droning flight,
And drowsy tinklings lull the distant folds;

Save that from yonder ivy-mantled tow'r
The moping owl does to the moon complain
Of such as, wand'ring near her secret bow'r,
Molest her ancient solitary reign.

Beneath those rugged elms, that yew-tree's shade,
Where heaves the turf in many a mould'ring heap,
Each in his narrow cell for ever laid,
The rude Forefathers of the hamlet sleep.

The breezy call of incense-breathing Morn,
The swallow twitt'ring from the straw-built shed,
The cock's shrill clarion, or the echoing horn,
No more shall rouse them from their lowly bed.

Thomas Gray (1716–1771)

NUALA NÍ DHOMHNAILL   106

Nuala Ní Dhomhnaill's choice: 'The Arrival of the Beebox'
by Sylvia Plath and 'Antarctica' by Derek Mahon

The Arrival of the Bee Box
I have to confess that I chose this poem because I am a bit of a Sylvia
Plath affectionado, especially of the later poems which many have
termed hysterical, and self-dramatising. I am not frightened or
repelled by these powerful poems; rather I find they are the nearest
thing I have ever read to some of my own states of mind, writ large. I
read these poems as extremely honest and clear-eyed expressions of
women's emotions in a society that frustrates the self-fulfilment of
women. Literary critics, men for the most part, and especially covert
upholders of the old order are particularly baffled by these poems.
They pretend to be irritated by them. Mostly, actually, they are
frightened out of their skins.
For all its seeming artlessness, this poem is actually very finely
crafted. Plath has come far from the careful, formal stylization of, say,

'The Colossus', but has lost nothing in transit. The poem fairly buzzes with energy, not the least of which is the energy of simple, colloquial words and phrases — 'coffin of a midget', 'a square baby', 'I have simply ordered a box of maniacs', yet the whole is greater than the parts, being as it is almost one long sustained metaphor. Muriel Rukeyser asked once

'What would happen if one woman told the truth about her
   life?
The world would split open.'

In the terrible tension of containing the clamour of the host of my own interior selves, so as not to destroy the world, I am often that bee box. I am like a walking keg of dynamite. As in Plath's poem a whole swarm of dark little angry things are barely contained within my skin. A great African Queen would loose her cohorts if I ever took the lid off. And nobody knows as well as I do how they can sting. It is perhaps interesting that the phrase used in Irish for acting on a sudden impulse is 'do phrioch an bheach mé, — 'the bee stung me.' In view of Sylvia Plath's untimely death the last line of the poem is particularly poignant and prophetic:— 'The box is only temporary.' It would make you wonder if the price to pay for leaving all the bees out is always as great as it had to be in her case.

The Arrival of the Bee Box

I ordered this, this clean wood box
Square as a chair and almost too heavy to lift.
I would say it was the coffin of a midget
Or a square baby
Were there not such a din in it.

The box is locked, it is dangerous.
I have to live with it overnight
And I can't keep away from it,
There are no windows, so I can't see what is in there
There is only a little grid, no exit.

I put my eye to the grid.
It is dark, dark,
With the swarmy feeling of African hands
Minute and shrunk for export,
Black on black, angrily clambering.

How can I let them out?
It is the noise that appals me most of all,
The unintelligible syllables.
It is like a Roman mob,
Small, taken one by one, but my god, together!

I lay my ear to furious Latin.
I am not a Caesar.
I have simply ordered a box of maniacs.
They can be sent back.
They can die, I need feed them nothing, I am the owner.

I wonder how hungry they are.
I wonder if they would forget me
If I just undid the locks and stood back and turned into a tree.
There is the laburnum, its blond colonnades,
And the petticoats of the cherry.

They might ignore me immediately
In my moon suit and funeral veil.
I am no source of honey
So why should they turn on me?
Tomorrow I will be sweet God, I will set them free.

The box is only temporary.

Sylvia Plath (1932–1963)

Antarctica

Now just to show that I have no particular prejudice against formalism as such, my second choice is, on the surface at least, a very different kind of poem — Derek Mahon's 'Antarctica'. Once before a reading I asked Derek to read this poem as a special favour and he said he felt a bit of a dolt reading it, hearing all those rhymes and repetitions clanging heavily about his ears. But he still read it for me, and then I knew at once why I loved this poem, because it suddenly dawned on me that the dull thud of the repetitions is an absolutely intrinsic part of the poem itself. If every poem, as opposed to every piece of verse, is an invocation or an evocation of the Muse then it must be the Goddess Durga who is called into being here, the Snow Queen, mistress of the cold impenetrable regions of the psyche, that inner tundra. It is a region I have travelled in myself, where the bouncing common-sense ego on which our civilization is built perishes in a vertiginous swoon. Therefore as Derek Mahon says himself, this is a feminist poem, because it chronicles the moment when the more-than-faintly-ridiculous heroic male ego finally snuffs it. The rigidity of the metre and the constant repetitions are a very symptom of the state of the soul. The psyche is an ice-box, a house in mid-winter with the heat turned off. In this state you wander about, metaphorically, in furs and highboots, in a frozen stupor, stamping your feet and repeating yourself constantly. The pipes, the conduits of emotion, are frozen solid, rigid like the lines of the poem. Thus for me 'Antarctica' is the supreme example of a formal poem that is not merely emptily so, but where the metre and strict rhyming scheme play an essential part in building up the reality enacted.

Ta súil agam go ndéanfaidh an méid seo cúis,
Nuala x x x

Antarctica

'I am just going outside and may be some time.'
The others nod, pretending not to know.
At the heart of the ridiculous, the sublime.

He leaves them reading and begins to climb,
Goading his ghost into the howling snow;
He is just going outside and may be some time.

The tent recedes beneath its crust of rime
And frostbite is replaced by vertigo:
At the heart of the ridiculous, the sublime.

Need we consider it some sort of crime,
This numb self-sacrifice of the weakest? No,
He is just going outside and may be some time —

In fact, for ever. Solitary enzyme,
Though the night yield no glimmer there will glow,
At the heart of the ridiculous, the sublime.

He takes leave of the earthly pantomime
Quietly, knowing it is time to go:—
'I am just going outside and may be some time.'
At the heart of the ridiculous, the sublime.

Derek Mahon (b. 1941)

KENNETH BLACKMORE   107

Wesley College
Dublin 16

Dear Julie, Jonathan and Duncan,
Thank you for inviting me to submit a favourite poem in the latest edition of Lifelines.
I chose 'Schoolmaster' because of the way I remember my days in the old St Patrick's Cathedral Grammar School (a new school is to be opened by the Taoiseach next month) and the variety of the teaching styles of Miss Dunbar and the schoolmasters there. All of them had at least one great gift in common — the ability to inspire. Albert Schweitzer has written 'I do not believe that we can put into anyone ideas which are not in him anyway. As a rule there are in everyone some good ideas, like tinder. But much of this tinder catches fire only when it meets some flame or spark from outside; that is, from some other person.'
With every good wish,

Yours sincerely,
Kenneth Blackmore

Schoolmaster

Oh yes, yes, I remember him well,
though I do not know if I would recognise him now:
nobody grows any younger, or better,
and boys grow into much the sort of men one would suppose
though sometimes the moustaches bewilder
and one finds it hard to reconcile one's memory of a small
    non-too-clean urchin lying his way unsuccessfully out of his
      homework
with a fierce and many-medalled sergeant-major with three
      children
or a divorced chartered accountant;
and it is hard to realise
that some little tousled rebellious youth whose only claim
to fame among his contemporaries was his undisputed right
to the championship of the spitting contest
is now perhaps one's own bank manager.
Oh yes, I remember him well, the boy you are searching for:
he looked like most boys, no better, brighter, or more
      respectful;
he cribbed, mitched, spilt ink, rattled his desk and
garbled his lessons with the worst of them;
he could smudge, hedge, smirk, wriggle, wince,
whimper, blarney, badger, blush, deceive, be
devious, stammer, improvise, assume
offended dignity or righteous indignation as though to the
      manner born;
sullenly and reluctantly he drilled, for some small
crime, under Sergeant Bird, so wittily nicknamed
Oiseau, on Wednesday half-holidays,
appeared regularly in detention classes,
hid in the cloakroom during algebra,
was, when a newcomer, thrown, into the bushes of the
Lower Playground by bigger boys;
and threw newcomers into the bushes of the Lower
Playground when *he* was a bigger boy;
he scuffled at prayers,
he interpolated, smugly, the time-honoured wrong
irreverent words into the morning hymns,
he helped to damage the headmaster's rhubarb,
was thirty third in trigonometry,
and, as might be expected, edited the School Magazine.

Dylan Thomas (1914–1953)

JOE LYNCH   108

Dear Julie, Jonathan and Duncan,
My favourite poem in English is 'The Listeners' by Walter de la
Mare. The best line has to be: 'And a bird flew up out of the turret
above the traveller's head'. The onomatopoeia of the 'flutter' of a fast-
rising bird is unparalleled in any language. When I studied de la
Mare in school, I did not realise that he was still very much alive (he
died in the early 1950s) and for me, he always lifted the veil of
mystery just enough to intrigue the readers.

Sincerely,
Joe Lynch

The Listeners

'Is there anybody there?' said the Traveller,
    Knocking on the moonlit door;
And his horse in the silence champed the grasses
    Of the forest's ferny floor:
And a bird flew up out of the turret,
    Above the Traveller's head:
And he smote upon the door again a second time;
    'Is there anybody there?' he said.
But no one descended to the Traveller;
    No head from the leaf-fringed sill
Leaned over and looked into his grey eyes,
    Where he stood perplexed and still.
But only a host of phantom listeners
    That dwelt in the lone house then
Stood listening in the quiet of the moonlight
    To that voice from the world of men:
Stood thronging the faint moonbeams on the dark stair,
    That goes down to the empty hall,
Hearkening in an air stirred and shaken
    By the lonely Traveller's call.
And he felt in his heart their strangeness,
    Their stillness answering his cry,
While his horse moved, cropping the dark turf,
    'Neath the starred and leafy sky;
For he suddenly smote on the door, even
    Louder, and lifted his head: —
'Tell them I came, and no one answered,
    That I kept my word,' he said.
Never the least stir made the listeners,
    Though every word he spake

Fell echoing through the shadowiness of the still house
    From the one man left awake:
Ay, they heard his foot upon the stirrup,
    And the sound of iron on stone,
And how the silence surged softly backward,
    When the plunging hoofs were gone.

Walter de la Mare (1873–1956)

LIFELINES III

ANTONY SHER   109

Sonnet 29

When, in disgrace with fortune and men's eyes,
I all alone beweep my outcast state,
And trouble deaf heaven with my bootless cries,
And look upon myself, and curse my fate,
Wishing me like to one more rich in hope,
Featured like him, like him with friends possessed,
Desiring this man's art and that man's scope,
With what I most enjoy contented least;
Yet in these thoughts myself almost despising,
Haply I think on thee — and then my state,
Like to the lark at break of day arising
From sullen earth, sings hymns at heaven's gate;
For thy sweet love rememb'red such wealth brings
That then I scorn to change my state with kings.

William Shakespeare (1564–1616)

One of my favourite poems is Shakespeare's Sonnet Number 29,
'When, in disgrace with fortune and men's eyes'. It was a favourite
piece of the actor Norman Henry, a dear friend and respected
colleague in the Royal Shakespeare Company who sadly died last
year. I read this sonnet at his Memorial Service at Trinity Church in
Stratford upon Avon.

Good luck with the book,
Antony Sher

PATRICK GRAHAM   110

3 January 1990

Dear Joann, Jacki and Carolyn,
That everything I know is a betrayal of what I ought to know.

Patrick Graham

Gnome

Spend the years of learning squandering
Courage for the years of wandering
Through a world politely turning
From the loutishness of learning

Samuel Beckett (1906–1989)

MARY FITZGERALD   111

RTE

Dear Lifelines,
Thank you for asking me to submit a poem for your anthology. I
enclose a poem which is my favourite called 'Snowman Sniffles' by
N M Bodecker. I like this poem for its simplicity and for the beautiful
winter picture it creates.
I hope this is of help to you. I wish you all every success with your
worthwhile venture.

Best wishes,
Mary FitzGerald

Snowman Sniffles

At winter's end
a snowman grows
a snowdrop
on his carrot nose,

a little, sad,
late-season sniff
dried by the spring
wind's handkerchief.

But day and night
the sniffles drop
like flower buds
— they never stop,

until you wake
and find one day
the cold, old man
has run away,

and winter's winds
that blow and pass
left drifts of snowdrops
in the grass,

reminding us:
where such things grow
a snowman sniffed
not long ago.

N M Bodecker

LARRY GOGAN   112

RTE

Dear Lifelines,
Sorry for delay in replying. It just went out of my head. When I was
in school in St Mary's College in Rathmines I used to enter
Feiseanna as a verse speaker. I never won but I did come second once
when I was about twelve and the poem I did on that occasion has
always been a favourite of mine ever since. It was called 'Connolly'
by Liam MacGabhann and was about the 1916 leader.
I wish you well with your project.

Kind regards,
Larry Gogan

Connolly

The son of a Welsh miner, a member of the firing squad that shot James
Connolly, was so impressed by the bravery of the great leader that afterwards
he paid a visit to Connolly's relatives to implore their forgiveness. The
following poem is an impression of the soldier's story to his comrades.

The man was all shot through that came today
Into the barrack square;
A soldier I — I am not proud to say
We killed him there;
They brought him from the prison hospital;
To see him in that chair
I thought his smile would far more quickly call
A man to prayer.

Maybe we cannot understand this thing
That makes these rebels die;
And yet all things love freedom — and the Spring
Clear in the sky;
I think I would not do this deed again
For all that I hold by;
Gaze down my rifle at his breast — but then
A soldier I.

They say that he was kindly — different, too,
Apart from all the rest;
A lover of the poor; and all shot through,
His wounds ill drest,
He came before us, faced us like a man,
He knew a deeper pain
Than blows or bullets — ere the world began;
Died he in vain?

Ready — present; And he just smiling — God!
I felt my rifle shake
His wounds were opened out and round that chair
Was one red lake;
I swear his lips said 'Fire!' when all was still
Before my rifle spat
That cursed lead — and I was picked to kill
A man like that!

Liam MacGabhann

RITA ANN HIGGINS   113

4 January 1990

Dear Joann, Jacki and Carolyn,
Many thanks for inviting me to participate in this worthy venture.
A favourite poem of mine is 'Coal for Mike' by Brecht. As I
understand it, the poem is about unconditional love, which is rare
enough.
Also the vivid imagery in the poem allows one to play back the story
of the poem again and again, whether standing in a queue waiting for
stamps, or going home on the bus.
Success to you.

Slán go fóill,
Rita Ann Higgins

Coal for Mike

I have heard that in Ohio
At the beginning of this century
A woman lived in Bidwell
Mary McCoy, widow of a railroad man
Mike McCoy by name, in poverty.

But every night from the thundering trains of the Wheeling
  Railroad
The brakemen threw a lump of coal
Over the picket fence into the potato patch
Shouting hoarsely in their haste:
For Mike!

And every night when the lump of coal for Mike
Hit the back wall of the shanty
The old woman got up, crept
Drunk with sleep into her dress and hid away the lump of coal
The brakemen's present to Mike, who was dead but
Not forgotten.

The reason why she got up so long before daybreak and hid
Their gifts from the sight of the world was so that
The brakemen should not get into trouble
With the Wheeling Railroad.

This poem is dedicated to the comrades
Of the brakeman Mike McCoy
(Whose lungs were too weak to stand
The coal trains of Ohio)
For comradeship.

Bertolt Brecht (1898–1956)
(Translated by Edith Anderson)

MARGARET ATWOOD   114

Dear Lifelines,
Your efforts on behalf of starving people are most commendable. I
don't have one favourite poem — I have many — but I'm sending
you this quite wonderful poem by Canadian poet P K Page. You may
not know the poet or the poem — but both are well known here —
and I have a particular affection for this poem, having read it at an
early age — and having built many a snowman in my day!

With best wishes for your project.
Margaret Atwood

The Snowman

Ancient nomadic snowman has rolled round.
His spoor: a wide swathe on the white ground
signs of a wintry struggle where he stands.

Stands? Yes, he stands. What snowman sat?
Legless, indeed, but more as if he had
legs than had not.

White double O, white nothing nothing, this
the child's first man on a white paper, his
earliest and fistful image is

now three-dimensional. Abstract. Everyman.
Of almost manna, he is still no man
no person, this so personal snowman.

O transient un-inhabitant, I know
no child who, on seeing the leprous thaw
undo your whitened torso and face of snow

would not, had he the magic
call you back
from that invisible attack

even knowing he can, with the new miracle
of another and softer and whiter snowfall
make you again, this time more wonderful.

Innocent single snowman. Overnight
brings him — a bright
omen — a thunderbolt of white.

But once I saw a mute in every yard
come like a plague; a stock-still multitude
and all stone-buttoned, bun-faced and absurd.

And next day they were still there but each
had changed a little as if all had inched
forward or back, I barely knew which;

and greyed a little too, grown sinister
and disreputable in their sooty fur,
numb, unmoving and nothing moving near.

And as far as I could see the snow was scarred
only with angels' wing marks or the feet of birds
like twigs broken upon the snow or shards

discarded. And I could hear no sound
as far as I could hear except a round
kind of echo without end

rung like a hoop below them and above
jarring the air they had no need of
in a landscape without love.

P K (Patricia Kathleen) Page (b. 1916)

KEN BOURKE   115

3 January 1990

Dear Joann, Jacki and Carolyn,
Thank you for your letter and for the chance to contribute to
Lifelines III.
My choice is 'On Raglan Road' *by Patrick Kavanagh. I like this*
poem for its romance, its tragedy, and its evocation of Dublin. I am
particularly fond of the sung version by Luke Kelly. I sing it myself,
often on my own, but also in company, when I'm let.
I wish you the best of luck with your enterprise.

Yours sincerely,
Ken Bourke

On Raglan Road

On Raglan Road on an autumn day I met her first and knew
That her dark hair would weave a snare that I might one day
  rue;
I saw the danger, yet I walked along the enchanted way,
And I said, let grief be a fallen leaf at the dawning of the day.

On Grafton Street in November we tripped lightly along the
  ledge
Of the deep ravine where can be seen the worth of passion's
  pledge,
The Queen of Hearts still making tarts and I not making hay —
O I loved too much and by such by such is happiness thrown
  away.

I gave her gifts of the mind I gave her the secret sign that's
  known
To the artists who have known the true gods of sound and
  stone
And word and tint. I did not stint for I gave her poems to say.
With her own name there and her own dark hair like clouds
  over fields of May.

On a quiet street where old ghosts meet I see her walking now
Away from me so hurriedly my reason must allow
That I had wooed not as I should a creature made of clay —
When the angel woos the clay he'd lose his wings at the dawn
  of day.

Patrick Kavanagh (1904 –1967)

ALICIA BOYLE   116

6 January 1990

Dear Joann, Jacki and Carolyn,
What a good omen for the New Year: your venture for the Third
World. Thank you for your invitation to me to choose a poem. But
what a problem, as I have many favourite poems. However, I select
Emily Dickinson as she speaks so vividly to me now; a person who
maintained her integrity as an artist, shown again and again in her
visual words.

Yours sincerely,
Alicia Boyle

I stepped from Plank to Plank
A slow and cautious way
The Stars about my Head I felt
About my Feet the sea.

I knew not but the next
Would be my final inch —
This gave me that precarious Gait
Some call Experience.

Emily Dickinson (1830–1886)

ROSALEEN LINEHAN   117

My favourite poem is 'Les Sylphides' by Louis MacNeice. He is my favourite poet. I love this poem because it is a strange mixture of the romantic and the sardonic. It is a warning not to be carried away by youthful infatuation and still it has an awareness of how beautiful such an infatuation is.

Rosaleen Linehan

Les Sylphides

Life in a day: he took his girl to the ballet;
Being shortsighted himself could hardly see it —
      The white skirts in the grey
      Glade and the swell of the music
      Lifting the white sails.

Calyx upon calyx, canterbury bells in the breeze
The flowers on the left mirror to the flowers on the right
      And the naked arms above
      The powdered faces moving
      Like seaweed in a pool.

Now, he thought, we are floating — ageless, oarless —
Now there is no separation, from now on
      You will be wearing white
      Satin and a red sash
      Under the waltzing trees.

But the music stopped, the dancers took their curtain,
The river had come to a lock — a shuffle of programmes —
      And we cannot continue down
      Stream unless we are ready
      To enter the lock and drop.

So they were married — to be the more together —
And found they were never again so much together,
    Divided by the morning tea,
    By the evening paper,
    By children and tradesmen's bills.

Waking at times in the night she found assurance
Due to his regular breathing but wondered whether
    It was really worth it and where
    The river had flowed away
    And where were the white flowers.

Louis MacNeice (1907–1963)

TOM McCAUGHREN   118

7 January 1990

Dear Joann, Jacki and Carolyn,
Thank you for your letter concerning your project in aid of the Third
World.
May I congratulate you on the success of your first two projects and
hope that your third one will be even more successful.
As your project is to help alleviate suffering in the Third World, I
think my favourite poem is particularly appropriate. It's called
'Stupidity Street' by Ralph Hodgson:

Stupidity Street

I saw with open eyes,
    singing birds sweet;
Sold in the shops
    for the people to eat.
Sold in the shops
    of Stupidity Street.

I saw in vision
    the worm in the wheat
And in the shops nothing
    for people to eat.
Nothing for sale
    in Stupidity Street.

This poem was given to me by Mr William Stewart, Headmaster of
Booterstown National Boys School in Dublin several years ago when
I visited the school to talk about books, in particular my wildlife
books. It seemed to say a lot of the things I was saying in my books
about the importance of maintaining a proper relationship with

nature, and maintaining the balance of nature. To me it also, by a slight stretch of the imagination, talks about the use of pesticides, instead of letting nature take its course, about crop failure and about hunger. To me it says that we in the rich farming countries of today, with all our inventions and progress, our modern techniques for providing greater yields, are out of step with nature; that we are all living in one great Stupidity Street. Hopefully the little bit of green we can see at the end of this drab street is our slow awakening to the damage we've been doing to our environment.
Wishing you every success with your project,

Yours sincerely,
Tom McCaughren

THOMAS McCARTHY   119

Dear Joann, Jacki and Carolyn,
My favourite poem is 'In Memory of Eva Gore-Booth and Con Markiewicz' *by W B Yeats.*
I like the poem for its spectacularly beautiful opening images, the kimono, the south-facing windows — but also for its maturity of insight and its underlying sadness. Yeats had a novelist's eye for detail, rather like Molly Keane or Elizabeth Bowen, but he has a poet's provocative tongue ('Conspiring among the ignorant') and he combines these perfectly to make a statement about time passing.
I hope all goes well with the anthology. It's a noble enterprise,

Love,
Tom McCarthy x x x

('*In Memory of Eva Gore-Booth and Con Markiewicz*' was also Justice Niall McCarthy's choice. The poem appears in full on page 128.)

MEDBH McGUCKIAN   120

Dear Pupils,
My favourite poem is 'No Coward Soul is Mine' *by Emily Brontë.*
It is a perfect expression of her nature, defying the death that would come in two years. It is full of feminine passion and courage. It vindicates all lives that are cut short with apparent meaninglessness and is the only poem I know worthy of this anthology.

Medbh McGuckian

No Coward Soul is Mine

No coward soul is mine,
No trembler in the world's storm-troubled sphere!
I see Heaven's glories shine,
And Faith shines equal, arming me from Fear

O God within my breast,
Almighty ever-present Deity!
Life, that in me hast rest,
As I, Undying Life, have power in thee!

Vain are the thousand creeds
That move men's hearts, unutterably vain;
Worthless as withered weeds,
Or idlest froth amid the boundless main,

To waken doubt in one
Holding so fast by thy infinity,
So surely anchored on
The steadfast rock of Immortality.

With wide-embracing love
Thy spirit animates eternal years,
Pervades and broods above,
Changes, sustains, dissolves, creates and rears.

Though earth and moon were gone,
And suns and universes ceased to be,
And thou wert left alone,
Every Existence would exist in thee.

There is not room for Death,
Nor atom that his might could render void;
Since thou art Being and Breath
And what thou art may never be destroyed.

Emily Brontë (1818–1848)

JEREMY IRONS   121

15 January 1990

Dear Joann, Jacki and Carolyn,
Thank you for your letter regarding Lifelines III. *Herewith my*
poem, the author is unknown to me. It is my favourite poem since it
deals with risk and trust and the magic that occurs sometimes when
you do either.

Appolinaire said
'Come to the edge'
'It is too high'
'Come to the edge'
'We might fall'
'Come to the edge'
And they came
And he pushed them
And they flew

I hope this will suffice and I wish you good luck in your efforts.

Yours sincerely,
Jeremy Irons

DESMOND HOGAN   122

I have many favourite poems but in this evening's mood I mention this one, by Sergei Essenin, the Russian poet, husband of Isadora Duncan, who died young. It reminds me of his American contemporary Hart Crane. Both these young men, who don't look dissimilar — there is a wonderful letter by Hart Crane about a performance of Isadora Duncan's in Cleveland — are haunted by a sense of life's brevity and yet, as in this poem, are continually astonished by the loveliness of the earth, by what D H Lawrence called the 'God-flame', the 'fourth dimension', the part where mortal things encounter a sense of transcendence, a sense of ecstasy, a sense of connection, of not just holding hands but binding hands against thought and terror.

Desmond Hogan

My Teper' Ukhodim Ponemnogu

One by one we gradually are leaving
For the land of quietness and bliss.
Soon perhaps I also shall be needing
To embrace the hour of my release.

O beloved birch-trees of the forest!
Mother earth! You sands upon the plain!
Contemplating those who died before us
I can't hide my longing and my pain.

In this world I was too much enamoured
Of the things that make our soul enslaved.
May the aspens find a peace untrammelled
As they gaze into the rosy waves.

Many thoughts in silence I have pondered,
Many songs I quietly conceived,
And upon this dark and gloomy planet
I am happy that I lived and breathed.

I am happy that I fondled women,
Crumpled flowers and tumbled in the grass,
And that animals, our little brethren,
Never felt the anger of my palms.

I'm aware that there we'll find no forest,
And no ringing of the swan-necked rye.
That is why all those who died before us
Always chill my heart until I cry.

I'm aware there won't be any meadows
Glowing golden in that misty land.
That is why the people are so precious
Who on earth walk with me hand in hand.

Sergei Essenin
Translated by Gordon McVay

(*My teper' ukhodim ponemnogu*: 'We are bound for the land of the pure and the holy.' Literally it means 'We are leaving slowly on the journey.')

ALICE TAYLOR   123

16 January 1990

Dear Joann, Jacki and Carolyn,
Thank you for your letter and congratulations on your worthwhile plan which I am pleased to be involved in.
'Free Soul' — Patrick Kavanagh
Here Kavanagh opens the windows of our mind and we look through his eyes to see the beauty of a farmyard. Even the humble dung-heap is viewed through a poetic mist. It is a poem to sharpen our senses.

Good luck with your project,
Alice Taylor

Free Soul

Yesterday I saw the Earth beautiful
Through the frosted glass of November's tree
I peered into an April country
Where love was day-dream free.

And in the steam rising from the dung-heap
Another firmament was blown
Dotted over with fairy worlds
And lamped with silver stone.

Over the bleak grey-bearded bogs
I looked and beheld the last Atlantis
And surely it was not November
But a time the freed souls grant us.

Patrick Kavanagh (1904–1967)

ELIZABETH COPE   124

2 January 1990

Dear Girls,
Thank you for your letter received today. It is a great honour for me
to be asked to contribute to Lifelines III.
William Blake is one of my favourite poets, and a poem I learned in
school always comes to mind; it is from the Songs of Innocence:
'Introduction'.
I don't really know why I like this poem, but instinctively I feel its
simplicity and its happiness. A child could understand it; it is not a
long poem. The best poetry to me seems to be short, flowing and easy
to say. I don't care much for Blake's paintings or etchings but a book
of Blake's poems would help fill the spiritual void for me.

Yours sincerely,
Elizabeth Cope

Songs of Innocence
Introduction

Piping down the valleys wild
Piping songs of pleasant glee
On a cloud I saw a child,
And he laughing said to me,

'Pipe a song about a Lamb';
So I piped with merry cheer.
'Piper, pipe that song again!'
So I piped, he wept to hear.

'Drop thy pipe thy happy pipe
Sing thy songs of happy cheer';
So I sung the same again
While he wept with joy to hear.

'Piper sit thee down and write
In a book that all may read' —
So he vanished from my sight
And I plucked a hollow reed,

And I made a rural pen,
And I stained the water clear,
And I wrote my happy songs
Every child may joy to hear.

William Blake (1757–1827)

BRIAN MOORE   125

11 January 1990

I have many favourite poems and I like them for varying reasons. But I would choose 'The Waste Land' *by T S Eliot over all the others because, from the time I first read it many years ago, it has seemed to me to be the poem of our age. It was one of the first 'modern' poems I ever read, so totally different from the poetry of my schoolbooks. It remains, for me, one of the best.*

Brian Moore

[Due to space restrictions we were unable to include *'The Waste Land'*. Brian Moore very kindly proposed a second choice. It is Derek Mahon's *A Disused Shed in Co. Wexford* which was also chosen by Seamus Deane and can be found on pages 278–279.]

A S BYATT   126

Dear Lifelines,
I am sorry not to have replied to your letter sooner but I have been abroad and also overwhelmed with work.
My favourite poem (or one of my favourite poems) is Andrew Marvell's The Garden. *I love it because of its wit, its clarity, its image of perfect vegetable peacefulness and the way it seems as new and surprising today as it must have done when it was written. I have always for some reason been drawn to images of the Paradise Garden and this is one of the most subtle and the most beautiful.*

Yours sincerely
A S Byatt

The Garden

I

How vainly men themselves amaze
To win the palm, the oak, or bays,
And their uncessant labours see
Crowned from some single herb or tree,
Whose short and narrow vergèd shade
Does prudently their toils upbraid,
While all flow'rs and all trees do close
To weave the garlands of repose.

II

Fair Quiet, have I found thee here,
And Innocence, thy sister dear!
Mistaken long, I sought you then
In busy companies of men.
Your sacred plants, if here below,
Only among the plants will grow.
Society is all but rude,
To this delicious solitude.

III

No white nor red was ever seen
So am'rous as this lovely green.
Fond lovers, cruel as their flame,
Cut in these trees their mistress' name.
Little, alas, they know, or heed,
How far these beauties hers exceed!
Fair trees! wheres'e'er your barks I wound,
No name shall but your own be found.

IV

When we have run our passion's heat,
Love hither makes his best retreat.
The gods, that mortal beauty chase,
Still in a tree did end their race.
Apollo hunted Daphne so,
Only that she might laurel grow.
And Pan did after Syrinx speed,
Not as a nymph, but for a reed.

V

What wondrous life is this I lead!
Ripe apples drop about my head;
The luscious clusters of the vine
Upon my mouth do crush their wine;
The nectarene, and curious peach,
Into my hands themselves do reach;
Stumbling on melons, as I pass,
Ensnared with flowers, I fall on grass.

VI
Meanwhile the mind, from pleasures less,
Withdraws into its happiness:
The mind, that ocean where each kind
Does straight its own resemblance find,
Yet it creates, transcending these,
Far other worlds, and other seas,
Annihilating all that's made
To a green thought in a green shade.

VII
Here at the fountain's sliding foot,
Or at some fruit-tree's mossy root,
Casting the body's vest aside,
My soul into the boughs does glide:
There like a bird it sits, and sings,
Then whets, and combs its silver wings;
And, till prepared for longer flight,
Waves in its plumes the various light.

VIII
Such was that happy garden-state,
While man there walked without a mate:
After a place so pure, and sweet,
What other help could yet be meet!
But 'twas beyond a mortal's share
To wander solitary there:
Two paradises 'twere in one
To live in paradise alone.

IX
How well the skilful gardener drew
Of flowers and herbs this dial new;
Where from above the milder sun
Does through a fragrant zodiac run;
And, as it works, the industrious bee
Computes its time as well as we.
How could such sweet and wholesome hours
Be reckoned but with herbs and flowers!

Andrew Marvell (1621–1678)

DAVID OWEN   127

Dear Lifelines,
Thank you for your letter about your project Lifelines, *and I am*
sorry to have not replied before now. In fact I have been busy myself
producing an anthology of poetry which is to be published in the

autumn by Michael Joseph, the proceeds of which will be donated to
Great Ormond Street Hospital.
I wish you success in your fundraising efforts with Lifelines *to raise*
funds for the Third World.
My favourite poem is Candles *by C P Cavafy, translated by Rae*
Dalven. It is a reminder that so many things in life fade or die and
that you must always look forward, not back. In politics,
particularly, there is a need to move on, learn from past mistakes or
achievements; but don't dwell in the past, live for the future. I have
found Rae Dalven's translation of the Greek poet's work particularly
beautiful.

Yours sincerely
David Owen
The Rt Hon Dr David Owen

Candles

The days of our future stand before us
like a row of little lighted candles —
golden, warm, and lively little candles.

The days gone by remain behind us,
a mournful line of burnt-out candles;
the nearest ones are still smoking,
cold candles, melted and bent.

I do not want to look at them; their form saddens me,
and it saddens me to recall their first light.
I look ahead at my lighted candles.

I do not want to turn back, lest I see and shudder —
how quickly the sombre line lengthens,
how quickly the burnt-out candles multiply.

C P Cavafy (1863–1933)
Translated by Rae Dalven

JAMES PLUNKETT   128

17 January 1990

Who my favourite poet is, and what my favourite poem, are questions
to be sidestepped as nimbly as good manners permit: the answers
vary almost from moment to moment. However, Patrick Kavanagh
and the poems of Patrick Kavanagh occupy an elevated place in the
list at all times.

*I came to know of him first in the 1940s when I read his epic poem
'The Great Hunger' and then in person when I met him during the
fifties in the company of Peadar O'Donnell who was editing* The Bell
*at the time. After that there were casual meetings in the coffee shops
of Bewleys and Mitchells and in Sunday Pubs. His work, in both
prose and poetry, became a must.*
The poem I have selected here is from Come Dance With Kitty
Stobling and Other Poems, *first published in 1960. It is* 'In
Memory of My Mother'. *I found it deeply moving when I first read
it and it continues to evoke the same admiration and emotion
whenever I return to it, especially on the repetition at the beginning
of the last verse of the line:*

O you are not lying in the wet clay. . . .

What a tender, brooding sorrow hovers over it.
With good wishes for the success of Lifelines III.

Sincerely,
James Plunkett

In Memory of My Mother

I do not think of you lying in the wet clay
Of a Monaghan graveyard; I see
You walking down a lane among the poplars
On your way to the station, or happily

Going to second Mass on a summer Sunday —
You meet me and you say:
'Don't forget to see about the cattle —'
Among your earthiest words the angels stray.

And I think of you walking along a headland
Of green oats in June,
So full of repose, so rich with life —
And I see us meeting at the end of a town

On a fair day by accident, after
The bargains are all made and we can walk
Together through the shops and stalls and markets
Free in the oriental streets of thought.

O you are not lying in the wet clay,
For it is a harvest evening now and we
Are piling up the ricks against the moonlight
And you smile up at us — eternally.

Patrick Kavanagh (1904–1967)

ADAM CLAYTON   129

4 Windmill Lane
Dublin 2

Dear Lifelines,
Thank you for your letter. I enclose a copy of Adam's chosen poem:
'Rock' by Charles Bukowski, an American writer on rock musicians.
With best wishes,

Yours sincerely
Suzanne Doyle

Rock

Here were all these males tuning their guitars
not a woman around
and they were content with that.

Then they started arguing about who was best
and what was wrong with the so called best:
and a couple of them had been famous,
and they sat there on my rug
drinking my wine and beer and smoking my cigarettes.

Two of them stood up to duke it out
and that's when I ran them off
with their guitars and their guitar cases
out into the moonlight
still arguing.

I closed the door then I leaned against the couch
and drained a beer fast and I gagged:
not a very good night:
it was full of ashes.

Charles Bukowski (b.1920)

FIONA SHAW   130

10 January 1990

Dear Joann, Jacki and Carolyn,
Thank you so very much for inviting me to be part of your anthology.
I am truly honoured particularly as I think your predecessors asked
me and due to my infinite moves my reply was never sent.

Anyway good luck with this and I do hope it's another sell-out.
You have asked a difficult question. 'Favourite' is always hard for a fanatic, so I have approached this by trying to narrow down the possibilities to a favourite poet.
I have decided that it is Yeats and I am full of trepidation that too many of your poems will be Yeats choices. Mine is either: 'The Song of Wandering Aengus' and I really don't know why. I don't intellectually understand the poem but I think it's great because the moment you start reading it you are transported to another place, the inside of someone else's vision and you travel swiftly through landscape and time even to the end of life with the yearning speaker and then you wake up at the end of the poem having had the beatific rest of unravelling sleep.
If too many chose that poem I would like to offer the alternative of 'The Second Coming'. I love this poem because it frightens me!
Best wishes,

Yours, with gratitude,
Fiona Shaw

The Song of Wandering Aengus

I went out to the hazel wood,
Because a fire was in my head,
And cut and peeled a hazel wand,
And hooked a berry to a thread;
And when white moths were on the wing,
And moth-like stars were flickering out,
I dropped the berry in a stream
And caught a little silver trout.

When I had laid it on the floor
I went to blow the fire aflame,
But something rustled on the floor,
And some one called me by my name:
It had become a glimmering girl
With apple blossom in her hair
Who called me by my name and ran
And faded through the brightening air.

Though I am old with wandering
Through hollow lands and hilly lands,
I will find out where she has gone,
And kiss her lips and take her hands;
And walk among long dappled grass,
And pluck till time and times are done
The silver apples of the moon,
The golden apples of the sun.

W B Yeats (1865–1939)

The Second Coming

Turning and turning in the widening gyre
The falcon cannot hear the falconer;
Things fall apart; the centre cannot hold;
Mere anarchy is loosed upon the world,
The blood-dimmed tide is loosed, and everywhere
The ceremony of innocence is drowned;
The best lack all conviction, while the worst
Are full of passionate intensity.

Surely some revelation is at hand;
Surely the Second Coming is at hand.
The Second Coming! Hardly are those words out
When a vast image out of *Spiritus Mundi*
Troubles my sight: somewhere in sands of the desert
A shape with lion body and the head of a man,
A gaze blank and pitiless as the sun,
Is moving its slow thighs, while all about it
Reel shadows of the indignant desert birds.
The darkness drops again; but now I know
That twenty centuries of stony sleep
Were vexed to nightmare by a rocking cradle,
And what rough beast, its hour come round at last,
Slouches towards Bethlehem to be born?

W B Yeats (1865–1939)

MARY BANOTTI   131

16 January 1990

Dear Ms Bradish,
Thank you for your letter and your invitation to contribute to Lifelines
III. *My two poems are:* 'From the Republic of Conscience' *by
Seamus Heaney and* 'Martha's Wall' *by Paul Durcan.*
When I first read 'From the Republic of Conscience' *which was
written for Amnesty International, I thought it would be an eloquent
and beautiful inspiration for everyone but particularly for politicians.*
Paul Durcan's 'Martha's Wall' *describes the south wall in Ringsend
which is near where I live and it movingly describes the magic and
special qualities which that lovely walk has for those who go there often,
as I do.*
*Thank you for inviting me to contribute to your book and I look
forward to seeing it.*
With every good wish.

Yours sincerely,
Mary Banotti

From the Republic of Conscience

I
When I landed in the republic of conscience
it was so noiseless when the engines stopped
I could hear a curlew high above the runway.

At immigration, the clerk was an old man
who produced a wallet from his homespun coat
and showed me a photograph of my grandfather.

The woman in customs asked me to declare
the words of our traditional cures and charms
to heal dumbness and avert the evil eye.

No porters. No interpreter. No taxi.
You carried your own burden and very soon
your symptoms of creeping privilege disappeared.

II
Fog is a dreaded omen there but lightning
spells universal good and parents hang
swaddled infants in trees during thunderstorms.

Salt is their precious mineral. And seashells
are held to the ear during births and funerals.
The base of all inks and pigments is seawater.

Their sacred symbol is a stylized boat.
The sail is an ear, the mast a sloping pen,
The hull a mouth-shape, the keel an open eye.

At their inauguration, public leaders
must swear to uphold unwritten law and weep
to atone for their presumption to hold office —

and to affirm their faith that all life sprang
from salt in tears which the sky-god wept
after he dreamt his solitude was endless.

III
I came back from that frugal republic
with my two arms the one length, the customs woman
having insisted my allowance was myself.

The old man rose and gazed into my face
and said that was official recognition
that I was now a dual citizen.

He therefore desired me when I got home
to consider myself a representative
and to speak on their behalf in my own tongue.

Their embassies, he said, were everywhere
but operated independently
and no ambassador would ever be relieved.

Seamus Heaney (b. 1939)

Martha's Wall

Her pleasure — what gave her pleasure — was to be walked
Down her wall, the South Wall, a skinny, crinkly, golden-
  stemmed wall
That contracts and expands, worms and unworms, in and out
  of Dublin Bay,
Across the sea's thighs pillowing in, besotted, under daisy-
  gartered skies.
She'd curl her finger around my finger and I'd lead her out on
  to it.
She liked it when the flowering sea was shedding spray across
  it.
She'd tense up with delight to see me get wet
And wetter still, and wetter — the wetter it was
The better she liked it, and me — and she wanted always
To get down, away down, to the very end of it
Where there is a deep-red lighthouse, and the deep-red
  lighthouse
Was hers also, hers, and we'd sit down on a bench under it
And she'd put her arm around my neck and we'd stop needing
  to speak
And we'd sit there, breathless, in silence, for a long time.

Paul Durcan (b. 1944)

IAN McKELLEN   132

15 January 1990

Dear Joann Bradish,
My favourite poem, perhaps, is by G M Hopkins — 'The Leaden
Echo and the Golden Echo'.
I admire Hopkins's use of language, strongly influenced by
Shakespeare's use of punning and metaphor. These lines were
originally intended to be part of a dramatic work and, when spoken
out loud, reveal a wonderful grasp of theatrical passion. Although I
am not Christian I always find the optimism of the second part of the
poem very moving indeed.
All best wishes to you and to Jacki Erskine and to Carolyn Gibson.

Yours ever,
Ian McKellen

The Leaden Echo and The Golden Echo

(Maiden's song from *St Winefred's Well*)

The Leaden Echo

How to kéep — is there ány any, is there none such, nowhere
  known some, bow or brooch or braid or brace, láce, latch or
  catch or key to keep
Back beauty, keep it, beauty, beauty, beauty, . . . from
  vanishing away?
Ó is there no frowning of these wrinkles, rankèd wrinkles
  deep,
Dówn? no waving off of these most mournful messengers, still
  messengers, sad and stealing messengers of grey?
No there's none, there's none, O no there's none,
Nor can you long be, what you now are, called fair,
Do what you may do, what, do what you may,
And wisdom is early to despair:
Be beginning; since, no, nothing can be done
To keep at bay
Age and age's evils, hoar hair,
Ruck and wrinkle, drooping, dying, death's worst, winding
  sheets, tombs and worms and tumbling to decay;
So be beginning, be beginning to despair.
O there's none; no no no there's none:
Be beginning to despair, to despair,
Despair, despair, despair, despair.

The Golden Echo

  Spare!
There ís one, yes I have one (Hush there!);
Only not within seeing of the sun,
Not within the singeing of the strong sun,
Tall sun's tingeing, or treacherous the tainting of the earth's
  air,
Somewhere elsewhere there is ah well where! one,
Ońe. Yes I cán tell such a key, I dó know such a place,
Where whatever's prized and passes of us, everything that's
  fresh and fast flying of us, seems to us sweet of us and
  swiftly away with, done away with undone,
Úndone, done with, soon done with, and yet dearly and
  dangerously sweet
Of us, the wimpled-water-dimpled, not-by-morning-matchèd
  face,
The flower of beauty, fleece of beauty, too too apt to, ah! to
  fleet,

Never fleets móre, fastened with the tenderest truth
To its own best being and its loveliness of youth: it is an ever-
    lastingness of, O it is an all youth!
Come then, your ways and airs and looks, locks, maiden gear,
    gallantry and gaiety and grace,
Winning ways, airs innocent, maiden manners, sweet looks,
    loose locks, long locks, lovelocks, gaygear, going gallant,
    girlgrace —
Resign them, sign them, seal them, send them, motion them
    with breath,
And with sighs soaring, soaring síghs deliver
Them; beauty-in-the-ghost, deliver it, early now, long before
    death
Give beauty back, beauty, beauty, beauty, back to God,
    beauty's self and beauty's giver.
See; not a hair is, not an eyelash, not the least lash lost; every
    hair
Is, hair of the head, numbered.
Nay, what we had lighthanded left in surly the mere mould
Will have waked and have waxed and have walked with the
    wind what while we slept,
This side, that side hurling a heavyheaded hundredfold
What while we, while we slumbered.
O then, weary then whý should we tread? O why are we so
    haggard at the heart, so care-coiled, care-killed, so fagged,
    so fashed, so cogged, so cumbered,
When the thing we freely fórfeit is kept with fonder a care,
Fonder a care kept than we could have kept it, kept
Far with fonder a care (and we, we should have lost it) finer,
    fonder
A care kept. — Where kept? Do but tell us where kept, where. —
Yonder. — What high as that! We follow, now we follow. —
    Yonder, yes yonder, yonder,
Yonder.

Gerard Manley Hopkins (1844–1889)

KINGSLEY AMIS   133

18 January 1990

Dear Misses Bradish, Erskine and Gibson,
Thank you for your letter about Lifelines. *My favourite poem is by*
A E Housman. It has no title but the first line is:

'Tell me not here, it needs not saying.'

*Why is it my favourite poem? I am afraid I would have to know much
more about myself than I do to answer that question. But I can say
that it is a piece of beautiful observation, precisely expressed and it
exactly expresses what I have myself sometimes felt in rural places.
I wish you the best of luck with* Lifelines III.

Yours sincerely,
Kingsley Amis

Tell Me Not Here, It Needs Not Saying

Tell me not here, it needs not saying,
    What tune the enchantress plays
In aftermaths of soft September
    Or under blanching mays,
For she and I were long acquainted
    And I knew all her ways.

On russet floors, by waters idle,
    The pine lets fall its cone;
The cuckoo shouts all day at nothing
    In leafy dells alone;
And traveller's joy beguiles in autumn
    Hearts that have lost their own.

On acres of the seeded grasses
    The changing burnish heaves;
Or marshalled under moons of harvest
    Stand still all night the sheaves;
Or beeches strip in storms for winter
    And stain the wind with leaves.

Possess, as I possessed a season,
    The countries I resign,
Where over elmy plains the highway
    Would mount the hills and shine,
And full of shade the pillared forest
    Would murmur and be mine.

For nature, heartless, witless nature,
    Will neither care nor know
What stranger's feet may find the meadow
    And trespass there and go,
Nor ask amid the dews of morning
    If they are mine or no.

A E Housman (1859–1936)

AMY CLAMPITT   134

16 January 1990

Dear Joann Bradish, Jacki Erskine, and Carolyn Gibson,
You ask me to name my favorite poem. Like many other people, I have
too many favorites to settle for very long on any single one. But since
I first encountered it at the age of four or five, one of those favorites
has always been 'Jabberwocky' from Through the Looking-Glass,
the second of the Alice books by Lewis Carroll. It is one of the few
poems I can recite from memory without stumbling, and that is
strange since it is studded with words that came out of nowhere and
mean nothing in particular. As Alice herself put it, '...it seems to fill
my head with ideas — only I don't know exactly what they are.'
Anyhow, the sound of those words is somehow magical and
ridiculous both at once. And the sound, after all, is what makes a
good poem worth remembering.

Sincerely yours,
Amy Clampitt

Jabberwocky

'Twas brillig, and the slithy toves
    Did gyre and gimble in the wabe:
All mimsy were the borogoves,
    And the mome raths outgrabe.

'Beware the Jabberwock, my son!
    The jaws that bite, the claws that catch!
Beware the Jubjub bird, and shun
    The frumious Bandersnatch!'

He took his vorpal sword in hand:
    Long time the manxome foe he sought —
So rested he by the Tumtum tree,
    And stood awhile in thought.

And, as in uffish thought he stood,
    The Jabberwock, with eyes of flame,
Came whiffling though the tulgey wood,
    And burbled as it came!

One, two! One, two! And through and through
    The vorpal blade went snicker-snack!
He left it dead, and with its head
    He went galumphing back.

'And, hast thou slain the Jabberwock?
    Come to my arms, my beamish boy!
O frabjous day! Callooh! Callay!'
    He chortled in his joy.

'Twas brillig, and the slithy toves
    Did gyre and gimble in the wabe:
All mimsy were the borogoves,
    And the mome raths outgrabe.

Lewis Carroll (1832–1898)

CAMILLE SOUTER   135

January 1990

Dear Joann, Jacki and Carolyn,
Thank you for your letter and invitation to contribute to Lifelines
III.
I have chosen 'After Night Offensive' *by James Farrar. He lost his*
life three months before his twenty-first birthday, in a Mosquito
aircraft on 26 July 1944, while attacking a V-I flying bomb, over the
English Channel.
His prose and poems are excitingly visual and grasp elusive truth. I
wish I could include all of his work.

Good luck,
Camille Souter

After Night Offensive

Glowed through the violet petal of the sky
Like a death's-head the calm summer moon
And all the distance echoed with owl-cry.

Hissing the white waves of grass unsealed
Peer of moon on metal, hidden men,
As the wind foamed deeply through the field.

Rooted to soil, remote and faint as stars,
Looking to neither side, they lay all night
Sunken in the murmurous seas of grass.

No flare burned upwards: never sound was shed
But lulling cries of owls beyond the world
As wind and moon played softly with the dead.

James Farrar (killed in action 1944)

ALICE MAHER   136

13 January 1990

Dear Joann Bradish, Jacki Erskine, Carolyn Gibson,
I enclose a photocopy of a scrap of paper I have carried around with
me for many years now. I cannot remember how it came into my
possession, why it was typed out, or who wrote the piece. The
sentence in Italian beneath it leads me to believe it may have been a
libretto to an Opera?
I am very attached to this scrap and every time I move to a new city
and set up home again, it goes up on the mantelpiece straight away.
There it sits amidst the photos and gegaws ready to make my own
blood freeze every time I catch sight of it.
Is there some way you can reproduce it in your book as it is, i.e. a
fragment? This is part of its importance for me. Even though it was
torn out of something else for its 'written' words, it has since then
become an 'object' too, a talisman.
Good luck with Lifelines III.

Sincerely yours,
Alice Maher

Pallid the Sun

Pallid the Sun
& turbid grows the Air.
Thy Soul'd imperilled;
Man, for Death prepare.
Thy Heart turns sick
With Terror & Remorse;
Thy Blood turns thick
& freezes in its Course.
Thy Life to Loathing turns,
Eclipsed by Sin:
Loathing thy Self,
Thine Enemy Within.

    Fino a sera la rosa cremata

    e sangue, sangue, un coro d'

    (Until the
    is bl. . . .)

ANDY O'MAHONY   137

RTE
6 February 1990

Dear Anthologists,
Thank you for your kind invitation to contribute to your anthology.
While I find it impossible to select one favourite poem in preference to
all others, what I have done is chosen a poem that I was reminded of
when recently reading Gabriel Marquez' novel Love in the Time of
Cholera.
This novel intoxicated me with its richness: there's a potent sense in
it of the plurality of things both natural and man-made. Reading it
brought to mind a phrase of Louis MacNeice, 'the drunkenness of
things being various', from a poem called 'Snow' written in January
1935.
On re-reading the poem I realised that I had forgotten the expression
'incorrigibly plural' which also captures (though clearly not as
memorably) my reaction to the world of Marquez. The occasion of
this epiphany for MacNeice was the peeling of a tangerine in a room
framed by a bay-window of snow and pink roses. It's only now it has
dawned on me the number of tangerines I enjoyed not in the snow
but in the sunshine while reading Love in the Time of Cholera.

Sincerely,
Andy O'Mahony

Snow

The room was suddenly rich and the great bay-window was
Spawning snow and pink roses against it
Soundlessly collateral and incompatible:
World is suddener than we fancy it.

World is crazier and more of it than we think,
Incorrigibly plural. I peel and portion
A tangerine and spit the pips and feel
The drunkenness of things being various.

And the fire flames with a bubbling sound for world
Is more spiteful and gay than one supposes —
On the tongue on the eyes on the ears in the palms of one's
    hands —
There is more than glass between the snow and the huge roses.

Louis MacNeice (1907–1963)

DAVID LODGE   138

22 January 1990

Dear Misses Bradish, Erskine and Gibson,
I would nominate as my favourite poem 'Among School Children'
by W B Yeats. It deals with some of the most fundamental human
emotions: love, nostalgia, regret, and the longing for what Yeats
called elsewhere 'unity of being', but which he figured here in the
wonderful final stanzas in the symbols of the chestnut tree and the
dancer. What I particularly admire about the poem is the
extraordinary range of diction, from the most down-to-earth and
colloquial, to the most sublime; and the way a natural-seeming
utterance is fitted into a most complex stanzaic form.

Yours sincerely,
David Lodge

Among School Children

I
I walk through the long schoolroom questioning;
A kind old nun in a white hood replies;
The children learn to cipher and to sing,
To study reading-books and histories,
To cut and sew, be neat in everything
In the best modern way — the children's eyes
In momentary wonder stare upon
A sixty-year-old smiling public man.

II
I dream of a Ledaean body, bent
Above a sinking fire, a tale that she
Told of a harsh reproof, or trivial event
That changed some childish day to tragedy —
Told, and it seemed that our two natures blent
Into a sphere from youthful sympathy,
Or else, to alter Plato's parable,
Into the yolk and white of the one shell.

III
And thinking of that fit of grief or rage
I look upon one child or t'other there
And wonder if she stood so at that age —
For even daughters of the swan can share
Something of every paddler's heritage —
And had that colour upon cheek or hair,
And thereupon my heart is driven wild:
She stands before me as a living child.

IV

Her present image floats into the mind —
Did Quattrocento finger fashion it
Hollow of cheek as though it drank the wind
And took a mess of shadows for its meat?
And I though never of Ledaean kind
Has pretty plumage once — enough of that,
Better to smile on all that smile, and show
There is a comfortable kind of old scarecrow.

V

What youthful mother, a shape upon her lap
Honey of generation had betrayed,
And that must sleep, shriek, struggle to escape
As recollection or the drug decide,
Would think her son, did she but see that shape
With sixty or more winters on its head,
A compensation for the pang of his birth,
Or the uncertainty of his setting forth?

VI

Plato thought nature but a spume that plays
Upon a ghostly paradigm of things;
Solider Aristotle played the taws
Upon the bottom of a king of kings;
World-famous golden-thighed Pythagoras
Fingered upon a fiddle-stick or strings
What a star sang and careless Muses heard:
Old clothes upon old sticks to scare a bird.

VII

Both nuns and mothers worship images,
But those the candles light are not as those
That animate a mother's reveries,
But keep a marble or a bronze repose.
And yet they too break hearts — O Presences
That passion, piety or affection knows,
And that all heavenly glory symbolise —
O self-born mockers of man's enterprise;

VIII

Labour is blossoming or dancing where
The body is not bruised to pleasure soul,
Nor beauty born out of its own despair,
Nor blear-eyed wisdom out of midnight oil.
O chestnut-tree, great-rooted blossomer,
Are you the leaf, the blossom or the bole?
O body swayed to music, O brightening glance,
How can we know the dancer from the dance?

W B Yeats (1865–1939)

SÉAMUS BRENNAN   139

Oifig an Aire Turasóireachta agus Iompair
(Office of The Minister for Tourism and Transport)
Baile Átha Cliath 2
(Dublin 2)
29 January 1990

Dear Joann, Jacki and Carolyn,
Thank you for your recent letter. It was nice hearing from you.
I will be glad to contribute to Lifelines and would like to
congratulate you on such a worthwhile venture.
I have been thinking since I received your letter about my favourite
poem. Different verses have come to mind, but I have opted for the
one which first struck me — 'The Song of Wandering Aengus' by
W B Yeats.
My reasons for nominating this poem are more difficult to articulate.
I am putting to paper some random thoughts which come to mind:
the words have stayed in my mind over so many years; they must
have impacted to a greater degree than I previously realised.
The opening lines:

> I went out to the hazel wood,
> Because a fire was in my head,
> And cut and peeled a hazel wand,
> And hooked a berry to a thread;
>
> . . . .
> And walk among long dappled grass,
> And pluck till time and times are done
> The silver apples of the moon,
> The golden apples of the sun.

The opening lines bring to my mind an image of a person confused,
but from that opening Yeats weaves a most serene, peaceful and
tranquil picture with absolute simplicity, in a manner only a master
poet can do.
Sorry for delay in replying. I will be looking forward to purchasing a
copy of Lifelines III.
With best wishes,

Yours sincerely,
Séamus
Séamus Brennan, TD
(Minister for Tourism and Transport)

CHARLES J HAUGHEY   140

9 February 1990

Dear Joann, Jacki and Carolyn,
I enclose the Taoiseach's contribution for Lifelines III — *the text of*
'The Song of Wandering Aengus' *by W B Yeats and the reasons*
why it is his favourite poem.
Wishing you every success with your project.

Yours sincerely,
Fionnuala O'Kelly
Head of Government Information Services

'The Song of Wandering Aengus' *by W B Yeats*
The language and imagery are exquisite. It is full of romance,
mystery and magic.

('*The Song of Wandering Aengus*' was also Fiona Shaw's and Séamus Brennan's
choice. The poem appears in full on page 173.)

THOMAS KINSELLA   141

'The Love Song of J Alfred Prufrock' *by T S Eliot, for its sensual*
and dramatic skills, and its powerful beginning to a great career.
Good luck to the project and looking forward to a copy of the book.

Thomas Kinsella

The Love Song of J Alfred Prufrock

S'io credessi che mia riposta fosse
a persona che mai tornasse al mondo,
questa fiamma staria senza più scosse.
Ma per ciò che giammai di questo fondo
non tornò vivo alcun, s'i'odo il vero,
senza tema d'infamia ti rispondo.

Let us go then, you and I,
When the evening is spread out against the sky
Like a patient etherised upon a table;
Let us go, through certain half-deserted streets,
The muttering retreats

Of restless nights in one-night cheap hotels
And sawdust restaurants with oyster-shells:
Streets that follow like a tedious argument
Of insidious intent
To lead you to an overwhelming question. . .
Oh, do not ask, 'What is it?'
Let us go and make our visit.

In the room the women come and go
Talking of Michelangelo.

The yellow fog that rubs its back upon the window-panes,
The yellow smoke that rubs its muzzle on the window-panes,
Licked its tongue into the corners of the evening,
Lingered upon the pools that stand in drains,
Let fall upon its back the soot that falls from chimneys,
Slipped by the terrace, made a sudden leap,
And seeing that it was a soft October night,
Curled once about the house, and fell asleep.

And indeed there will be time
For the yellow smoke that slides along the street
Rubbing its back upon the window-panes;
There will be time, there will be time
To prepare a face to meet the faces that you meet;
There will be time to murder and create,
And time for all the works and days of hands
That lift and drop a question on your plate;
Time for you and time for me,
And time yet for a hundred indecisions,
And for a hundred visions and revisions,
Before the taking of a toast and tea.

In the room the women come and go
Talking of Michelangelo.

And indeed there will be time
To wonder, 'Do I dare?' and, 'Do I dare?'
Time to turn back and descend the stair,
With a bald spot in the middle of my hair —
(They will say: 'How his hair is growing thin!')
My morning coat, my collar mounting firmly to the chin,
My necktie rich and modest, but asserted by a simple pin —
(They will say: 'But how his arms and legs are thin!')
Do I dare
Disturb the universe?
In a minute there is time
For decisions and revisions which a minute will reverse.

For I have known them all already, known them all —
Have known the evenings, mornings, afternoons,
I have measured out my life with coffee spoons;

I know the voices dying with a dying fall
Beneath the music from a farther room.
    So how should I presume?

And I have known the eyes already, known them all —
The eyes that fix you in a formulated phrase,
And when I am formulated, sprawling on a pin,
When I am pinned and wriggling on the wall,
Then how should I begin
To spit out all the butt-ends of my days and ways?
    And how should I presume?

And I have known the arms already, known them all —
Arms that are braceleted and white and bare
(But in the lamplight, downed with light brown hair!)
Is it perfume from a dress
That makes me so digress?
Arms that lie along a table, or wrap about a shawl.
    And should I then presume?
    And how should I begin?

       .   .   .   .   .

Shall I say, I have gone at dusk through narrow streets
And watched the smoke that rises from the pipes
Of lonely men in shirt-sleeves, leaning out of windows? . . .

I should have been a pair of ragged claws
Scuttling across the floors of silent seas.

       .   .   .   .   .

And the afternoon, the evening, sleeps so peacefully!
Smoothed by long fingers,
Asleep . . . tired . . . or it malingers,
Stretched on the floor, here beside you and me.
Should I, after tea and cakes and ices,
Have the strength to force the moment to its crisis?
But though I have wept and fasted, wept and prayed,
Though I have seen my head (grown slightly bald)
    brought in upon a platter,
I am no prophet — and here's no great matter;
I have seen the moment of my greatness flicker,
And I have seen the eternal Footman hold my coat, and
  snicker,
And in short, I was afraid.

And would it have been worth it, after all,
After the cups, the marmalade, the tea,
Among the porcelain, among some talk of you and me,
Would it have been worth while,
To have bitten off the matter with a smile,
To have squeezed the universe into a ball

To roll it towards some overwhelming question,
To say: 'I am Lazarus, come from the dead,
Come back to tell you all, I shall tell you all' —
If one, settling a pillow by her head,
    Should say: 'That is not what I meant at all.
    That is not it, at all.'

And would it have been worth it, after all,
Would it have been worth while,
After the sunsets and the dooryards and the sprinkled streets,
After the novels, after the teacups, after the skirts that trail
    along the floor —
And this, and so much more? —
It is impossible to say just what I mean!
But as if a magic lantern threw the nerves in patterns on a
  screen:
Would it have been worth while
If one, settling a pillow or throwing off a shawl,
And turning toward the window, should say:
    'That is not it at all,
    That is not what I meant, at all.'

       .   .   .   .   .

No! I am not Prince Hamlet, nor was meant to be;
Am an attendant lord, one that will do
To swell a progress, start a scene or two,
Advise the prince; no doubt, an easy tool,
Deferential, glad to be of use,
Politic, cautious, and meticulous;
Full of high sentence, but a bit obtuse;
At times, indeed, almost ridiculous —
Almost, at times, the Fool.

I grow old . . . I grow old . . .
I shall wear the bottoms of my trousers rolled.

Shall I part my hair behind? Do I dare to eat a peach?
I shall wear white flannel trousers, and walk upon the beach.
I have heard the mermaids singing, each to each.

I do not think that they will sing to me.

I have seen them riding seaward on the waves
Combing the white hair of the waves blown back
When the wind blows the water white and black.

We have lingered in the chambers of the sea
By sea-girls wreathed with seaweed red and brown
Till human voices wake us, and we drown.

T S Eliot (1888–1965)

DEIRDRE PURCELL   142

Dear Joann, Jacki and Carolyn,
My favourite poem is a piece of doggerel (some would say) by H Belloc: 'Tarantella'.
It is the very first piece of literature I can remember. Probably from school, although I can't be sure. I think I 'hear' language and writing — rather than 'see' or 'read' it. The sounds in this poem are fabulous to me. The words themselves suggest the pictures and sounds. I've never forgotten them. (And this is almost the only poem I can remember by rote.)

Deirdre Purcell

Tarantella

Do you remember an Inn,
Miranda?
Do you remember an Inn?
And the tedding and the spreading
Of the straw for a bedding,
And the fleas that tease in the High Pyrenees,
And the wine that tasted of the tar?
And the cheers and the jeers of the young muleteers
(Under the vine of the dark verandah)?
Do you remember an Inn, Miranda,
Do you remember an Inn?
And the cheers and the jeers of the young muleteers
Who hadn't got a penny,
And who weren't paying any,
And the hammer at the doors and the Din?
And the Hip! Hop! Hap!
Of the clap
Of the hands to the twirl and the swirl
Of the girl gone chancing,
Glancing,
Dancing,
Backing and advancing,
Snapping of a clapper to the spin
Out and in —
And the Ting, Tong, Tang of the Guitar
Do you remember an Inn,
Miranda?
Do you remember an Inn?

    Never more;
    Miranda,
    Never more.

Only the high peaks hoar:
And Aragon a torrent at the door.
No sound
In the walls of the Halls where falls
The tread
Of the feet of the dead to the ground
No sound:
But the boom
Of the far Waterfall like Doom.

Hilaire Belloc (1870–1953)

FRANCIS STUART   143

16 February 1990

Dear Joann Bradish and colleagues,
In reply to your letter of January 1 which I would have answered
sooner but for having been away.
One of my favourite poems is by William Blake called, I think,
'Under the Hill'. *This is because of these lines:*

  Though thou art worshipped by the names divine
  Of Jesus and Jehova, thou art still
  The son of Morn in weary night's decline
  And the lost traveller's dream under the hill.

Yours sincerely,
Francis Stuart

Epilogue from *For the Sexes the Gates of Paradise*
To the Accuser Who is the God of This World

Truly My Satan thou art but a Dunce
And dost not know the Garment from the Man
Every Harlot was a Virgin once
Nor canst thou ever change Kate into Nan

Tho thou art Worshipped by the Names Divine
Of Jesus & Jehovah: thou art still
The Son of Morn in weary Nights decline
The lost Travellers Dream under the Hill

William Blake (1757–1827)

MACDARA WOODS   144

14 January 1990

Dear Editors,
Thank you for your letter — I am delighted to be asked to name a
favourite poem for Lifelines III. *Having said that let me add that I*
have a lot of favourite poems, the perspective changes every so often
and in naming one I'd be afraid of reneging on others that have kept
me going at various bad or good times. At the minute I am very taken
with the Jennifer Warnes tape, Famous Blue Raincoat, *though I*
must admit I feel Cohen's own version of that particular song is
better. Her version of 'Joan of Arc' — with him — is chilling.
Wonderful. In fact the whole tape is. The point about songs, though,
is that a lot of one's reaction depends on the time and circumstance in
which one first hears them, or who does the introductions.
I'd like to crave — if I may — a few more days to think it over. I
reckon in the end I may get back to an old favourite like Marvell's
'To His Coy Mistress', but we'll see.
I saw Lifelines I *and* Lifelines II *and thought them a marvellous*
idea, quite apart from enjoying them, which I also did, immensely. I
hope you sell a half a million — at least.

Yours sincerely,
Macdara Woods

3 March 1990

Andrew Marvell's 'To His Coy Mistress' *is a poem I keep coming*
back to because it is one of those texts, like Thomas Mann's Death In
Venice, *which goes on quietly growing by itself while you are away*
from it. Which may be just another way of saying that the older I get
the more relevant this poem appears to become. It is about human
contact and human vulnerability, with an acute perception of
mortality and decay, and yet it is hopeful — and even heroic —
because it says that human contact and the full endorsement of it,
despite the inevitability of heartbreak, is all we have got and is
worthwhile. This is all we can do in the end, be human, and courage
lies in being human in spite of that. In Beckett's words: 'You must go
on. I can't go on. I'll go on.' Somehow, in spite of logic, age, decay
and death do not rob life — or love — of meaning.

Macdara Woods

('To His Coy Mistress' was also Ita Daly's choice. The poem appears in full on
pages 94–95.)

BRYAN MacMAHON   145

Liostuathail
16 January 1990

*Selecting one poem from a lifetime of reading poetry can be difficult.
'Byzantium', by W B Yeats, though incompletely understood, acts on
my imagination like fire.*

*However, I tend to forsake the Middle East in favour of the Irish
West. From there I select 'Pádraic Ó Conaire, Gaelic Storyteller'
by F R Higgins. This is a poem I find myself chanting on the most
unlikely occasions and to an audience only of myself.*

*The poet, now buried in Laracor in County Meath, imagines himself
alone in the wake room where Sean-Phádraic is laid out. The other
mourners have gone: alone, Higgins remains beside the corpse until
the break of a cold dawn.*

*For me the poem is full of the nostalgic memory of oldsters telling me
that they knew Sean-Phádraic, the picaresque personality who, with
Pádraic Pearse, brought a new measure of reality to literature in
Irish.*

*Again I hear the voice of those oldsters telling me of the rambler tying
his Kinvara-bought donkey to a pole outside a pub in the Coombe or
climbing the railings of the Park in St Stephen's Green to bed down
among the ducks on the little island in the lake.*

*Image piles on vivid image as I recite. I observe the sea-cold eyes of
the old writer, hear the tap of his heavy stick, find the west in his soft
speech, or watch him step through the Spanish Arch in Galway City.
I seem to see him 'exploring' the countryside: I also meet his
comrades 'to whom our heights of race belong' — men who practise
'the secret joinery of song'.*

*Finally, I am back again in the wake room as the candlelight fades
with the coming of morning. 'Death mars the parchment of the old
writer's forehead' while the poet drinks to his eternal peace for the
last time.*

*The funeral dirge is chanted by young winds rising on the barren
countryside.*

I strongly recommend the learning of this poem by heart.

I am certain that by doing so the student will gain a comrade for life.

With compliments agus le dea-mhéin,
Bryan MacMahon

Pádraic Ó Conaire, Gaelic Storyteller

They've paid the last respects in sad tobacco
And silent is this wakehouse in its haze;
They've paid the last respects; and now their whiskey
Flings laughing words on mouths of prayer and praise;
And so young couples huddle by the gables,
O let them grope home through the hedgy night —
Alone I'll mourn my old friend, while the cold dawn
Thins out the holy candlelight.

Respects are paid to one loved by the people;
Ah, was he not — among our mighty poor —
The sudden wealth cast on those pools of darkness,
Those bearing, just, a star's faint signature;
And so he was to me, close friend, near brother,
Dear Pádraic of the wide and sea-cold eyes —
So lovable, so courteous and noble,
The very West was in his soft replies.

They'll miss his heavy stick and stride in Wicklow —
His story-talking down Winetavern Street,
Where old men sitting in the wizen daylight
Have kept an edge upon his gentle wit;
While women on the grassy streets of Galway,
Who hearken for his passing — but in vain,
Shall hardly tell his steps as shadows vanish
Through archways of forgotten Spain.

Ah, they'll say: Pádraic's gone again exploring;
But now down glens of brightness, O he'll find
An alehouse overflowing with wise Gaelic
That's braced in vigour by the bardic mind,
And there his thoughts shall find their own forefathers —
In minds to whom our heights of race belong,
In crafty men, who ribbed a ship or turned
The secret joinery of song.

Alas, death mars the parchment of his forehead;
And yet for him, I know, the earth is mild —
The windy fidgets of September grasses
Can never tease a mind that loved the wild;
So drink his peace — this grey juice of the barley
Runs with a light that ever pleased his eye —
While old flames nod and gossip on the hearthstone
And only the young winds cry.

F R Higgins (1896–1941)

PATRICIA HURL   146

14 February 1990

Dear Joann, Jacki and Carolyn,
Delighted to be invited to contribute to your Anthology. The poem
that jumps to mind initially is 'my father moved through dooms of
love' by e e cummings. I was very close to my father and it evokes his
memory vividly.
However the poem I have picked for you has to be 'Without
Touching' by Leland Bardwell and which she dedicated to me. It was
written while she was writer-in-residence in Maggie's Farm, a
cottage attached to the Tyrone Guthrie Centre, Annaghmakerrig, a
place which holds happy memories for me.

I hope you enjoy it.

Best wishes,
Patricia Hurl

Without Touching

How she lay with her true love in bed without touching
how her hand journeyed to the drumlin of his hip
her pelvis aching
but just like two saints or priests or nuns
the true loves lay without touching

How she would long for the brush of a kiss
to travel her cheek or the cheek of her groin
her heart aching
but just like two saints or priests or nuns
two true loves lay without touching

Last night in her dream she spoke to his wife
his once-love who'd left him surely as they lay without
   touching
her thoughts on her turning
for like two saints or priests or nuns
the once-loves had lain without touching

But the dream of her faded before concentrating
each to each in their innocent mutual hating
their hands aching
to blind each other with bullets to stop them from pining
for a once-love they'd longed for and lay without touching

Now their true love lies in the mutton of madness
'I was always troubled by sex' he says with great sadness
with the two women aching
in their cold single beds with many seas dividing
as they think of the years that they spent without touching.

Leland Bardwell (b. 1928)

EILÍS O'CONNELL   147

17 March 1990

Dear Joann, Jacki and Carolyn,
Thank you for your invitation and please forgive me for taking so
long to answer but I've had a very hectic spring. I hope it's not too
late. I like your idea very much and I'm sure it will be a great
success.
My favourite poem changes all the time but these days it's 'Poem' by
Seamus Heaney. I like it because it is about a subject usually
discussed by women and Heaney is well able to cross the role barrier
and talk about this deep desire. I particularly enjoy the visual images,
muck and clabber etc. Hope you like it too.

Yours sincerely,
Eilís O'Connell

Poem
For Marie

Love, I shall perfect for you the child
Who diligently potters in my brain
Digging with heavy spade till sods were piled
Or puddling through muck in a deep drain.

Yearly I would sow my yard-long garden.
I'd strip a layer of sods to build the wall
That was to exclude sow and pecking hen.
Yearly, admitting these, the sods would fall.

Or in the sucking clabber I would splash
Delightedly and dam the flowing drain
But always my bastions of clay and mush
Would burst before the rising autumn rain.

Love, you shall perfect for me this child
Whose small imperfect limits would keep breaking:
Within new limits now, arrange the world
Within our walls, within our golden ring.

Seamus Heaney (b. 1939)

MICHAEL VINEY   148

4 January 1990

Dear Joann, Jacki and Carolyn,
Thank you for letting me share in Lifelines III *— I hope it's very successful.*
My favourite poem is Dylan Thomas's 'Poem in October'. *I love it for its lyricism and its strong and singing language. It's about the exuberance and abundance of Nature and the sweet pain of turning thirty — experiences, alas, that millions of Third World children die without ever knowing.*

Best wishes,
Michael Viney

('*Poem in October*' was also Theodora FitzGibbon's choice. The poem appears in full on pages 44–45.)

GREG DELANTY   149

17 January 1990

Dear Joann, Jacki and Carolyn,
Thank you for giving me the privilege to take part in your blessed and much needed work. Outside of the essential purpose of helping the Third World, you've also given poetry a purpose and prove it can make something happen.
It's impossible for me to pick a single favourite poem. I must have hundreds. Instead of picking a poem by well-known authors from the Old Sod, I thought I'd choose a poem from ones I've read recently, which are mostly by US poets. I would have liked to have put in Hayden Carruth's 'Marshall Washer', John Engels's 'The Comet', and Donald Hall's 'Kicking the Leaves' but they are all too long. I would also have liked to have chosen poems written in Irish given me by Louis de Paor.... I could go on and on.
In the end I don't know whether I'll send Kenneth Rexroth's 'Blues' or Carolyn Forché's 'The Colonel'. They both seem fitting, especially the latter for the Colonels are everywhere, including Ireland, not just in El Salvador. And the Colonels are certainly partly responsible for the plight of the Third World. 'Blues' is a flower of art which nourishes us and helps us keep going when we are brought low by whatever circumstances.

Best wishes,
Greg Delanty

Blues

The tops of the higher peaks
Of the Sierra Nevada
Of California are
Drenched in the perfume of
A flower which grows only there —
The blue *Polemonium*
Confertum eximium,
Soft, profound blue, like the eyes
Of impregnable innocence;
The perfume is heavy and
Clings thickly to the granite
Peaks, even in violent wind;
The leaves are clustered,
Fine, dull green, sticky, and musky.
I imagine that the scent
Of the body of Artemis
That put Endymion to sleep
Was like this and her eyes had the
Same inscrutable color.
Lawrence was lit into death
By the blue gentians of Kore.
Vanzetti had in his cell
A bowl of tall blue flowers
From a New England garden.
I hope that when I need it
My mind can always call back
This flower to its hidden senses.

Kenneth Rexroth (1905–1982)

The Colonel

WHAT YOU HAVE HEARD is true. I was in his house. His
wife carried a tray of coffee and sugar. His daughter filed her
nails, his son went out for the night. There were daily papers,
pet dogs, a pistol on the cushion beside him. The moon swung
bare on its black cord over the house. On the television was a
cop show. It was in English. Broken bottles were embedded in
the walls around the house to scoop the kneecaps from a man's
legs or cut his hands to lace. On the windows there were
gratings like those in liquor stores. We had dinner, rack of
lamb, good wine, a gold bell was on the table for calling the
maid. The maid brought green mangoes, salt, a type of bread. I
was asked how I enjoyed the country. There was a brief
commercial in Spanish. His wife took everything away. There
was some talk then of how difficult it had become to govern.

The parrot said hello on the terrace. The colonel told it to shut up, and pushed himself from the table. My friend said to me with his eyes: say nothing. The colonel returned with a sack used to bring groceries home. He spilled many human ears on the table. They were like dried peach halves. There is no other way to say this. He took one of them in his hands, shook it in our faces, dropped it into a water glass. It came alive there. I am tired of fooling around he said. As for the rights of anyone, tell your people they can go fuck themselves. He swept the ears to the floor with his arm and held the last of his wine in the air. Something for your poetry, no? he said. Some of the ears on the floor caught this scrap of his voice. Some of the ears on the floor were pressed to the ground.

Carolyn Forché (b. 1950)

WILLIAM TREVOR   150

14 January 1990

'The Lady of Shalott' *is one of the poems I most enjoy, but to attempt to explain why that is would be like trying to explain why a certain food is a particular favourite. You cannot describe the taste of bananas or fresh peas. You cannot describe the magic of poetry.*

Best wishes for your splendid project.
William Trevor

The Lady of Shalott

Part I

On either side the river lie
Long fields of barley and of rye,
That clothe the wold and meet the sky;
And through the field the road runs by
    To many-towered Camelot;
And up and down the people go,
Gazing where the lilies blow
Round an island there below,
    The island of Shalott.

Willows whiten, aspens quiver,
Little breezes dusk and shiver
Through the wave that runs forever
By the island in the river
    Flowing down to Camelot.

Four grey walls, and four grey towers,
Overlook a space of flowers,
And the silent isle imbowers
    The Lady of Shalott.

By the margin, willow-veiled,
Slide the heavy barges trailed
By slow horses; and unhailed
The shallop flitteth silken-sailed
    Skimming down to Camelot:
But who hath seen her wave her hand?
Or at the casement seen her stand?
Or is she known in all the land,
    The Lady of Shalott?

Only reapers, reaping early
In among the bearded barley,
Hear a song that echoes cheerly
From the river winding clearly,
    Down to towered Camelot;
And by the moon the reaper weary,
Piling sheaves in uplands airy,
Listening, whispers ' 'Tis the fairy
    Lady of Shalott.'

Part II

There she weaves by night and day
A magic web with colours gay.
She has heard a whisper say,
A curse is on her if she stay
    To look down to Camelot.
She knows not what the curse may be,
And so she weaveth steadily,
And little other care hath she,
    The Lady of Shalott.

And moving through a mirror clear
That hangs before her all the year,
Shadows of the world appear.
There she sees the highway near
    Winding down to Camelot;
There the river eddy whirls,
And there the surly village-churls,
And the red cloaks of market girls,
    Pass onward from Shalott.

Sometimes a troop of damsels glad,
An abbot on an ambling pad,
Sometimes a curly shepherd-lad
Or long-haired page in crimson clad,
    Goes by to towered Camelot;

And sometimes through the mirror blue
The knights come riding two and two:
She hath no loyal knight and true,
　　The Lady of Shalott.

But in her web she still delights
To weave the mirror's magic sights,
For often through the silent nights
A funeral, with plumes and lights,
　　And music, went to Camelot;
Or when the moon was overhead,
Came two young lovers lately wed;
'I am half sick of shadows,' said
　　The Lady of Shalott.

Part III

A bowshot from her bower-eaves,
He rode between the barley-sheaves,
The sun came dazzling through the leaves,
And flamed upon the brazen greaves
　　Of bold Sir Lancelot.
A red-cross knight forever kneeled
To a lady in his shield,
That sparkled on the yellow field,
　　Beside remote Shalott.

The gemmy bridle glittered free,
Like to some branch of stars we see
Hung in the golden Galaxy.
The bridle bells rang merrily
　　As he rode down to Camelot;
And from his blazoned baldric slung
A mighty silver bugle hung,
And as he rode his armor rung,
　　Beside remote Shalott.

All in the blue unclouded weather
Thick-jewelled shone the saddle-leather,
The helmet and the helmet-feather
Burned like one burning flame together,
　　As he rode down to Camelot;
As often through the purple night,
Below the starry clusters bright,
Some bearded meteor, trailing light,
　　Moves over still Shalott.

His broad clear brow in sunlight glowed;
On burnished hooves his war-horse trode;
From underneath his helmet flowed
His coal-black curls as on he rode,
　　As he rode down to Camelot.

From the bank and from the river
He flashed into the crystal mirror,
'Tirra lirra', by the river
      Sang Sir Lancelot.

She left the web, she left the loom,
She made three paces through the room,
She saw the water-lily bloom,
She saw the helmet and the plume,
      She looked down to Camelot.
Out flew the web and floated wide;
The mirror cracked from side to side;
'The curse is come upon me,' cried
      The Lady of Shalott.

Part IV

In the stormy east-wind straining,
The pale yellow woods were waning,
The broad stream in his banks complaining,
Heavily the low sky raining
      Over towered Camelot;
Down she came and found a boat
Beneath a willow left afloat,
And round about the prow she wrote
      The Lady of Shalott.

And down the river's dim expanse —
Like some bold seër in a trance,
Seeing all his own mischance —
With a glassy countenance
      Did she look to Camelot.
And at the closing of the day
She loosed the chain, and down she lay;
The broad stream bore her far away,
      The Lady of Shalott.

Lying, robed in snowy white
That loosely flew to left and right —
The leaves upon her falling light —
Through the noises of the night
      She floated down to Camelot;
And as the boat-head wound along
The willowy hills and fields among,
They heard her singing her last song,
      The Lady of Shalott.

Heard a carol, mournful, holy,
Chanted loudly, chanted lowly,
Till her blood was frozen slowly,
And her eyes were darkened wholly,
      Turned to towered Camelot;

For ere she reached upon the tide
The first house by the waterside,
Singing in her song she died,
        The Lady of Shalott.

Under tower and balcony,
By garden-wall and gallery,
A gleaming shape she floated by,
Dead-pale between the houses high,
        Silent into Camelot.
Out upon the wharfs they came,
Knight and burgher, lord and dame,
And round the prow they read her name,
        The Lady of Shalott.

Who is this? and what is here?
And in the lighted palace near
Died the sound of royal cheer;
And they crossed themselves for fear,
        All the knights at Camelot:
But Lancelot mused a little space;
He said, 'She has a lovely face;
God in his mercy lend her grace,
        The Lady of Shalott.'

Alfred, Lord Tennyson (1809–1892)

BARBARA BUSH   151

The White House
Washington
19 March 1990

Dear Friends,
On behalf of Mrs Bush, thank you for your message. She appreciates
your interest.
Mrs Bush has always enjoyed the works of William Wordsworth,
especially his 'Ode — Intimations of Immortality' *from*
Recollections of Early Childhood.
I know Mrs Bush would want me to convey her best wishes.

Sincerely,
Joan C DeCain
Director of Correspondence for Mrs Bush

From *Ode — Intimations of Immortality from Recollections of Early Childhood*

> The Child is father of the Man;
> And I could wish my days to be
> Bound each to each by natural piety.

I

There was a time when meadow, grove, and stream,
The earth, and every common sight,
    To me did seem
    Apparelled in celestial light,
The glory and the freshness of a dream.
It is not now as it hath been of yore —
    Turn whereso'er I may,
      By night or day,
The things which I have seen I now can see no more.

II

    The Rainbow comes and goes,
    And lovely is the Rose,
    The Moon doth with delight
Look round her when the heavens are bare,
      Waters on a starry night
      Are beautiful and fair;
    The sunshine is a glorious birth;
    But yet I know, where'er I go,
That there hath passed away a glory from the earth.

V

Our birth is but a sleep and a forgetting:
The Soul that rises with us, our life's Star,
    Hath had elsewhere its setting,
      And cometh from afar:
    Not in entire forgetfulness,
    And not in utter nakedness,
But trailing clouds of glory do we come
    From God, who is our home:
Heaven lies about us in our infancy!
Shades of the prison-house begin to close
    Upon the growing Boy,
      But He
Beholds the light, and whence it flows,
    He sees it in his joy;
The Youth, who daily farther from the east
    Must travel, still is Nature's Priest,
    And by the vision splendid
    Is on his way attended;
At length the Man perceives it die away,
And fade into the light of common day.

XI
And O, ye Fountains, Meadows, Hills and Groves,
Forebode not any severing of our loves!
Yet in my heart of hearts I feel your might;
I only have relinquished one delight
To live beneath your more habitual sway.
I love the Brooks which down their channels fret,
Even more than when I tripped lightly as they;
The innocent brightness of a newborn Day
     Is lovely yet;
The Clouds that gather round the setting sun
Do take a sober colouring from an eye
That hath kept watch o'er man's mortality;
Another race hath been, and other palms are won.
Thanks to the human heart by which we live,
Thanks to its tenderness, its joys, and fears,
To me the meanest flower that blows can give
Thoughts that do often lie too deep for tears.

William Wordsworth (1770–1850)

HELEN VENDLER   152

Harvard University
Department of English and American Literature and Language
4 March 1990

Dear Students of Wesley College,
I am sorry to be answering you so late. I was in Japan for a month,
and am only catching up.
My favorite poem is 'The Auroras of Autumn' by Wallace Stevens
(1879–1955), our American great modernist poet. In it, Stevens
confronts the exhaustion and destruction of everything we hold dear,
and praises the sublimity of the human mind, which rises to meet and
master, if only by imagination, the disasters of reality. This great
hymn to change, even if change entails our own destruction, is
Stevens's summarium in excelsis: *'Hear what he says, The*
dauntless master, as he starts the human tale.' This quotation, from
Stevens's poem 'Puella Parvula', always comes to my mind when I
re-read 'The Auroras of Autumn': it is the human tale of the
innocent human being pitted against an impersonal but innocent
necessitarian law of change.

Yours truly,
Helen Vendler
Kenan Professor of English

from *The Auroras of Autumn*

II
Farewell to an idea . . . A cabin stands,
Deserted, on a beach. It is white,
As by a custom or according to

An ancestral theme or as a consequence
Of an infinite course. The flowers against the wall
Are white, a little dried, a kind of mark

Reminding, trying to remind, of a white
That was different, something else, last year
Or before, not the white of an aging afternoon,

Whether fresher or duller, whether of winter cloud
Or of winter sky, from horizon to horizon.
The wind is blowing the sand across the floor.

Here, being visible is being white,
Is being of the solid of white, the accomplishment
Of an extremist in an exercise. . .

The season changes. A cold wind chills the beach.
The long lines of it grow longer, emptier,
A darkness gathers though it does not fall

And the whiteness grows less vivid on the wall.
The man who is walking turns blankly on the sand.
He observes how the north is always enlarging the change,

With its frigid brilliances, its blue-red sweeps
And gusts of great enkindlings, its polar green,
The color of ice and fire and solitude.

III
Farewell to an idea . . . The mother's face,
The purpose of the poem, fills the room.
They are together, here, and it is warm,

With none of the prescience of oncoming dreams,
It is evening. The house is evening, half dissolved.
Only the half they can never possess remains,

Still-starred. It is the mother they possess,
Who gives transparence to their present peace.
She makes that gentler that can gentle be.

And yet she too is dissolved, she is destroyed.
She gives transparence. But she has grown old.
The necklace is a carving not a kiss.

The soft hands are a motion not a touch.
The house will crumble and the books will burn.
They are at ease in a shelter of the mind

And the house is of the mind and they and time,
Together, all together. Boreal night
Will look like frost as it approaches them

And to the mother as she falls asleep
And as they say good-night, good-night. Upstairs
The windows will be lighted, not the rooms.

A wind will spread its windy grandeurs round
And knock like a rifle-butt against the door.
The wind will command them with invincible sound.

VII
Is there an imagination that sits enthroned
As grim as it is benevolent, the just
And the unjust, which in the midst of summer stops

To imagine winter? When the leaves are dead,
Does it take its place in the north and enfold itself,
Goat-leaper, crystalled and luminous, sitting

In highest night? And do these heavens adorn
And proclaim it, the white creator of black, jetted
By extinguishings, even of planets as may be,

Even of earth, even of sight, in snow,
Except as needed by way of majesty,
In the sky, as crown and diamond cabala?

It leaps through us, through all our heavens leaps,
Extinguishing our planets, one by one,
Leaving, of where we were and looked, of where

We knew each other and of each other thought,
A shivering residue, chilled and foregone,
Except for that crown and mystical cabala.

But it dare not leap by chance in its own dark.
It must change from destiny to slight caprice.
And thus its jetted tragedy, its stele

And shape and mournful making move to find
What must unmake it and, at last, what can,
Say, a flippant communication under the moon.

Wallace Stevens (1879–1955)

MICHAEL O'LOUGHLIN   153

Dear Joann, Jacki and Carolyn,
Auden called poetry 'the wholly human instrument', and I know no
better example than this poem by César Vallejo, one of my favourites.

César Vallejo was a poet from Peru who died in Paris in 1938. He was a deeply unhappy man, and had a difficult life, but he never lost his belief in humanity, even when confronted by poverty and death. This poem is about a soldier in the Spanish Civil War. Wars, like famines, are illustrations of Yeats's idea that 'Man has created death'. Whenever I read this miraculous poem, I catch a glimpse of a possible world where war and famine could be eliminated by mankind working together to the end. And even if that vision only lasts a moment, that is enough to begin with.

With all best wishes,
Michael O'Loughlin

XII *Masa*

Al fin de la batalla,
y muerto el combatiente, vino hacia él un hombre
y le dijo: «¡ No mueras; te amo tanto !»
Pero el cadáver ¡ ay ! siguió muriendo.

Se le acercaron dos y repitiéronle:
«¡ No nos dejes! ¡ Valor ! ¡ Vuelve a la vida !»
Pero el cadáver ¡ ay ! siguió muriendo.

Acudieron a él veinte, cien, mil, quinientos mil,
clamando: «¡ Tanto amor, y no poder nada contra la muerte !»
Pero el cadáver ¡ ay ! siguió muriendo.

Le rodearon millones de individuos,
con un ruego común: «¡ Quédate hermano !»
Pero el cadáver ¡ ay ! siguió muriendo.

Entonces todos los hombres de la tierra
le rodearon; les vió el cadáver triste, emociónado;
incorporóse lentamente,
abrazó al primer hombre; echóse a andar. . . .

XII *Mass*

At the end of the battle,
with the combatant dead, a man came up
and told him: 'Don't die, I love you so much!'
But the corpse, alas! went on dying.

Two others came up and said to him again:
'Don't leave us! Courage! Come back to life!'
But the corpse, alas! went on dying.

Twenty, a hundred, a thousand, five hundred thousand ran up
   to him,
crying out: 'So much love and no way of countering death!'
But the corpse, alas! went on dying.

Millions of individuals stood round him,
with a common plea: 'Stay here brother!'
But the corpse, alas! went on dying.

Then all the men on earth
stood round him; the sad corpse saw them, with emotion;
he got up slowly,
embraced the first man; began to walk . . .

César Vallejo (1892–1938)
(Translated from the Spanish by Ed Dorn)

NIAMH CUSACK   154

31 January 1990

Dear Joann, Jacki and Carolyn,
I think these anthologies are a wonderful idea. Not only are they
helping a very worthy cause but they're a grand old read. It's so
interesting to learn of people's choices and their reasons for choosing
certain poems.
I love poetry. I have crushes on different poets depending on my
frame of mind. I think Shakespeare sonnets are great for exercising
your brain and plumbing the depths of human emotions and finding
words and images that depict the grandeur of those emotions. All the
sonnets I love. And Donne's. Yeats, Heaney, and Manley Hopkins
are poets I dip into regularly. Oh yes and Philip Larkin. There's a
lovely collection by Wendy Cope called Making Cocoa for Kingsley
Amis. *But if I have to choose one poem it would be a very simple one*
called 'The Road Not Taken' by Robert Frost. I first read it when I
was about thirteen and even then it struck a chord deep within me.
First, I found it so lovely to speak and the image of the two roads in a
yellow wood was clear for me to see. But it was the idea of choices
changing your life forever that has made this poem stick with me. At
thirteen I wished myself a kindred spirit of Frost's when he wrote:

Two roads diverged in a wood, and I —
I took the one less traveled by,
And that has made all the difference.

I hope I'm not too late for inclusion in Lifelines.

Good luck, and thank you for asking me.
Niamh Cusack

('*The Road Not Taken*' was also chosen by Eithne Hand and Margaret Heckler.
The poem appears in full on page 78.)

JOHN BAYLEY

155

5 January 1990

My favourite poem is Pushkin's 'Ruslan and Lyudmila' because it is a wonderful fairy-story anyone can read and enjoy — in Russian or in translation — from the time they learn to read till the time they die.

Very best wishes to Lifelines.
John Bayley

Пролог к «Руслану и Людтиле»

У лукоморья дуб зелёный;
Элатая цепь на дубе том:
И днём и ночью кот учёный
Всё ходит по цепи кругом;
Идёт направо — песнь заводит,
Налево — сказку говорит.

Там чудеса: там леший бродит,
Русалка на ветвях сидит;
Там на неведомых дорожках
Следы невиданных зверей;
Избушка там на курьих ножках
Стоит без окон, без дверей;

Там лес и дол видений полны;
Там о заре прихлынут волны
На брег песчаный и пустой,
И тридцать витязей прекрасных
Чредой из вод выходят ясных,
И с ними дядька их морской;
Там королевич мимоходом
Пленяет грозного царя;
Там в облаках перед народом
Через леса, через моря
Колдун несёт богатыря;
В темнице там царевна тужит,
А бурый волк ей верно служит;
Там ступа с Бабою Ягой
Идёт, бредёт сама собой;
Там царь Кащей над златом чахнет;
Там русский дух ... там Русью пахнет!
И там я был, и мёд я пил;
У моря видел дуб зелёный;
Под ним сидел, и кот учёный
Свои мне сказки говорил.
Одну я помню: сказку эту
Поведаю теперь я свету ...

Aleksandr Pushkin (1799–1837)

Prologue to *Ruslan and Lyudmila*

By the shores of a bay there is a green oak-tree; there is a
golden chain on that oak; and day and night a learned cat
ceaselessly walks round on the chain; as it moves to the right,
it strikes up a song, as it moves to the left, it tells a story.

There are marvels there: the wood-sprite roams, a mermaid
sits in the branches; there are tracks of strange animals on
mysterious paths; a hut on hen's legs stands there, without
windows or doors; forest and vale are full of visions; there at
dawn the waves come washing over the sandy and deserted
shore, and thirty fair knights come out one by one from the
clear water, attended by their sea-tutor; a king's son, passing
on his way, takes a dreaded king prisoner; there, in full view of
the people, a sorcerer carries a knight through the clouds,
across forests and seas; a princess pines away in prison, and a
brown wolf serves her faithfully; a mortar with Baba-Yaga in it
walks along by itself. There King Kashchey grows sickly
beside his gold; there is a Russian odour there . . . it smells of
Russia! And I was there, I drank mead, I saw the green oak-
tree by the sea and sat under it, while the learned cat told me
its stories. I remember one — and this story I will now reveal
to the world . . . .

BRIAN LENIHAN   156

Oifig an Tánaiste
Office of the Tánaiste
24 April 1990

Dear Ms Bradish,
I have been asked by An Tánaiste and Minister for Defence, Mr
Brian Lenihan, TD, to refer to your letter of 1 January 1990
requesting information from An Tánaiste in relation to his favourite
poem.
An Tánaiste very much regrets the delay in replying to you and he
trusts that it is not too late to be included in Lifelines.
An appropriate poem favoured by An Tánaiste is by William Butler
*Yeats and is titled '*Among School Children'. *The last few lines*
read:

O chestnut-tree, great-rooted blossomer,
Are you the leaf, the blossom or the bole?
O body swayed to music, O brightening glance,
How can we know the dancer from the dance?

The lines relate to the unity of being, embracing the harmony of existence, which gives meaning to life.
The essential message for children to learn and retain for life is the unity of being. This is the basis of conviction, integrity and the rejection of anarchy, insecurity and fragmentation. It emphasises the harmony of existence which gives meaning and purpose to life.

Yours sincerely,
Brian Spain
Private Secretary
An Tánaiste and Minister for Defence

('*Among School Children*' was also David Lodge's choice. The poem appears in full on pages 184–185.)

SUE TOWNSEND   157

Leicester
April 1990

Dear Joann, Jacki and Carolyn,
My favourite poem is very short but, I think, powerful. I'm not even sure that it is a poem though it reads like poetry.

First they came for the Jews
and I did not speak out —
because I was not a Jew.
Then they came for the communists
and I did not speak out —
because I was not a communist.
Then they came for the trade unionists
and I did not speak out —
because I was not a trade unionist.
Then they came for me —
and there was no one left
to speak out for me.

Pastor Niemoeller (victim of the Nazis)

I wish you all well in your fundraising. All three of you obviously have kind hearts — the very best thing to have.

Very best wishes,
Sue Townsend

MOTHER TERESA   158

LDM

Missionaries of Charity
54A A J C Bose Road
Calcutta 700016
13 February 1990

Dear Joann Bradish, Jacki Erskine and Carolyn Gibson,
Thank you for your letter of 1 January 1990. I am sure God is very
pleased with your desire to serve the sick and save the lives of
children through Lifelines. *I feel nothing can be better than Christ's*
own words: 'Whatever you do to the least of my brothers you
do it to ME.' *Jesus cannot deceive us — we can be sure that*
whatever we do for His poor, sick and suffering people, we do it for
Him, and to Him. The same applies if we are unkind, uncharitable
and unforgiving, we do it to Christ.
I am praying for you and wish you a year of true Peace — that comes
from loving and caring and from respecting the rights of every
human being — even the unborn child.

God bless you
Mother Teresa, MC

[All contributors to the original *Lifelines* were contacted and their permission
sought to include them in the *Collected* edition. Mother Teresa of Calcutta
asked that the following paragraph be added to her first letter.]

12 June 1992

The prayer for Peace of St Francis of Assisi is so beautiful and simple
that we pray it daily after Mass. I would like to include it now. My
prayer for you is that you may make this prayer your own and put it
into your life and so become an instrument of Jesus's peace — the
true peace that comes from loving and sharing and respecting
everyone as a child of God — my Brother — my Sister.

God bless you
Mother Teresa, MC

Prayer for Peace

Lord, make me a channel of Thy peace that, where there is
hatred, I may bring love; that where there is wrong, I may
bring the spirit of forgiveness; that where there is discord, I
may bring harmony; that, where there is error, I may bring

truth; that, where there is doubt, I may bring faith; that, where there is despair, I may bring hope; that, where there are shadows, I may bring light; that where there is sadness, I may bring joy.

Lord, grant that I may seek rather to comfort than to be comforted, to understand than to be understood; to love than to be loved; for it is by forgetting self that one finds; it is by forgiving that one is forgiven; it is by dying that one awakens to eternal life.

Amen.

PETER FALLON   159

9 May 1990

To: The Editors of Lifelines
I don't know how I'd single out one poem as a favourite. So many verses are central to my life as a writer, an editor, a reader. Still I appreciate opportunities to attempt to direct people to patterns of words which I've come to love. Perhaps, in this case, I am asking that familiar words be reconsidered, thought about again. Thousands of times I've heard the 'Hail Mary' transformed into, at best, a kind of mantra, at worst, the sound of no sense. Yet the words are lovely in their pure praise of a woman, a mother — maybe all women — and the phrase which has always delighted me, that is 'the fruit of thy womb', for an offspring, a welcomed child, has again and again been submerged in the interminable decades of a million galloping rosaries. One thoughtful recitation of this prayer would be worth those millions. Perhaps it's the editor in me which would propose to alter the order of the first section of the piece so that it ends 'Blessed is Jesus, the fruit of thy womb', to recover its special emphasis.
Now I'm no holy Joe but the plain beauty of this homage came to me first on my uncle's farm when I was a boy, when we congregated each evening and slumped as much as we were allowed on the arms of the drawing-room chairs and my brother Bernard (or BP if you like), on holidays from Prep School in England, knelt straight upright and spoke his pieces with the clear impression that he'd be a bishop at least if not the Pope! Somehow the arch loveliness of the words and ideas filtered through to me then. I thought them perfectly married. I still do.
Thank you for asking me.

Very best wishes,
Peter Fallon

Hail Mary, full of grace,
the Lord is with thee.
Blessed art thou amongst women
and blessed is the fruit of thy womb, Jesus.

Holy Mary, mother of God,
pray for us sinners,
now and at the hour of our death. Amen.

LIFELINES IV

ANTHONY CLARE   160

When You Are Old

When you are old and grey and full of sleep,
And nodding by the fire, take down this book,
And slowly read, and dream of the soft look
Your eyes had once, and of their shadows deep;

How many loved your moments of glad grace,
And loved your beauty with love false or true,
But one man loved the pilgrim soul in you,
And loved the sorrows of your changing face;

And bending down beside the glowing bars,
Murmur, a little sadly, how Love fled
And paced upon the mountains overhead
And hid his face amid a crowd of stars.

W B Yeats (1865–1939)

*I choose it because it never fails to move me when I read it, because it
evokes the sweet, aching agony of nostalgia and ageing and the
elusive, endlessly sought human love that every one of us seeks and
because when I recite it myself I immediately feel my kinship,
however slight, with the greatest poet in the English language in this
century.*

Best wishes,
Anthony W Clare   24 January 1992

DOROTHY CROSS   161

3 January 1992

Dear Nicola, Paula and Alice,
Thank you for your invitation to participate in your next volume of
Lifelines. *The poem I have chosen is 'Contusion' by Sylvia Plath.*
I chose this poem because it is like standing on the edge of a sea-cliff.
Good luck with your project.

All the best,
Dorothy Cross

Contusion

Colour floods to the spot, dull purple.
The rest of the body is all washed out,
The colour of pearl.

In a pit of rock
The sea sucks obsessively,
One hollow the whole sea's pivot.

The size of a fly,
The doom mark
Crawls down the wall.

The heart shuts,
The sea slides back,
The mirrors are sheeted.

Sylvia Plath (1932–1963)

ANNA SCHER   162

6 January 1992

Dear Nicola, Paula and Alice,
Speaking as an Irish Jewish integrationist this poem really appeals to
the warts-and-all in me as it celebrates individuality, its uniqueness
and all the 'oddballness' that goes with it.

Pied Beauty

Glory be to God for dappled things —
  For skies of couple-colour as a brinded cow;
    For rose-moles all in stipple upon trout that swim;
Fresh-firecoal chestnut-falls; finches' wings;
  Landscape plotted and pieced — fold, fallow, and plough;
And áll trádes, their gear and tackle and trim.

All things counter, original, spare, strange;
  Whatever is fickle, freckled (who knows how?)
    With swift, slow; sweet, sour; adazzle, dim;
He fathers-forth whose beauty is past change:
        Praise him.

Gerard Manley Hopkins (1844–1889)

All the best with your excellent project,

Shalom for '92,
Anna Scher

MICHEAL O'SIADHAIL   163

6 January 1992

Dear Editors,
Thank you for your letter inviting me to name a favourite poem for your Lifelines IV.
I love the passion and precision of much Elizabethan poetry, so I've chosen the Shakespearean sonnet 'They that have power to hurt, and will do none'. This is a wonderful meditation on power which is as sparkling and as actual as it was the day it was written. Its cadence contains a core wisdom about all our human endeavours: the corruption of the best is worst.

Yours sincerely,
Micheal O'Siadhail

XCIV

They that have power to hurt and will do none,
That do not do the thing they most do show,
Who, moving others, are themselves as stone,
Unmoved, cold, and to temptation slow;
They rightly do inherit heaven's graces
And husband nature's riches from expense;
They are the lords and owners of their faces,
Others but stewards of their excellence.
The summer's flower is to the summer sweet,
Though to itself it only live and die;
But if that flower with base infection meet,
The basest weed outbraves his dignity:
    For sweetest things turn sourest by their deeds;
    Lilies that fester smell far worse than weeds.

William Shakespeare (1564–1616)

SEBASTIAN BARRY   164

6 January 1992

Dear Nicola, Paula, and Alice,
Happy to respond to your kind invitation. A splendid enterprise. Hope this will suffice.

With all best wishes,
Sebastian Barry

Saint Judas

When I went out to kill myself, I caught
A pack of hoodlums beating up a man.
Running to spare his suffering, I forgot
My name, my number, how my day began,
How soldiers milled around the garden stone
And sang amusing songs; how all that day
Their javelins measured crowds; how I alone
Bargained the proper coins, and slipped away.

Banished from heaven, I found the victim beaten,
Stripped, kneed, and left to cry. Dropping my rope
Aside, I ran, ignored the uniforms:
Then I remembered bread my flesh had eaten,
The kiss that ate my flesh. Flayed without hope,
I held the man for nothing in my arms.

James Wright (1927–1980)

I read this poem first in 1987, in America. James Wright isn't that well known here but in America, his home place, he is almost accorded greatness. He had to struggle out of an early Yeatsian influence to the sort of slightly rhetorical simplicity found in this poem. It's the last line that makes the sonnet unforgettable, a characteristic of sonnets more or less. The feeling also that Wright is writing about something in his life amplifies the effect — but this notion of some forgotten act of Judas going a long way to redeeming him is very potent on its own.

Sebastian Barry

ROBIN EAMES   165

8 January 1992

Dear Editors,
Thank you for your recent letter. I would like to wish you every success in your venture. I am particularly pleased to know that the proceeds of the book will go to the Third World at this time when so many are suffering hunger and homelessness.
I have long regarded the Book of Psalms as one of the greatest collections of poetry in the world. While I enjoy poetry I often find myself returning to the Psalms for the beauty of their language as much as their meaning. Psalm 121 holds particular interest for me:

I will lift up mine eyes unto the hills:
from whence cometh my help.

This language reminds me of the eternal strength of God and is reflected in the magnificent scenery we have in Ireland.

All good wishes,
Robin Eames
Archbishop of Armagh and Primate of All Ireland

Psalm 121

I will lift up mine eyes unto the hills, from whence cometh my help. My help cometh from the Lord, which made heaven and earth. He will not suffer thy foot to be moved: he that keepeth thee will not slumber. Behold, he that keepeth Israel shall neither slumber nor sleep. The Lord is thy keeper; the Lord is thy shade upon thy right hand. The sun shall not smite thee by day, nor the moon by night. The Lord shall preserve thee from all evil; he shall preserve thy soul. The Lord shall preserve thy going out and thy coming in from this time forth, and even for evermore.

Authorised King James Version

LYNN BARBER   166

8 January 1992

Dear Nicola, Paula and Alice,
Thank you for your letter. Your Lifelines *project sounds very worthwhile though I wish you had said exactly which Third World charities you support: as an atheist, I prefer not to be associated with any which have a religious basis.*
My favourite poem is Shelley's 'Ozymandias' because it creates such an unforgettable picture of the ruined statue in the desert and quietly reminds us that all human pomp and power is transient and that even the greatest self-importance ends in dust. I love the commonplace, buttonholing, way it opens, and then the grandeur of its climax. A few years ago I saw the ruined Pharaonic statue near Luxor which the poem is supposed to be based on: a bitter disappointment because it is beside a busy tourist road. But the glory of the poem remains.

Yours sincerely,
Lynn Barber

Ozymandias

I met a traveller from an antique land
Who said — Two vast and trunkless legs of stone
Stand in the desert. Near them on the sand,
Half sunk a shatter'd visage lies, whose frown
And wrinkled lip and sneer of cold command
Tell that its sculptor well those passions read
Which yet survive, stamp'd on these lifeless things,
The hand that mock'd them, and the heart that fed;
And on the pedestal these words appear:
'My name is Ozymandias, king of kings:
Look on my works, ye Mighty, and despair!'
Nothing beside remains. Round the decay
Of that colossal wreck, boundless and bare,
The lone and level sands stretch far away.

Percy Bysshe Shelley (1792–1822)

SHANE CONNAUGHTON   167

11 January 1992

Girls,
My favourite poem has no name and only one line and isn't normally thought of as poetry at all.

  'I ain't got no quarrel with them Vietcong.'

It was spoken by Muhammad Ali, the greatest boxer and sportsman this century. He said it to the US Government when refusing to join the Army to fight in Vietnam.
The line comes from the heart where all poetry comes from and has a real beat to it when you recite it aloud. It is pure rap. Rap is the street poetry of Black America. 'I ain't got no quarrel with them Vietcong.' It has music and truth. He stood against the Establishment like Byron, Shelley and Blake before him. And he was proven right! By saying that line he risked all. How many poets today can say the same?
Good luck to you all.

Sincerely,
Shane Connaughton

DORIS LESSING   168

8 January 1992

Dear Nicola Hughes, Paula Griffin and Alice McEleney,
Yeats's poem 'Memory' has always been a favourite.

Memory

One had a lovely face,
And two or three had charm,
But charm and face were in vain
Because the mountain grass
Cannot but keep the form
Where the mountain hare has lain.

This short and apparently simple poem has something of the quality
of a Japanese haiku — a great deal said in a few words, on whatever
level it is being understood.

With good wishes,
Doris Lessing

NOËL BROWNE   169

Thank you for asking me.

my way is in the sand flowing
between the shingle and the dune
the summer rain rains on my life
on me my life harrying fleeing
to its beginning to its end.

my peace is there in the receding mist
when I may cease from treading these long shifting
        thresholds
and live the space of a door
that opens and shuts

Samuel Beckett (1906–1989)

Why? Because with Beckett and Pascal I believe that Life is 'a Prison
from which daily human kind is released to die'. Our function is to
make life tolerable for ourselves and for all our fellow Prisoners.

Love,
Noël Browne

JILLY COOPER   170

Thank you for your lovely letter.
I'm very proud to be asked to be part of Lifelines *and I enclose a copy*
of my favourite poem, which is an extract from 'The Ancient
Mariner'. It's obviously far too long a poem for you to publish the
whole thing, but I just think that this bit is particularly beautiful
because it tells people that the only thing that really matters in life is
to be kind and only if we can be kind to the smallest creatures will we
learn to be kind to each other. I think it's a very beautiful poem and
still when I read it, it makes the hair prickle on the back of my neck.
I hope you like it too.

Lots of love,
Jilly Cooper

from *The Ancient Mariner*

Beyond the shadow of the ship,
I watched the water snakes:
They moved in tracks of shining white,
And when they reared, the elfish light
Fell off in hoary flakes.

Within the shadow of the ship
I watched their rich attire:
Blue, glossy green, and velvet black,
They coiled and swam; and every track
Was a flash of golden fire.

O happy living things! no tongue
Their beauty might declare:
A spring of love gushed from my heart,
And I blessed them unaware:
Sure my kind saint took pity on me,
And I blessed them unaware.

The selfsame moment I could pray;
And from my neck so free
The Albatross fell off, and sank
Like lead into the sea.

Samuel Taylor Coleridge (1772–1834)

AILBHE SMYTH   171

13 January 1992

Dear Nicola, Paula and Alice,
Many thanks for your nice letter. I'm delighted to choose a poem for
Lifelines IV *and wish you the best of success with the collection.*
I don't have a favourite poem, or rather I have a very great many
favourites which inspire, console or illuminate me in different ways
at different moments. This one by Eithne Strong I like especially
because it expresses something of the experience of growing into
womanhood, its awkward confusions and difficulties as much as its
quick pleasures and delights. 'Identity' is both grave and witty and
inspires us all (I think) to avoid 'rectangular requisite' — a
wonderful phrase.

With warmest wishes,
Ailbhe Smyth

Identity

One-eyed Spring gone wrong and a rather
crazy — by district style — neighbour
having a go at her lawn, long-abandoned:
things just here are not in approved plan;
her odd-bod shave leaves behind
long swathes lumpily lying where,
quick, the small girls — newbreed mites,
latter-day, unfathered kind — rush to play;
quick into it they run, not letting
lie but running lumps of lying grass
abandonedly into the sky; high,
jumbling sky; wildish things these —
little newbreed Irish girls, scarce
parented, not to be grooved into
rectangular requisite, and I,
long tooth of expected sanity, see,
from my high seat, my supposed sober
chair, second storey; see, and feel,
in sudden flash, newfleshed;
rejoice, identified with bastards,
grass, odd-bod, confused sky; I, seeing me
not at all made to regular shape,
who privately am
according to suburban norm
quite ab.

Eithne Strong

V S PRITCHETT   172

One of my favourite poets is Arthur Hugh Clough — 'Amours de Voyage'. It delights me. His dates are 1819–1861. I love its appeal to courage and its autobiographical tone.

V S Pritchett

from *Amours de Voyage*

Canto I

I. Claude to Eustace

Dear Eustatio, I write that you may write me an answer,
Or at the least to put us again en rapport with each other.
Rome disappoints me much, — St Peter's, perhaps, in especial;
Only the Arch of Titus and view from the Lateran please me:
This, however, perhaps is the weather, which truly is horrid.
Greece must be better, surely; and yet I am feeling so spiteful
That I could travel to Athens, to Delphi, and Troy, and Mount
    Sinai,
Though but to see with my eyes that these are vanity also.
  Rome disappoints me much; I hardly as yet understand, but
Rubbishy seems the word that most exactly would suit it.
All the foolish destructions, and all the sillier savings,
All the incongruous things of past incompatible ages,
Seem to be treasured up here to make fools of present and
    future.
Would to Heaven the old Goths had made a cleaner sweep of it;
Would to Heaven some new ones would come and destroy
    these churches!
However, one can live in Rome as also in London.
It is a blessing, no doubt, to be rid, at least for a time,
All one's friends and relations, — yourself (forgive me!)
    included, —
All the assujettissement of having been what one has been,
What one thinks one is, or thinks that others suppose one;
Yet, in despite of all, we turn like fools to the English.
Vernon has been my fate; who is here the same that you knew
    him, —
Making the tour, it seems, with friends of the name of
    Trevellyn.

Arthur Hugh Clough (1819–1861)

MARY BECKETT   173

13 January 1992

Dear Alice, Nicola and Paula,
I hope you have a lovely time with your book of poetry. Good luck
with it.

Yours sincerely,
Mary Beckett

When I was in my twenties I taught in a primary school in Ardoyne,
Belfast. At one time I had a class of 13-year-old girls who were to
leave school at 14 and work in the mills. They are all closed now, the
mills. And I did not know at that time that their homes would be
burnt, bombed, wrecked. However, I thought it more profitable to
neglect algebra, for instance, and fill their minds with good novels
and poetry. So we read Lorna Doone, The Mill on the Floss, Pride
and Prejudice, *and we learned rafts of poetry. I loved that time and I*
think the girls enjoyed it. The poem that stays most clearly in my
mind from then is T S Eliot's 'Ash Wednesday'. We did not learn it
all off by heart — just clumps of it. But the rhythm made it easy to
remember and the words are simple if the thought is not. The mystery
in it appealed to us.
A line in it now strikes a chord for me:

'Why should the agèd eagle stretch its wings?'

Mary Beckett

lines from *Ash Wednesday*

Lady, three white leopards sat under a juniper-tree
In the cool of the day, having fed to satiety
On my legs my heart my liver and that which had been
  contained
In the hollow round of my skull. And God said
Shall these bones live? shall these
Bones live? And that which had been contained
In the bones (which were already dry) said chirping:
Because of the goodness of this Lady
And because of her loveliness, and because
She honours the Virgin in meditation,
We shine with brightness. And I who am here dissembled
Proffer my deeds to oblivion, and my love
To the posterity of the desert and the fruit of the gourd.

T S Eliot (1888–1965)

LOUIS LE BROCQUY   174

16 January 1992

Dear Three,
Thank you for writing to me.
The poem which means most to me, after all, is Yeats's 'The Second
Coming'. What are my reasons? Yeats himself replies with his own
question in 'Stream and Sun at Glendalough':

   What motion of the sun or stream
   Or eyelid shot the gleam
   That pierced my body through?

Need I say I wish you ever greater success in your wonderful effort.

Yours gratefully,
Louis Le Brocquy

('*The Second Coming*' was also Fiona Shaw's choice. The poem appears in full
on page 174.)

FERDIA MacANNA   175

13 January 1992

Dear Paula,
My favourite poem of the moment is 'Buying Winkles' from Paula
Meehan's collection The Man who was Marked by Winter. *I like*
it because it is direct, simple and beautiful, and because it conjures
up images of a child's experience of the adult world. Each time I read
it, I find something new to savour. Most of all though, I like this
poem because of its strong cinematic flavour. Reading it is a bit like
being inside an imaginary Fellini film set in Dublin — there is
colour, dash, charm, light and character as well as an ever-present
tinge of danger.
I love this kind of work. I think it gives Poetry a good name. Also, I
think Paula Meehan is a great writer.
I hope all the above is helpful. Good luck with the project.

Regards,
Ferdia MacAnna

Buying Winkles

My mother would spare me sixpence and say,
'Hurry up now and don't be talking to strange
men on the way.' I'd dash from the ghosts
on the stairs where the bulb had blown
out into Gardiner Street, all relief.
A bonus if the moon was in the strip of sky
between the tall houses, or stars out,
but even in rain I was happy — the winkles
would be wet and glisten blue like little
night skies themselves. I'd hold the tanner tight
and jump every crack in the pavement,
I'd wave up to women at sills or those
lingering in doorways and weave a glad path through
men heading out for the night.

She'd be sitting outside the Rosebowl Bar
on an orange-crate, a pram loaded
with pails of winkles before her.
When the bar doors swung open they'd leak
the smell of men together with drink
and I'd see light in golden mirrors.
I envied each soul in the hot interior.

I'd ask her again to show me the right way
to do *it*. She'd take a pin from her shawl —
'Open the eyelid. So. Stick it in
till you feel a grip, then slither him out.
Gently, mind.' The sweetest extra winkle
that brought the sea to me.
'Tell yer Ma I picked them fresh this morning.'

I'd bear the newspaper twists
bulging fat with winkles
proudly home, like torches.

Paula Meehan (b. 1955)

SIMON ARMITAGE   176

Dear Nicola, Paula and Alice,
Many thanks for your invitation. Good luck with the project.
'The More Loving One' by W H Auden (1907–1973). *Favourite
poems come and go, and although I wouldn't claim that this is the
greatest piece ever written, it has stayed with me longer than most.
On the face of it I'm attracted to its casual but compelling tone, its
shifting rhythms and acoustics, its brevity, as well as its sentiments,*

*which I can more or less subscribe to. The second stanza is
exceptional — my heart goes off like a flash-bulb every time I read it.
More than this, whilst the poem would be at home in any anthology
of modern verse, it would be equally as comfortable on a toilet door or
the back of a bus seat, and none the worse for it.*

Very best,
Simon Armitage

The More Loving One

Looking up at the stars, I know quite well
That, for all they care, I can go to hell.
But on earth indifference is the least
We have to dread from man or beast.

How should we like it were stars to burn
With a passion for us we could not return?
If equal affection cannot be,
Let the more loving one be me.

Admirer as I think I am
Of stars that do not give a damn,
I cannot, now I see them, say
I missed one terribly all day.

Were all stars to disappear or die
I should learn to look at an empty sky
And feel its total dark sublime,
Though this might take me a little time.

W H Auden (1907–1973)

THEO DORGAN   177

Dear Nicola, Paula and Alice,
I'm glad to hear that Lifelines IV *is to appear, and I wish you the
very best of luck with it — if it's as good as previous incarnations it
will be a pleasure to have and to hold.*
*A favourite poem is a rare and elusive beast — I find that
circumstances of the daily life prompt different poems at different
times to stir in the memory.*
*A poem I can never shake from memory, however, is an untitled poem
by the late, great Russian poet Osip Mandelstam. The version I have
carried around with me for years is in origin a translation by the
American Clarence Brown, but like a song in the traditional idiom I
suspect it has mutated into my own version by now:*

What shall I do with the body that has been given me,
so much at one with me, so much my own?

For the calm happiness of breathing, for the joy
of being alive, tell me where should I be grateful?

I am garden and gardener too,
and un-alone in this vast dungeon.

My breath, my glow you can already see
on the windowpane of eternity.

A pattern is imprinted there,
Unknown till now.

Let this muddle die down, the sediment flow out —
the lovely pattern cannot be crossed out.

Best wishes,
Theo Dorgan

JOSEPH O'CONNOR   178

28 January 1992

Dear Nicola, Paula, Alice,
Thanks very much for your recent note about the Lifelines IV *book.*
It sounds like a good idea, and I'm happy to be involved.

Warmest best wishes,
Joseph O'Connor

I don't really have one favourite poem but I like Raymond Carver's
'Happiness' a lot. I like the clarity of it. It's lucid and atmospheric
and very moving. For me, what makes a poem work is the sense that
it had to be written. Carver's poems and short stories are alive with
that quality.

Happiness

So early it's still almost dark out.
I'm near the window with coffee,
and the usual early morning stuff
that passes for thought.
When I see the boy and his friend
walking up the road
to deliver the newspaper.
They wear caps and sweaters,

and one boy has a bag over his shoulder.
They are so happy
they aren't saying anything, these boys.
I think if they could, they would take
each other's arm.
It's early in the morning ,
and they are doing this thing together.
They come on, slowly.
The sky is taking on light,
though the moon still hangs pale over the water.
Such beauty that for a minute
death and ambition, even love,
doesn't enter into this.
Happiness. It comes on
unexpectedly. And goes beyond, really,
any early morning talk about it.

Raymond Carver (1938–1988)

WILLIAM CROZIER   179

Dear Nicola, Paula and Alice,
Thank you for your letter regarding my favourite poem.
My 'favourite' poem can be one I have just read and can change from
week to week or from day to day.
However, I send you the last seven verses of a poem which has been
with me all my adult life and has become part of me. It is the poem
called 'Liberté' by the French poet Paul Eluard.
My best wishes to you and for Lifelines.

Yours sincerely,
William Crozier

Liberté (an excerpt)

Sur le tremplin de ma porte
Sur les objets familiers
Sur le flot du feu béni
J'écris ton nom

Sur toute chair accordée
Sur le font de mes amis
Sur chaque main qui se tend
J'écris ton nom

Sur la vitre des surprises
Sur les lèvres attentives
Bien au-dessus du silence
J'écris ton nom

Sur mes refuges détruits
Sur mes phares écroulés
Sur les murs de mon ennui
J'écris ton nom

Sur l'absence sans désir
Sur la solitude nue
Sur les marches de la mort
J'écris ton nom

Sur la santé revenue
Sur le risque disparu
Sur l'espoir sans souvenir
J'écris ton nom

Et par le pouvoir d'un mot
Je recommence ma vie
Je suis né pour te connaître
Pour te nommer

Liberté

Paul Eluard (1895–1952)

Translation:

Liberty (an excerpt)

On the threshold of my door
On familiar things
On the surge of blessed fire
I write your name

On all accordant flesh
On the foreheads of my friends
On every hand held out
I write your name

On the window of surprises
On attentive lips
High above the silence
I write your name

On my devastated shelters
On my perished beacons
On the walls of my fatigue
I write your name

On absence without desire
On barren solitude
On the steps of death
I write your name

On health returned
On vanished risk
On hope without remembrance
I write your name

And by the power of a word
I begin my life again
I was born to know you
To name you

Liberty

DARINA ALLEN   180

16 January 1992

Dear Nicola, Paula and Alice,
Thank you for inviting me to contribute to Lifelines IV.
My favourite poem is 'The Lake Isle of Innisfree' *by W B Yeats.*
This is a wonderfully evocative poem. I can escape in my mind's eye
to this idyllic peaceful isle where peace comes dropping slow and
there are no telephones.
Congratulations on the great success of Lifelines *in the past and I*
hope this issue will also be a sell-out.
Keep up the good work.

Yours sincerely,
M Darina Allen

('*The Lake Isle of Innisfree*' was also Chaim Herzog's choice. The poem appears
in full on page 143.)

ANNE FINE   181

Dear Nicola, Paula and Alice,
I'm delighted to be part of Lifelines, *because I was so impressed with*
the two I have, and you all work on it for such good reasons. I've
given up trying to choose a favourite *poem. Here's George Barker's*
'Summer Song I', *which I'm not sure I understand, but the last*

three verses haunted me all through my late childhood, and after.
And 'A Slice of Wedding Cake', by Robert Graves. I really don't
know why I like it so much, except that Graves is one of my favourite
poets, and this one should amuse people your age!

All good wishes,
Yours sincerely,
Anne Fine

Summer Song I

I looked into my heart to write
    And found a desert there.
But when I looked again I heard
Howling and proud in every word
    The hyena despair.

Great summer sun, great summer sun,
    All loss burns in trophies;
And in the cold sheet of the sky
Lifelong the fish-lipped lovers lie
    Kissing catastrophes.

O loving garden where I lay
    When under the breasted tree
My son stood up behind my eyes
And groaned: Remember that the price
    Is vinegar for me.

Great summer sun, great summer sun,
    Turn back to the designer:
I would not be the one to start
The breaking day and the breaking heart
    For all the grief in China.

My one, my one, my only love,
    Hide, hide your face in a leaf,
And let the hot tear falling burn
The stupid heart that will not learn
    The everywhere of grief.

Great summer sun, great summer sun,
    Turn back to the never-never
Cloud-cuckoo, happy, far-off land
Where all the love is true love, and
    True love goes on for ever.

George Barker (1913–1991)

A Slice of Wedding Cake

Why have such scores of lovely, gifted girls
    Married impossible men?
Simple self-sacrifice may be ruled out,
    And missionary endeavour, nine times out of ten.

Repeat 'impossible men': not merely rustic,
    Foul-tempered or depraved
(Dramatic foils chosen to show the world
    How well women behave, and always have behaved).

Impossible men: idle, illiterate,
    Self-pitying, dirty, sly,
For whose appearance even in City parks
    Excuses must be made to casual passers-by.

Has God's supply of tolerable husbands
    Fallen, in fact, so low?
Or do I always over-value woman
    At the expense of man?
                    Do I?
                        It might be so.

Robert Graves (1895–1985)

PATRICIA SCANLAN   182

7 January 1992

Dear Nicola, Paula and Alice,
The name of my favourite poem is Rudyard Kipling's 'The Thousandth Man'. I particularly like this poem because of the way it describes a true and real friendship where a person is accepted for who and what they are, warts and all. In this poem a friend is always there to share the good times and the bad 'to the gallows foot — and after!'
I am lucky to have some great friends and I like this poem so much I used it as my theme for my first novel City Girl. *I hope this will suit your requirements and wish you the very best of success with your task. I look forward to the publishing of your book and congratulations on your initiative.*

Best wishes and Happy New Year,
Patricia Scanlan

('The Thousandth Man' was also Jeffrey Archer's choice. The poem appears in full on pages 118–119.)

GLENDA JACKSON   183

January 1992

Dear Nicola, Paula and Alice,
Thank you for your letter.
I don't really have a favourite poem, but I would choose 'Not Waving,
but Drowning' *by Stevie Smith, because I share her feeling.*
Best wishes for your book and I hope it will raise a wonderful sum of
money.

Yours sincerely,
Glenda Jackson

('*Not Waving, but Drowning*' was also Sara Berkeley's choice. The poem appears
in full on page 82.)

CHRISTY MOORE   184

12 January 1992

Dear Nicola, Paula and Alice,
My father Christy Moore asked me to write, sending the poem 'The
Cuckoo' *by Seán Lysaght in reply to your letter.*

Yours sincerely,
James Moore

P.S.   I think it would be fitting if you could include the title of the
collection from which this poem I read, also the publishers, thus
allowing your readers the opportunity to read some more.

Sincerely,
Christy

Cuckoo

Scarcer now
than when he named himself
to every meadow in the townland
when the hay was down,

as I stood on the butt of the wain,
bedding in what tumbled from the pikes
with *cuck-oo*
repeated from the next acre.

So I drifted off
to stalk nearer the bird.
The song got louder
along the bristly edge of the headland.

I hadn't said a word
when my uncle came
calling 'Seán!'
and so I lost the cuckoo.

Seán Lysaght (b. 1957)
(From *The Clare Island Survey,* The Gallery Press, 1991)

CHRISTOPHER RICKS   185

Boston University
11 February 1992

Dear Nicola Hughes, Paula Griffin and Alice McEleney,
Sorry about the delay; have been away. (Poet but he doesn't know it.)
Lifelines: *A good thing about the word 'favourite' (my favourite*
poem) is that it doesn't have to be the same as the poem you think the
best. *So: Alfred Tennyson, 'To E FitzGerald' (note the capital G in*
the middle . . .). A lovely poem from a great poet to a true poet, the
translator of the Rubaiyat of Omar Khayyam; *an act of friendship,*
over the years (they had been college friends, and are now in their
seventies); no condescension (Tennyson the Poet Laureate, *for*
Victoria's sake): one sentence rippling through 56 lines, but never
unravelling; and coming to rest with the word 'praise' — which it so
deserves itself.

Best wishes,
Christopher Ricks

To E FitzGerald

Old Fitz, who from your suburb grange,
    Where once I tarried for a while,
Glance at the wheeling Orb of change,
    And greet it with a kindly smile;
Whom yet I see as there you sit
    Beneath your sheltering garden-tree,
And while your doves about you flit,
    And plant on shoulder, hand and knee,
Or on your head their rosy feet,
    As if they knew your diet spares

Whatever moved in that full sheet
    Let down to Peter at his prayers;
Who live on milk and meal and grass;
    And once for ten long weeks I tried
Your table of Pythagoras,
    And seemed at first 'a thing enskied'
(As Shakespeare has it) airy-light
    To float above the ways of men,
Then fell from that half-spiritual height
    Chilled, till I tasted flesh again
One night when earth was winter-black,
    And all the heavens flashed in frost;
And on me, half-asleep, came back
    That wholesome heat the blood had lost,
And set me climbing icy capes
    And glaciers, over which there rolled
To meet me long-armed vines with grapes
    Of Eshcol hugeness; for the cold
Without, and warmth within me, wrought
    To mould the dream; but none can say
That Lenten fare makes Lenten thought,
    Who reads your golden Eastern lay,
Than which I know no version done
    In English more divinely well;
A planet equal to the sun
    Which cast it, that large infidel
Your Omar; and your Omar drew
    Full-handed plaudits from our best
In modern letters, and from two,
    Old friends outvaluing all the rest,
Two voices heard on earth no more;
    But we old friends are still alive,
And I am nearing seventy-four,
    While you have touched at seventy-five,
And so I send a birthday line
    Of greeting; and my son, who dipt
In some forgotten book of mine
    With sallow scraps of manuscript,
And dating many a year ago,
    Has hit on this, which you will take
My Fitz, and welcome, as I know
    Less for its own than for the sake
Of one recalling gracious times,
    When, in our younger London days,
You found some merit in my rhymes,
    And I more pleasure in your praise.

Alfred Lord Tennyson (1809–1892)

JULIAN BARNES   186

26 January 1992

Dear Nicola Hughes, Paula Griffin and Alice McEleney
Thank you for your letter about Lifelines IV. *I am enclosing one of*
my favourite poems, by A E Housman, with a few lines about it.
Good luck with your project.

Yours sincerely
Julian Barnes

XII

The laws of God, the laws of man,
He may keep that will and can;
Not I: let God and man decree
Laws for themselves and not for me;
And if my ways are not as theirs
Let them mind their own affairs.
Their deeds I judge and much condemn,
Yet when did I make laws for them?
Please yourselves, say I, and they
Need only look the other way.
But no, they will not; they must still
Wrest their neighbour to their will,
And make me dance as they desire
With jail and gallows and hell-fire.
And how am I to face the odds
Of man's bedevilment and God's?
I, a stranger and afraid
In a world I never made.
They will be master, right or wrong;
Though both are foolish, both are strong.
And since, my soul, we cannot fly
To Saturn nor to Mercury,
Keep we must, if keep we can,
These foreign laws of God and man.

A E Housman (1859–1936)

This untitled poem, number XII *from Housman's* Last Poems, *was*
written in circa 1900, and could have been addressed to our whole
century. It is a passionate plea for individualism, for the right to be
oneself, against the bullyings of religion and one's fellow-men,
against those who are sure they know all the answers. It uses simple

words, and is in simple couplets, but is far from being a cool, 'argument' poem: listen for the rage, the protest, the hurt, the stoicism. Listen, in particular, to the implications of that sly phrase in the penultimate line, 'if keep we can'.

Julian Barnes

KENNETH BRANAGH   187

30 January 1992

Dear Nicola Hughes, Paula Griffin and Alice McEleney,
Thank you for your letter to Kenneth Branagh.
His favourite poem/song is 'Fear No More the Heat o' the Sun' *from Shakespeare's* Cymbeline.
He feels it is the most moving and beautiful commentary on life and death. Simple and profound.
Wishing you every success with Lifelines.

Yours sincerely,
Tamar Thomas
Assistant to Mr Branagh

Fear No More The Heat O' The Sun

Fear no more the heat o' the sun,
     Nor the furious winter's rages;
Thou thy worldly task hast done,
     Home art gone, and ta'en thy wages;
Golden lads and girls all must
     As chimney-sweepers, come to dust.

Fear no more the frown o' the great,
     Thou art past the tyrant's stroke:
Care no more to clothe and eat;
     To thee the reed is as the oak;
The sceptre, learning, physic, must
     All follow this, and come to dust.

Fear no more the lightning-flash,
     Nor the all-dreaded thunder-stone;
Fear not slander, censure rash;
     Thou hast finish'd joy and moan:
All lovers young, all lovers must
     Consign to thee, and come to dust.

No exorcizer harm thee!
   Nor no witchcraft charm thee!
Ghost unlaid forbear thee!
   Nothing ill come near thee!
Quiet consummation have;
   And renowned be thy grave!

William Shakespeare (1564–1616)

MARY HARNEY   188

Oifig an Aire um Chaomhnú Comhshaoil
(Office of the Minister for Environmental Protection)
Baile Átha Cliath 1
(Dublin 1)
20 February 1992

Dear Paula,
I wish to acknowledge receipt of your letter received in early January
which unfortunately got mislaid during renovations to my office.
You asked for my favourite poem and the reasons why and I hope I
am not too late with my contribution for Lifelines IV. *My favourite*
poem is 'Stony Grey Soil' by Patrick Kavanagh and I first
encountered this poem while studying English for my Leaving Cert.
at the Presentation Convent, Clondalkin.
As an 18 year old I immediately identified with the theme of the
love/hate relationship between the poet and his native Monaghan soil.
The stony grey soil of the title reminds me of the terrain of East
Galway where I was born and where I have spent many happy
holidays. It is symbolic of the way of life associated with the land —
harsh, mundane and full of strife. Yet this same land has also
produced his poetic inspirations.
What I particularly like about the poem is the way in which
Kavanagh manages to link up the sterility and frustration of farm life
with the physical beauty and grace that only working so close to
nature can produce.
The first five verses are very accusing in tone — he blames the stony
grey soil of Monaghan for his lack of freedom and spontaneity as a
child, yet in the final three verses he acknowledges, very calmly, the
significance of his early environment as a major influence on his
early development.
Hope the above is of benefit to you.

Sincerely,
Mary Harney
Minister for Environmental Protection

[We were pleased to note that Minister Harney's letter came, appropriately, on
recycled paper — Compilers]

Stony Grey Soil

O stony grey soil of Monaghan
The laugh from my love you thieved;
You took the gay child of my passion
And gave me your clod-conceived.

You clogged the feet of my boyhood
And I believed that my stumble
Had the poise and stride of Apollo
And his voice my thick-tongued mumble.

You told me the plough was immortal!
O green-life-conquering plough!
Your mandril strained, your coulter blunted
In the smooth lea-field of my brow.

You sang on steaming dunghills
A song of cowards' brood,
You perfumed my clothes with weasel itch,
You fed me on swinish food.

You flung a ditch on my vision
Of beauty, love and truth.
O stony grey soil of Monaghan
You burgled by bank of youth!

Lost the long hours of pleasure
All the women that love young men.
O can I still stroke the monster's back
Or write with unpoisoned pen

His name in these lonely verses
Or mention the dark fields where
The first gay flight of my lyric
Got caught in a peasant's prayer.

Mullahinsha, Drummeril, Black Shanco —
Wherever I turn I see
In the stony grey soil of Monaghan
Dead loves that were born for me.

Patrick Kavanagh (1904–1967)

SEAN McMAHON   189

5 January 1992

Dear Nicola, Paula and Alice,
Thank you for your letter and invitation to contribute to Lifelines
IV. I have the earlier volumes and I am very pleased that a collected

Lifelines *will be available in October.*

Asking for my favourite poem sets me a poser. I have lots of favourite poems; 'Fear No More the Heat O' the Sun' from Cymbeline, *'The Planter's Daughter' by Austin Clarke, 'Meeting Point' by Louis MacNeice, 'Caiseal Mumhan', bits of Herbert, Donne, Crashaw, Marvell, Pope, Keats, Yeats and hectares of Shakespeare. The one I've chosen as if on Desert Island Discs is not well known but has been a favourite since I first found it thirty-five years ago. It was written by Helen Waddell, a woman who for all her academic distinction did not seem to have a very happy life. Yet I find its simple beauty and alternative theology very consoling. It is called* 'I Shall Not Go to Heaven'.

I hope Lifelines IV *repeats the success of the others.*

Le gach dea-ghuí,
Sean McMahon

I Shall Not Go To Heaven

I shall not go to Heaven when I die,
　　But if they let me be
I think I'll take the road I used to know
　　That goes by Shere-na-garagh and the sea.
And all day breasting me the wind shall blow,
　　And I'll hear nothing but the peewits cry
And the waves talking in the sea below.

I think it will be winter when I die
　　For no one from the North could die in spring —
And all the heather will be dead and grey
　　And the bog-cotton will have blown away,
And there will be no yellow on the whin.

But I shall smell the peat,
　　And when it's almost dark I'll set my feet
Where a white track goes glimmering to the hills,
　　And see far up a light . . . .
Would you think Heaven could be so small a thing
　　As a lit window on the hills at night?
And come in stumbling from the gloom,
　　Half-blind, into a fire-lit room,
Turn, and see you,
　　And there abide.

If it were true
　　And if I thought they would let me be
I almost wish it were tonight I died.

Helen Waddell (1889–1965)

THOMAS DOCHERTY   190

Trinity College
Dublin 2
8 January 1992

Dear Nicola, Paula, Alice,
Very many thanks for your most kind invitation to select a poem for
inclusion in Lifelines IV. *Living surrounded by poetry, as I do,*
makes it difficult to select a single favourite. Others — those to whom
the volume is dedicated — have to live surrounded by poverty and
injustice; their difficulties are much greater. It would be easy for me
to choose a poem with some obvious political point, but in this
instance I would prefer to propose a text which is not in any sense
directly political. John Ashbery's 'Crazy Weather' is, like all his
writing, difficult and obscure. My sense when I read it is that I am
somehow reading a poem in a foreign language: it makes the world I
thought I knew seem less sure, less clear, less known. Like all the best
poetry, it deploys its own art, its aesthetic, to produce a shift in the
everyday world, the political world; like all the best writing, it offers a
second world, adjacent to but different from our own. May it also
give something to a Third World.
With very best wishes for the success of the volume,

Yours sincerely,
Thomas Docherty

Crazy Weather

It's this crazy weather we've been having:
Falling forward one minute, lying down the next
Among the loose grasses and soft, white, nameless flowers.
People have been making a garment out of it,
Stitching the white of lilacs together with lightning
At some anonymous crossroads. The sky calls
To the deaf earth. The proverbial disarray
Of morning corrects itself as you stand up.
You are wearing a text. The lines
Droop to your shoelaces and I shall never want or need
Any other literature than this poetry of mud
And ambitious reminiscences of times when it came easily
Through the then woods and ploughed fields and had
A simple unconscious dignity we can never hope to
Approximate now except in narrow ravines nobody
Will inspect where some late sample of the rare,
Uninteresting specimen might still be putting out shoots,
    for all we know.

John Ashbery (b. 1927)

ANTHONY CRONIN   191

20 January 1992

Dear Editors,
I never know what my favourite poem of all is because there are so
many and I am constantly being bowled over by new discoveries.
My favourite poem of the moment is a poem about the great Irish
writer Francis Stuart by Anne Haverty. It will, I believe, be
published in a Canadian university publication in celebration of
Francis's 90th birthday. You may find it difficult to get a copy of the
magazine so I am enclosing a typescript copy of the poem.
Anne Haverty's 'Whenever I Think of Francis' is a lovely poem
about a great writer which manages to do honour to its subject while
being very tender, personal and moving at the same time.

Yours sincerely,
Anthony Cronin

Whenever I Think of Francis

Whenever I think of Francis
Stuart I think of Easter.
In a warm wind blowing from the west
he is going with his mediaeval monk's
face to feed a young goat
leaping on the rock.
Actually he is walking in the direction
of Nassau Street when the October
evening is drawing in but
it seems the light glows longer
than it did yesterday and
flowers in the far North that were
dying out during the afternoon
are beginning to bloom again.
For the last of the great
Christian festivals left to us
uncolonised by commerce, we are
preparing a frugal and sweet repast,
almonds, chocolate and spring lamb.
Whenever I think of Francis
limping like a boy
who fell out of a tree,
I think of the feast of Resurrection.

Anne Haverty

MICHAEL LONGLEY   192

19 January 1992

I hope the enclosed will be of some use to you.

Best wishes
Michael Longley

Voyages (II) *by Hart Crane*
A favourite poem is not necessarily the best poem by a poet whom one admires more than all — or even most — other poets. For me it is a piece which took me completely by surprise once, and continues to do so without my ever being able to comprehend its 'meaning' or follow its processes. A spell has been cast. 'Fern Hill' by Dylan Thomas; Yeats's 'Byzantium'; 'Tall Nettles' by Edward Thomas; 'Innocence' by Patrick Kavanagh; 'Mayfly' by Louis MacNeice; D.H. Lawrence's 'Bavarian Gentians' are all candidates for the dubious privilege of being My Favourite Poem. (And I have confined myself to this century.)
I choose 'Voyages II' by the American poet Hart Crane. It is the high-point of a sequence of lyrics, each one a great psalm to the sea. Sensuous yet spiritual, unabashed in its erotic embrace, unembarrassed by its own over-reaching rhetoric, Crane's incantation risks failing ludicrously. Instead, here is a poem which has everything. After hundreds of readings it remains for me a revelation. When Hart Crane wrote at this altitude his genius became a small part of the universe, one of its wonders.

II
— And yet this great wink of eternity,
Of rimless floods, unfettered leewardings,
Samite sheeted and processioned where
Her undinal vast belly moonward bends,
Laughing the wrapt inflections of our love;

Take this Sea, whose diapason knells
On scrolls of silver snowy sentences,
The sceptred terror of whose sessions rends
As her demeanors motion well or ill,
All but the pieties of lovers' hands.

And onward, as bells off San Salvador
Salute the crocus lustres of the stars,
In these poinsettia meadows of her tides, —
Adagios of islands, O my Prodigal,
Complete the dark confessions her veins spell.

Mark how her turning shoulders wind the hours,
And hasten while her penniless rich palms
Pass superscription of bent foam and wave, —
Hasten, while they are true, — sleep, death, desire,
Close round one instant in one floating flower.

Bind us in time, O Seasons clear, and awe.
O minstrel galleons of Carib fire,
Bequeath us to no earthly shore until
Is answered in the vortex of our grave
The seal's wide spindrift gaze toward paradise.

Hart Crane (1899–1932)

P.S. My favourite line of poetry is the last line of 'Voyages III':
   'Permit me voyage, love, into your hands . . .'

AMELIA STEIN   193

14 February 1992

Dear Nicola, Paula and Alice,
I am sorry for taking such a long time to reply to your letter — or
rather that I have written several times and changed my mind the
next morning and not posted the letter to you.
It is a difficult decision — I have so many pieces of poetry which
reflect different times in my life — poems that I use when I am
unhappy, poems to explain, to soothe — to cheer me up. So. I have
chosen something for none of these reasons — 'The Man with Five
Penises' by Paul Durcan. It was read to me first by the painter Gene
Lambert when he was painting a piece inspired by this poem. It
marked my introduction to modern Irish poetry and the start of a long
and special friendship.
Why do I like it so much? I have bathaholic tendencies at times myself
so I can identify with the father in retreat in the bathroom — but also
with the sense of the notion of something rather than the actuality.
I suppose it is to do with the demystifying of people, incidences and
relationships as time passes, the pure fantasy that just a glimpse gives
and the little boy has his mind made up on the 'fact' of what he saw.
Such is life. It becomes vaguely clearer the harder one looks — or does
it?
I thank you for asking me to contribute. I wish you every success with
this project. If I have not made myself clear (this is usual) please call
me and I will try to unmuddle my thoughts.

Good luck,
Amelia (Stein)

The Man with Five Penises

My father was a man with five penises.
I caught a glimpse of him in the bath one morning,
A Sunday morning after Mass and Holy Communion
(Normally he went to Golf after Mass and Holy
    Communion
But owing probably to weather conditions
— Sand-bunkers flooded and greens waterlogged —
There was no Golf on the Sunday morning in question).
I stepped into the bathroom, thinking it empty:
There he was, immobile as a crocodile,
In communion with waters that looked immensely fishy.
He peered at me out of his amphibious eyes;
I stepped back out, as out of a jungle comic.
'I am having a bath' he growled fretfully.
I could have sworn I saw, as I say,
At least four or five penises floating about,
Possibly six or seven.
For a long time after that, I used feel sorry for him,
Concerned as well as sorry:
He must have a right old job on his hands every morning
Stuffing that lot into his pants.
And imagine what he must feel
When he has to use the public toilets,
Holding himself together for fear
All that lot might spill out —
What would the blokes in the next stalls say to him?
But also I began to worry about myself:
Maybe it was me who was all missing,
Me with my solitary member.
Over the next years I watched anxiously
For signs of new members
But membership remained steadfastly at zero.
Now that I know the score
— Or at least now that I think I know the score —
I am inclined to think
One penis is more than enough.
Although I will always cherish the notion
Of my father as the man with five penises,
Initially I interpreted it as a sinister spectacle
And frankly it comes as a relief to discover
That there was in fact only one of them.
Unquestionably, one penis is more than enough.

Paul Durcan (b. 1944)

RICHARD MURPHY   194

5 January 1992

Dear Nicola, Paula and Alice,
Thank you for your New Year's Day letter about your anthology. I
hope it will be successful.
I enclose my contribution: a poem by Pasternak called 'Bread' in an
English version by Michael Harari, followed by my comments.

With best wishes,
Richard Murphy

Bread

With half a century to pile,
    Unwritten, your conclusions,
    By now, if you're not a halfwit,
You should have lost a few illusions,

    Grasped the pleasure of study,
The laws and secrets of success,
The curse of idleness, the heroism
    Needed for happiness;

    That the powerful kingdom of beasts,
The sleepy kingdom of vegetation
    Await their heroes, giants,
Their altars and their revelation;

That first of all the revelations,
    Father of living and dead,
Gift to the generations, growth
    Of the centuries, is bread;

And a harvest field is not just wheat
    But a page to understand,
    Written about yourself
In your remote forefather's hand,

His very word, his own amazing
Initiative among the birth,
    Sorrow and death that circle
    Their set ways round the earth.

Boris Pasternak (1890–1960)
(English version by Michael Harari)

Boris Pasternak's poem 'Bread' in the English version by Michael Harari has been a favourite poem of mine since a friend showed it to me about fifteen years ago. It was then a purifying antidote to the toxic effects of creative writing at Iowa during the coldest winter on record. It still seems to have a mysterious power to say everything under the sun in a way that sounds new. I can't imagine what gets lost in this translation, apart from rhyme, because the poetry comes through with visionary force.

If that sounds grandiloquent, it's because I think Pasternak has taken a high risk in daring to make a conclusive comment on what life seems to him to be all about. Wisely he uses the admonishing tone of voice of an alter ego or a conscience or the muse. He addresses himself as 'you': and you as a reader feel yourself drawn inside his thought process, becoming transformed into a better person as you read.

The great metaphor of the harvest field, as 'a page to understand, written about yourself in your remote forefather's hand' is, at least, an original way of seeing the link between the discovery of agriculture and the invention of writing. The biblical word forefather *may suggest God, but at earth level it projects our unknown primitive ancestors, perhaps in the valleys of the Jordan and the Euphrates, whose 'amazing initiative' began the process that has enabled us to probe beyond the farthest visible stars.*

The word forefather, *like* mankind, *may disturb readers affected by the feminist assault on sexist vocabulary. Since seed was cast in a fenced field, and bread baked, women have done much of the work, while men have been waging war. I don't think Pasternak, or his translator, intended the word* forefather *to exclude the idea of motherhood, but to be inclusive. If he'd used a neuter word, such as 'originator', humanity would have been drained out of his poem at its climax. Instead, without losing his foothold on the ground, he rises to a new affirmation of the mythical link between bread and the word, or logos. To express the search through the self and the cosmos for salvation, he uses a tone of voice unflawed by religiosity.*

Before he works this beneficial magic, he rings bells as common as those that chime from village or city clock towers. If the clichés in the first two stanzas sound banal, their banality is soon transmuted into the poem's myth. And the bread is revealed as the truth. Pasternak had suffered through the famine caused by Stalin's policy of collectivisation, the terror under Stalin, and the horrors of war. He had earned the moral authority with which he speaks of 'the heroism needed for happiness'.

'Bread' was written in the mid-fifties. Bearing this in mind while reading the final stanza, I recall the first sputnik moving across the sky before dawn over Dublin, where I watched it from the cattle-markets. Russia was then winning the space race by an 'amazing initiative', putting a dog into orbit. The unfortunate creature received a lethal injection when its job of contributing to a triumph of human technology was finished. In a sense that is literal and shocking, the dog on its doomed voyage underscores and confirms

Pasternak's final metaphor of the 'birth, sorrow and death that circle their set ways round the earth'. The poem has become all the more relevant in the winter of 1991–1992, when a great number of desperate people in Russia and the Third World cannot obtain enough bread.

Richard Murphy

CONOR CRUISE O'BRIEN   195

14 January 1992

Dear Nicola, Paula and Alice,
Here goes:
My favourite poem is Milton's 'Ode on the Morning of Christ's Nativity', which I usually read aloud to my family on Christmas Day. I love the poem mainly because of the splendour of the language and imagery and my love of all that is tinged with incredulous horror, both at Christian redemption theology in itself and also at the association of that theology with baroque grandeur.
Best wishes for the New Year,

Yours sincerely,
Conor Cruise O'Brien

On the Morning of Christ's Nativity

I
This is the Month, and this the happy morn
Wherin the Son of Heav'ns eternal King,
Of wedded Maid, and Virgin Mother born,
Our great redemption from above did bring
For so the holy sages once did sing,
    That he our deadly forfeit should release,
And with his Father work us a perpetual peace.

II
That glorious Form, that Light unsufferable,
And that far-beaming blaze of Majesty,
Wherwith he wont at Heav'ns high Councel-Table,
To sit the midst of Trinal Unity,
He laid aside; and here with us to be,
    Forsook the Courts of everlasting Day,
And chose with us a darksom House of mortal Clay.

III
Say Heav'nly Muse, shall not thy sacred vein
Afford a present to the Infant God?
Hast thou no vers, no hymn, or solemn strein,
To welcom him to this his new abode,
Now while the Heav'n by the Suns team untrod,
     Hath took no print of the approaching light,
And all the spangled host keep watch in squadrons bright?

IV
See how from far upon the Eastern rode
The Star-led Wisards haste with odours sweet,
O run, prevent them with thy humble ode,
And lay it lowly at his blessed feet;
Have thou the honour first, thy Lord to greet,
     And joyn thy voice unto the Angel Quire,
From out his secret Altar toucht with hallow'd fire.

The Hymn

I
It was the Winter wilde,
While the Heav'n-born-childe,
     All meanly wrapt in the rude manger lies;
Nature in aw to him
Had doff't her gawdy trim,
     With her great Master so to sympathize:
It was no season then for her
To wanton with the Sun her lusty Paramour.

II
Only with speeches fair
She woo's the gentle Air
     To hide her guilty front with innocent Snow,
And on her naked shame,
Pollute with sinfull blame,
     The Saintly Vail of Maiden white to throw,
Confounded, that her Makers eyes
Should look so neer upon her foul deformities.

III
But he her fears to cease,
Sent down the meek-eyd Peace,
     She crown'd with Olive green, came softly sliding
Down through the turning sphear
His ready Harbinger,
     With Turtle wing the amorous clouds dividing,
And waving wide her mirtle wand,
She strikes a universall Peace through Sea and Land.

IV
No War, or Battails sound
Was heard the World around,
    The idle spear and shield were high up hung;
The hooked Chariot stood
Unstain'd with hostile blood,
    The Trumpet spake not to the armed throng,
And Kings sate still with awfull eye,
As if they surely knew their sovran Lord was by.

V
But peacefull was the night
Wherin the Prince of light
    His raign of peace upon the earth began:
The Windes with wonder whist,
Smoothly the waters kist,
    Whispering new joyes to the milde Ocean,
Who now hath quite forgot to rave,
While Birds of Calm sit brooding on the charmed wave.

VI
The Stars with deep amaze
Stand fixt in steadfast gaze,
    Bending one way their pretious influence,
And will not take their flight,
For all the morning light,
    Or *Lucifer* that often warn'd them thence;
But in their glimmering Orbs did glow,
Untill their Lord himself bespake, and bid them go.

VII
And though the shady gloom
Had given day her room,
    The Sun himself with-held his wonted speed,
And hid his head for shame,
As his inferiour flame ,
    The new enlightn'd world no more should need;
He saw a greater Sun appear
Then his bright Throne, or burning Axletree could bear.

VIII
The Shepherds on the Lawn,
Or ere the point of dawn,
    Sate simply chatting in a rustick row;
Full little thought they than,
That the might *Pan*
    Was kindly com to live with them below;
Perhaps their loves, or els their sheep,
Was all that did their silly thoughts so busie keep.

IX
When such musick sweet
Their hearts and ears did greet,
    As never was by mortall finger strook,
Divinely-warbled voice
Answering the stringed noise,
    As all their souls in blisfull rapture took:
The Air such pleasure loth to lose,
With thousand echo's still prolongs each heav'nly close.

X
Nature that heard such sound
Beneath the hollow round
    Of *Cynthia's* seat, the Airy region thrilling,
Now was almost won
To think her part was don,
    And that her raign had here its last fulfilling;
She knew such harmony alone
Could hold all Heav'n and Earth in happier union.

XI
At last surrounds their sight
A Globe of circular light,
    That with long beams the shame-fac't night array'd
The helmed Cherubim
And sworded Seraphim,
    Are seen in glittering ranks with wings displaid,
Harping in loud and solemn quire,
With unexpressive notes to Heav'ns new-born Heir.

XII
Such Musick (as 'tis said)
Before was never made,
    But when of old the sons of morning sung,
While the Creator Great
His constellations set,
    And the well-ballanc't world on hinges hung,
And cast the dark foundations deep,
And bid the weltring waves their oozy channel keep.

XIII
Ring out ye Crystall sphears,
Once bless our human ears,
    (If ye have power to touch our senses so)
And let your silver chime
Move in melodious time;
    And let the Base of Heav'ns deep Organ blow,
And with your ninefold harmony
Make up full consort to th'Angelike symphony.

XIV
For if such holy Song
Enwrap our fancy long,
    Time will run back, and fetch the age of gold,
And speckl'd vanity
Will sicken soon and die,
    And leprous sin will melt from earthly mould,
And Hell it self will pass away,
And leave her dolorous mansions to the peering day.

XV
Yea Truth, and Justice then
Will down return to men,
    Orb'd in a Rain-bow; and like glories wearing
Mercy will sit between,
Thron'd in Celestiall sheen,
    With radiant feet the tissued clouds down stearing,
And Heav'n as at som festivall,
Will open wide the Gates of her high Palace Hall.

XVI
But wisest Fate sayes no,
This must not yet be so,
    The Babe lies yet in smiling Infancy,
That on the bitter cross
Must redeem our loss;
    So both himself and us to glorifie:
Yet first to those ychain'd in sleep,
The wakefull trump of doom must thunder through the deep.

XVII
With such a horrid clang
As on mount *Sinai* rang
    While the red fire, and smouldring clouds out brake:
The aged Earth agast
With terrour of that blast,
    Shall from the surface to the center shake;
When at the worlds last session,
The dreadfull Judge in middle Air shall spread his throne.

XVIII
And then at last our bliss
Full and perfect is,
    But now begins; for from this happy day
Th'old Dragon under ground
In straiter limits bound,
    Not half so far casts his usurped sway,
And wrath to see his Kingdom fail,
Swindges the scaly Horrour of his foulded tail.

XIX

The Oracles are dumm,
No voice or hideous humm
 Runs through the arched roof in words deceiving.
Apollo from his shrine
Can no more divine,
 With hollow shreik the steep of *Delphos* leaving.
No nightly trance, or breathed spell,
Inspire's the pale-ey'd Priest from the prophetic cell.

XX

The lonely mountains o're,
And the resounding shore,
 A voice of weeping heard, and loud lament;
From haunted spring, and dale
Edg'd with poplar pale,
 The parting Genius is with sighing sent,
With flowre-inwov'n tresses torn
The Nimphs in twilight shade of tangled thickets mourn.

XXI

In consecrated Earth,
And on the holy Hearth,
 The *Lars*, and *Lemures* moan with midnight plaint,
In Urns, and Altars round,
A drear, and dying sound
 Affrights the *Flamins* at their service quaint;
And the chill Marble seems to sweat,
While each peculiar power forgoes his wonted seat.

XXII

Peor, and *Baalim*
Forsake their Temples dim,
 With that twise-batter'd god of *Palestine*,
And mooned *Ashtaroth*,
Heav'ns Queen and Mother both,
 Now sits not girt with Tapers holy shine,
The Libyc *Hammon* shrinks his horn,
In vain the *Tyrian* Maids their wounded *Thamuz* mourn.

XXIII

And sullen *Moloch* fled,
Hath left in shadows dred,
 His burning Idol all of blackest hue,
In vain with Cymbals ring,
They call the grisly king,
 In dismall dance about the furnace blue;
The brutish gods of *Nile* as fast,
Isis and *Orus*, and the Dog *Anubis* hast.

XXIV
Nor is *Osiris* seen
In *Memphian* Grove, or Green,
    Trampling the unshowr'd Grasse with lowings loud;
Nor can he be at rest
Within his sacred chest,
    Naught but profoundest Hell can be his shroud,
In vain with Timbrel'd Anthems dark
The sable-stoled Sorcerers bear his worshipt Ark.

XXV
He feels from *Juda's* Land
The dredded Infants hand,
    The rayes of *Bethlehem* blind his dusky eyn;
Nor all the gods beside,
Longer dare abide,
    Not *Typhon* huge ending in snaky twine:
Our Babe to shew his Godhead true,
Can in his swadling bands controul the damned crew.

XXVI
So when the Sun in bed,
Curtain'd with cloudy red,
    Pillows his chin upon an Orient wave,
The flocking shadows pale,
Troop to th'infernall jail,
    Each fetter'd Ghost slips to his severall grave,
And the yellow-skirted *Fayes*,
Fly after the Night-steeds, leaving their Moon-lov'd maze.

XXVII
But see the Virgin blest,
Hath laid her Babe to rest,
    Time is our tedious Song should here have ending:
Heav'ns youngest teemed Star,
Hath fixt her polisht Car,
    Her sleeping Lord with Handmaid Lamp attending:
And all about the Courtly Stable,
Bright-harnest Angels sit in order serviceable.

John Milton (1608–1674)

WENDY COPE   196

Dear Nicola, Paula and Alice,
Thank you for your letter. I am asked for my favourite poem at least
once a year and it would be boring to choose the same one every time.
This, along with several other poems by Housman, is certainly in my
top twenty.

We would all like to believe that love is stronger than death.
Housman can't go that far. Conceding that love doesn't last for ever,
he has written a very powerful love-poem.

Yours sincerely,
Wendy Cope

Additional Poems IV

It is no gift I tender,
    A loan is all I can;
But do not scorn the lender;
    Man gets no more from man.

Oh, mortal man may borrow
    What mortal man can lend;
And 'twill not end tomorrow,
    Though sure enough 'twill end.

If death and time are stronger,
    A love may yet be strong;
The world will last for longer
    But this will last for long.

A E Housman (1859–1936)

JOAN McBREEN   197

Dear Nicola, Paula and Alice,
Thank you for inviting me to contribute to Lifelines IV *and every*
good wish to the project. I hope it sells a million. My favourite poem
is called 'The Envy of Poor Lovers' by Austin Clarke (1896–1974).
Although the words are simple the theme is not. It appeals to me for I
feel it expresses all the sorrow of those who must hide their love.

Love from
Joan McBreen

The Envy of Poor Lovers

Pity poor lovers who may not do what they please
With their kisses under a hedge, before a raindrop
Unhouses it; and astir from wretched centuries,
Bramble and briar remind them of the saints.

Her envy is the curtain seen at night-time,
Happy position that could change her name.
His envy — clasp of the married whose thoughts can be alike,
Whose nature flows without the blame or shame.

Lying in the grass as if it were a sin
To move, they hold each other's breath, tremble,
Ready to share that ancient dread — kisses begin
Again — of Ireland keeping company with them.

Think, children, of institutions mured above
Your ignorance, where every look is veiled,
State-paid to snatch away the folly of poor lovers
For whom, it seems, the sacraments have failed.

Austin Clarke (1896–1974)

ALAN HOLLINGHURST   198

12 January 1992

Dear Mss Hughes, Griffin and McEleney,
Thank you for your invitation to nominate a favourite poem for your
Lifelines *anthology. When I settled down to think what it might be, I*
realised that I had at least thirty favourite poems; but some of them
were very long and some so obvious that they have doubtless been
chosen by many other contributors. So in the end I set aside my Pope
and Wordsworth and Tennyson and my Yeats and Hopkins and
Heaney and Elizabeth Bishop, and picked a rather less well-known
item by Thom Gunn (it comes from his book The Passages of Joy
published by Faber and Faber in 1982).
With all good wishes for your project.

Yours sincerely,
Alan Hollinghurst

Night Taxi
for Rod Taylor,
wherever he is

Open city
uncluttered as a map.
I drive through empty streets
scoured by the winds
of midnight. My shift
is only beginning and I am fresh
and excitable, master of the taxi.
I relish my alert reflexes
where all else
is in hiding. I have
by default it seems
conquered me a city.

My first address: I
press the doorbell, I lean back
against the hood, my headlights
scalding a garage door, my engine
drumming in the driveway,
the only sound on the block.
There the fare finds me
like a date, jaunty,
shoes shined, I am
proud of myself, on my toes,
obliging but not subservient.

I take short cuts, picking up
speed, from time to time
I switch on the dispatcher's
litany of addresses,
China Basin to Twin Peaks,
Harrison Street to the Ocean.

I am thinking tonight
my fares are like affairs
— no, more like tricks to turn:
quick, lively, ending up
with a cash payment.
I do not anticipate a holdup.
I can make friendly small talk.
I do not go on about Niggers,
women drivers or the Chinese.
It's all on my terms but
I let them think it's on theirs.

Do I pass through the city
or does it pass through me?
I know I have to be loose,
like my light embrace of the wheel,
loose but in control
— though hour by hour I tighten
minutely in the routine,
smoking my palate to ash,
till the last hour of all
will be drudgery, nothing else.

I zip down Masonic Avenue,
the taxi sings beneath the streetlights
a song to the bare city, it is
my instrument, I woo with it,
bridegroom and conqueror.

I jump out to open the door,
fixing the cap on my head
to, you know, firm up my role,
and on my knuckle
feel a sprinkle of wet.

Glancing upward I see
high above the lamppost
but touched by its farthest light
a curtain of rain already blowing
against black eucalyptus tops.

Thom Gunn (b. 1929)

*I know of no more beautiful evocation of a city at night than that in
'Night Taxi'. In this case the city is San Francisco, where Thom
Gunn lives, and to read these fluent but watchful lines is to see again
its plunging hills and the glittering panorama of its bay. 'Loose but
in control' might sum up the poet's technique: the voice is natural,
unforced, though capable of a kind of exaltation; and the subject-
matter, if rare — even unprecedented — in poetry, is deliberately
routine. Yet it seems to me a great elegiac poem, the stronger and the
more poignant for the way it only glances at its theme, which I take
to be the transience of experience, of sexual happiness, of our brief
tenancy of our spot on earth. The poet, the taxi-driver, the dedicatee
('wherever he is') have made their passage through this ghostly
cityscape. The last lines hauntingly combine imagery of radiance and
of dissolution.*

Alan Hollinghurst

MARTIN AMIS   199

Dear Nicola Hughes,
Thank you for your letter. In reply:
*As my twenty-first birthday neared, my then stepmother Elizabeth
Jane Howard cunningly asked me: 'What's your favourite stanza in
English poetry?' Stanza three of the following poem subsequently
appeared on the book-plate that was her present to me, above the
words* ex libris:

Hear the voice of the Bard!
Who Present, Past, & Future sees
Whose ears have heard,
The Holy Word
That walk'd among the ancient trees,

Calling the lapsed Soul
And weeping in the evening dew
That might control,
The starry pole;
And fallen fallen light renew!

O Earth O Earth, return!
Arise from out the dewy grass;
Night is worn,
And the morn
Rises from the slumberous mass.

Turn away no more:
Why wilt thou turn away
The starry floor,
The watry shore
Is giv'n thee till the break of day.

These lines — from Blake's 'Introduction' to The Songs of
Experience *— expressed my belief that poetry could awaken our
prelapsarian soul. That belief is now inevitably weakened, though
these lines will always make me remember what that belief felt like.*

With best wishes,
Martin Amis

PAULA MEEHAN   200

9 January 1992

Dear Nicola, Paula and Alice,
I came across the earlier Lifelines *and they were invariably good
reads and I'm delighted to put my own spake in. I tend to get haunted
by poems — they won't let me alone and hang around in my head for
ages. At any given time there will be a number clamouring for
attention. Some insinuate themselves so completely that when I'm
making my own poems stray lines will cross over and I'll even think
I've written them myself. This must be what they mean by influence.*
*A poem I go back to again and again is Eavan Boland's 'The
Journey' from the collection of the same name. It gives me a huge
amount of comfort and courage, apart altogether from its music,
which I love. It calls up all the great poems about guided
underground quests and also challenges the tradition, for the shades
the speaker meets on her journey with Sappho are not the dead heroes
but ordinary women and children who have largely been edited out of
history.*

Good luck with your project. I hope you make a rake of money.
Paula x
Paula Meehan

The Journey
For Elizabeth Ryle

Immediately cries were heard. These were the loud wailing of infant souls
weeping at the very entrance-way; never had they had their share of life's
sweetness for the dark day had stolen them from their mothers' breasts and
plunged them to a death before their time.

— Virgil, *The Aeneid*, Book VI

And then the dark fell and 'there has never'
I said 'been a poem to an antibiotic:
never a word to compare with the odes on
the flower of the raw sloe for fever

'or the devious Africa-seeking tern
or the protein treasures of the sea-bed.
Depend on it, somewhere a poet is wasting
his sweet uncluttered metres on the obvious

'emblem instead of the real thing.
Instead of sulpha we shall have hyssop dipped
in the wild blood of the unblemished lamb,
so every day the language gets less

'for the task and we are less with the language.'
I finished speaking and the anger faded
and dark fell and the book beside me
lay open at the page Aphrodite

comforts Sappho in her love's duress.
The poplars shifted their music in the garden,
a child startled in a dream,
my room was a mess —

the usual hardcovers, half-finished cups,
clothes piled up on an old chair —
and I was listening out but in my head was
a loosening and sweetening heaviness,

not sleep, but nearly sleep, not dreaming really
but as ready to believe and still
unfevered, calm and unsurprised
when she came and stood beside me

and I would have known her anywhere
and I would have gone with her anywhere
and she came wordlessly
and without a word I went to her

down down down without so much as
ever touching down but always, always
with a sense of mulch beneath us,
the way of stairs winding down to a river

and as we went on the light went on
failing and I looked sideways to be certain
it was she, misshapen, musical —
Sappho — the scholiast's nightingale

and down we went, again down
until we came to a sudden rest
beside a river in what seemed to be
an oppressive suburb of the dawn.

My eyes got slowly used to the bad light.
At first I saw shadows, only shadows.
Then I could make out women and children
and, in the way they were, the grace of love.

'Cholera, typhus, croup, diptheria'
she said, 'in those days they racketed
in every backstreet and alley of old Europe.
Behold the children of the plague'.

Then to my horror I could see to each
nipple some had clipped a limpet shape —
suckling darknesses — while others had their arms
weighed down, making terrible pietàs.

She took my sleeve and said to me, 'be careful.
Do not define these women by their work:
not as washerwomen trussed in dust and sweating,
muscling water into linen by the river's edge

'nor as court ladies brailled in silk
on wool and woven with an ivory unicorn
and hung, nor as laundresses tossing cotton,
brisking daylight with lavender and gossip.

'But these are women who went out like you
when dusk became a dark sweet with leaves,
recovering the day, stooping, picking up
teddy bears and rag dolls and tricycles and buckets —

'love's archaeology — and they too like you
stood boot deep in flowers once in summer
or saw winter come in with a single magpie
in a caul of haws, a solo harlequin'.

I stood fixed. I could not reach or speak to them.
Between us was the melancholy river,
the dream water, the narcotic crossing
and they had passed over it, its cold persuasions.

I whispered, 'let me be
let me be at least their witness,' but she said
'what you have seen is beyond speech,
beyond song, only not beyond love;

'remember it, you will remember it'
and I heard her say but she was fading fast
as we emerged under the stars of heaven,
'there are not many of us; you are dear

'and stand beside me as my own daughter.
I have brought you here so you will know forever
the silences in which are our beginnings,
in which we have an origin like water,'

and the wind shifted and the window clasp
opened, banged and I woke up to find
the poetry books stacked higgledy piggledy,
my skirt spread out where I had laid it —

nothing was changed; nothing was more clear
but it was wet and the year was late.
The rain was grief in arrears; my children
slept the last dark out safely and I wept.

Eavan Boland (b. 1944)

MARTIN WADDELL   201

21 January 1992

Dear Alice McEleney,
Martin has asked me to write to you about the Lifelines *book which*
you hope to produce this year.
Apologies for the delay in replying to you and he hopes that he has
not left it too late.
The poem he would choose is from Tarry Flynn *by Patrick*
Kavanagh. He chooses it because of 'the sense of freshness and energy
and wonder in and around the commonplace things of life'.
I hope that this is of some use to you. All best wishes with your
project.

Yours sincerely,
Rosaleen Waddell

from *Tarry Flynn*

On an apple-ripe September morning
Through the mist-chill fields I went
With a pitch-fork on my shoulder
Less for use than for devilment.

The threshing mill was set-up, I knew,
In Cassidy's haggard last night,
And we owed them a day at the threshing
Since last year. O it was delight

To be paying bills of laughter
And chaffy gossip in kind
With work thrown in to ballast
The fantasy-soaring mind.

As I crossed the wooden bridge I wondered
As I looked into the drain
If ever a summer morning should find me
Shovelling up eels again.

And I thought of the wasps' nest in the bank
And how I got chased one day
Leaving the drag and the scraw-knife behind,
How I covered my face with hay.

The wet leaves of the cocksfoot
Polished my boots as I
Went round by the glistening bog-holes
Lost in unthinking joy.

I'll be carrying bags to-day, I mused,
The best job at the mill
With plenty of time to talk of our loves
As we wait for the bags to fill.

Maybe Mary might call round . . .
And then I came to the haggard gate,
And I knew as I entered that I had come
Through fields that were part of no earthly estate.

Patrick Kavanagh (1904–1967)

MICHELE SOUTER   202

Dear Nicola, Paula and Alice,
*Thank you for writing to me. I have enjoyed reading the past editions
of* Lifelines *and my choice for your next edition is Oscar Wilde's
poem* 'The Ballad of Reading Gaol'. *I find it so moving and
evocative of the circumstances in which he found himself. I only hope
it isn't too long for inclusion in your book.*
All the very best,

Yours sincerely,
Michele Souter

The Ballad of Reading Gaol
(an excerpt — the original poem is over six hundred lines long)

I know not whether Laws be right,
    Or whether Laws be wrong;
All that we know who lie in gaol
    Is that the wall is strong;
And that each day is like a year,
    A year whose days are long.

But this I know, that every Law
    That men hath made for Man,
Since first Man took his brother's life,
    And the sad world began,
But straws the wheat and saves the chaff
    With a most evil fan.

This too I know — and wise it were
    If each could know the same —
That every prison that men build
    Is built with bricks of shame,
And bound with bars lest Christ should see
    How men their brothers maim.

With bars they blur the gracious moon,
    And blind the goodly sun;
And they do well to hide their Hell,
    For in it things are done
That Son of God nor son of Man
    Ever should look upon!

Oscar Wilde (1854–1900)

FELIM EGAN 203

Dear Nicola, Paula and Alice,
Thank you for your letter and invitation to participate in your
publication. I enclose a poem by Seamus Heaney. This work has a
special place for me as it launched a four-year collaboration which
came to light last November as a book Squarings.
The poem opened for me an approach to land/nature, the spiritual
aspects, the lightness, airyness being close to my attempts in
painting.
The work also reflects the act of creation, and then the act of change
and re-creation. When I paint, my flat canvas on the floor, I find
myself 'walking round and round a space / utterly a source'.

Yours sincerely,
Felim Egan

8

I thought of walking round and round a space
Utterly empty, utterly a source
Where the decked chestnut tree had lost its place
In our front hedge above the wallflowers.
The white chips jumped and jumped and skited high.
I heard the hatchet's differentiated
Accurate cut, the crack, the sigh
And collapse of what luxuriated
Through the shocked tips and wreckage of it all.
Deep planted and long gone, my coeval
Chestnut from a jam jar in a hole,
Its heft and hush become a bright nowhere,
A soul ramifying and forever
Silent, beyond silence listened for.

Seamus Heaney (b. 1939)
(From the sonnet sequence 'Clearances': In memoriam M.K.H. 1911–1984)

BEN ELTON   204

Dear Nicola, Paula and Alice,
To tell you the truth I have read very little poetry since leaving
school. It is an omission I regret but one cannot do everything. I find
it difficult enough keeping up with the prose I wish to read. Therefore
I'm afraid I do not have a favourite poem. I know this is not a very
helpful reply, but there you go. Were you to ask me to name my
favourite poet I would answer Shakespeare, but to choose one piece
from his endlessly inspiring work would be impossible.
Favourites aside, you might be surprised to hear that the single piece
of verse that has most moved me is a quote from the lyric of Cliff
Richard's old hit 'The Young Ones'. It was in 1984 when the
Young Ones TV show which I had co-written was a big hit. Rik
Mayall and I were on tour together. After the show we always signed
autographs for those that wanted them. One night a mother came
back with her son, he was about eleven and was, she explained, a
colossal Young Ones fan, adding that he did not have long to live.
The boy was embarrassed and tongue-tied, and of course nobody
really knew what to say, so his mother asked Rik to write something
for the boy on a tour poster. I did not envy Rik at that moment; what
can you write, off the cuff, to a dying boy who adores you? In what I
feel was a moment of inspiration Rik wrote a quote from Cliff's old
song which Rik had sung over the titles of the series. He wrote
'Young Ones shouldn't be afraid'. The boy and his mother seemed
much moved by this thought, as indeed was I.
Not great poetry I'll admit, but good writing can sometimes be as

much about context as content and I shall always remember that line.
As Noël Coward (whose lyrics I also adore) once said 'strange how
potent cheap music can be'.
Huge best wishes for the book,

Yours sincerely,
Ben Elton

MICHAEL McGLYNN   205

14 January 1992

Dear Lifelines,
Thanks for your letter.
My favourite poem comes from Rimbaud's Les Illuminations *and is*
called 'Aube'. Although I've set many great poems nothing caused
me so much trouble as this one. My love of Rimbaud came about after
hearing Benjamin Britten's incredible setting of various poems of his
in his song cycle Les Illuminations. *I've set four Rimbaud poems,*
and 'Aube', begun in 1984, wasn't finished until 1990 and it takes
three minutes to sing!
French is a very easy language to set with its soft vowels and
consonants. I found the visual imagery of 'Aube' influencing the
setting to such an extent that I could get away with no short cuts, no
composer's gimmicks. I could only set it the way it finished up!
There is an incredible sense of motion through the poem: the short
bright images are only asides in the chase. The Dawn runs through a
fabulous landscape, loaded with cool sensuality. The final paragraph
still sends a shiver down my spine and I find it very hard to explain
why! Possibly it's the mingling of space, innocence, sexuality and the
great control Rimbaud exerts on this passage with its shockingly
abrupt 'Au réveil il était midi' snatching us back from his incredible
images.
I wish you luck Lifelines.

All the best,
Michael McGlynn

Aube

J'ai embrassé l'aube d'été.
Rien ne bougeait encore au front des palais. L'eau était morte.
Les camps d'ombres ne quittaient pas la route du bois.
J'ai marché, réveillant les haleines vives et tièdes, et les
    pierreries regardèrent, et les ailes se levèrent sans bruit.
La première entreprise fut, dans le sentier déjà empli de frais et
    blêmes éclats, une fleur qui me dit son nom.

Je ris au wasserfall blond qui s'échevela à travers les sapins: à la
  cime argentée je reconnus la déesse.
Alors je levai un à un les voiles. Dans l'allée, en agitant les bras.
  Par la plaine, où je l'ai dénoncée au coq. A la grand'ville, elle
  fuyait parmi les clochers et les dômes, et, courant comme un
  mendiant sur les quais de marbre, je la chassais.
En haut de la route, près d'un bois de lauriers, je l'ai entourée
  avec ses voiles amassées, et j'ai senti un peu son immense
  corps. L'aube et l'enfant tombèrent au bas du bois.
Au réveil il était midi.

Dawn

I have held the summer dawn in my arms.
Nothing moved as yet on the fronts of the palaces. The water
  was dead. Swarms of shadows refused to leave the road to the
  wood. I walked along, awakening the warm, alive air. Stones
  looked up, and wings rose up silently.
The first occurrence, in the path already filled with cool white
  shimmerings, was a flower which told me its name.
I laughed at the blond waterfall which tumbled down through
  the pine trees. At its silver top I recognized the goddess. Then I
  took off her veils one by one. In the path, where I waved my
  arms. In the field, where I gave away her name to the cock. In
  the city, she fled between steeples and domes; and running
  like a thief along the marble wharves, I chased her.
Where the road mounts, near a laurel wood, I wrapped her in
  all her veils and felt something of the immensity of her body.
  Dawn and the child collapsed at the edge of the wood.
On waking, it was midday.

Arthur Rimbaud (1854-1891)

MARY O'DONNELL   206

9 January 1992

Dear Nicola, Paula and Alice,
I find it hard to pin down an overall favourite poem, as what I think
is my favourite poem one year, changes to something completely
different the next.
However, lurking at the back of my mind forever and ever is
Matthew Arnold's 'Dover Beach' which I fell in love with as a
student when I heard it read aloud in 1974 by the Professor of
English in Maynooth College, Fr John McMacken. The poem was
read with passion and feeling and love and that's exactly what I've
carried within me about it ever since.

It's like listening to a Beethoven symphony — deeply romantic and probing, and even if Arnold mourns the demise of 'The Sea of Faith' which once 'round earth's shore/Lay like the folds of a bright girdle furled', the whole emotional sweep and mood of the poem carries the reader to the climactic pain and resolution of the final stanza — still for me, utterly believable, magnificent and something you live your way into!

> Ah, love, let us be true
> To one another! for the world, which seems
> To lie before us like a land of dreams . . .

Good luck with Lifelines IV *— it's a wonderful idea and I hope it's every bit as successful as previous editions.*

Sincerely,
Mary O'Donnell

Dover Beach

The sea is calm tonight.
The tide is full, the moon lies fair
Upon the straits — on the French coast the light
Gleams and is gone; the cliffs of England stand,
Glimmering and vast, out in the tranquil bay.
Come to the window, sweet is the night air!
Only, from the long line of spray
Where the sea meets the moon-blanched land,
Listen! you hear the grating roar
Of pebbles which the waves draw back, and fling,
At their return, up the high strand,
Begin, and cease, and then again begin,
With tremulous cadence slow, and bring
The eternal note of sadness in.

Sophocles long ago
Heard it on the Aegean, and it brought
Into his mind the turbid ebb and flow
Of human misery; we
Find also in the sound a thought,
Hearing it by this distant northern sea.

The Sea of Faith
Was once, too, at the full, and round earth's shore
Lay like the folds of a bright girdle furled.
But now I only hear
Its melancholy, long, withdrawing roar,
Retreating to the breath
Of the night wind, down the vast edges drear
and naked shingles of the world.

Ah, love, let us be true
To one another! for the world, which seems
To lie before us like a land of dreams,
So various, so beautiful, so new,
Hath really neither joy, nor love, nor light,
Nor certitude, nor peace, nor help for pain;
And we are here as on a darkling plain
Swept with confused alarms of struggle and flight,
Where ignorant armies clash by night.

Matthew Arnold (1822–1888)

NEIL RUDENSTINE   207

Harvard University
Office of the President
Massachusetts Hall,
Cambridge
Massachusetts 02138
9 January 1992

Dear Ms Hughes et al:
I am happy to contribute to Lifelines, *but I should say that I have no single favorite poem — and many of the poems that are most important to me are not quite 'poems' in the usual sense, and are much too long for an anthology.* The Iliad, The Canterbury Tales, The Divine Comedy, Paradise Lost, *and many other works would fall into this category.*
Poems shift their meanings — and their importance — at different times, in different periods of our life, and on different occasions. So no single poem — or even a few — will really be adequate. Choosing one poem is impossible, but it would be possible at least to say that John Keats's 'Ode to Autumn' is one of the very great poems in English, and is very important to me personally: it says much about growth and maturity; age and death and bleakness; richness and fruition and indulgence; and finally about the way in which all these perceptions, feelings, and ideas can be held together in consciousness, in such a way as to evoke their power and yet reconcile and give resolution to what may seem irreconcilable in them. It also does this, not so much by explicit statement, but by the wonderfully modulated tones of the poet, the images captured, and the implicit meanings that those images suggest.

Sincerely,
Neil Rudenstine

To Autumn

I
Season of mists and mellow fruitfulness,
    Close bosom friend of the maturing sun,
Conspiring with him how to load and bless
    With fruit the vines that round the thatch-eves run:
To bend with apples the mossed cottage-trees,
    And fill all fruit with ripeness to the core;
        To swell the gourd, and plump the hazel shells
    With a sweet kernel; to set budding more,
And still more, later flowers for the bees,
Until they think warm days will never cease,
    For summer has o'er-brimmed their clammy cells.

II
Who hath not seen thee oft amid thy store?
    Sometimes whoever seeks abroad may find
Thee sitting careless on a granary floor,
    Thy hair soft-lifted by the winnowing wind;
Or on a half-reaped furrow sound asleep,
    Drowsed with the fume of poppies, while thy hook
        Spares the next swath and all its twinèd flowers;
And sometimes like a gleaner thou dost keep
    Steady thy laden head across a brook;
    Or by a cyder-press, with patient look,
        Thou watchest the last oozings hours by hours.

III
Where are the songs of spring? Aye, where are they?
    Think not of them, thou hast thy music too —
While barrèd clouds bloom the soft-dying day,
    And touch the stubble-plains with rosy hue.
Then in a wailful choir the small gnats mourn
    Among the river sallows, borne aloft
        Or sinking as the light wind lives or dies;
And full-grown lambs loud bleat from hilly bourn;
    Hedge-crickets sing; and now with treble soft
    The red-breast whistles from a garden-croft;
        And gathering swallows twitter in the skies.

John Keats (1795–1821)

VIVIENNE ROCHE   208

22 January 1992

Dear Nicola, Alice and Paula,
Thank you for the invitation to nominate my favourite poem for
Lifelines IV *which I am very pleased to do.*
My favourite book of poems is Crow *by Ted Hughes which is really*
one long poem and selecting one single poem from the book is like
selecting a verse from a song. However, I have chosen 'Lineage' *(the*
second poem) — because it leads into the book. I can never imagine
hearing this poem read aloud because for me the strength of the poem
is in the image of the words on paper. It is almost like scaffolding
around a building, which helps you to understand the struggle of
that building. The poem is very precise and powerful.
Good luck with your excellent venture.

Yours sincerely,
Vivienne (Roche)

Lineage

In the beginning was Scream
Who begat Blood
Who begat Eye
Who begat Fear
Who begat Wing
Who begat Bone
Who begat Granite
Who begat Violet
Who begat Guitar
Who begat Sweat
Who begat Adam
Who begat Mary
Who begat God
Who begat Nothing
Who begat Never
Never Never Never

Who begat Crow

Screaming for Blood
Grubs, crusts
Anything

Trembling featherless elbows in the nest's filth

Ted Hughes (b. 1930)

SEAMUS DEANE   209

22 January 1992

Dear Nicola, Paula, Alice,
Thank you for your letter and my apologies for the delay in replying.
I don't know that I have a favourite poem; but certainly among my
favourites, I would include Derek Mahon's 'A Disused Shed in Co.
Wexford'.
The reasons? It is a poem that heartbreakingly dwells on and gives
voice to all those peoples and civilisations that have been lost and/or
destroyed. Since it is set in Ireland, with all the characteristic
features of an Irish 'Big House' ruin, it speaks with a special
sharpness to the present moment and the fear, rampant in Northern
Ireland, of communities that fear they too might perish and be lost,
with none to speak for them.

Yours sincerely,
Seamus Deane

A Disused Shed in Co. Wexford

Let them not forget us, the weak souls among the asphodels. —
Seferis, *Mythistorema*

For J G Farrell

Even now there are places where a thought might grow —
Peruvian mines, worked out and abandoned
To a slow clock of condensation,
An echo trapped for ever, and a flutter
Of wildflowers in the lift-shaft,
Indian compounds where the wind dances
And a door bangs with diminished confidence,
Lime crevices behind rippling rainbarrels,
Dog corners for bone burials;
And in a disused shed in Co. Wexford,

Deep in the grounds of a burnt-out hotel,
Among the bathtubs and the washbasins
A thousand mushrooms crowd to a keyhole.
This is the one star in their firmament
Or frames a star within a star.
What should they do there but desire?
So many days beyond the rhododendrons
With the world waltzing in its bowl of cloud,
They have learnt patience and silence
Listening to the rooks querulous in the high wood.

They have been waiting for us in a foetor
Of vegetable sweat since civil war days,
Since the gravel-crunching, interminable departure
Of the expropriated mycologist.
He never came back, and light since then
Is a keyhole rusting gently after rain.
Spiders have spun, flies dusted to mildew
And once a day, perhaps, they have heard something —
A trickle of masonry, a shout from the blue
Or a lorry changing gear at the end of the lane.

There have been deaths, the pale flesh flaking
Into the earth that nourished it;
And nightmares, born of these and the grim
Dominion of stale air and rank moisture.
Those nearest the door grow strong —
'Elbow room! Elbow room!'
The rest, dim in a twilight of crumbling
Utensils and broken flower-pots, groaning
For their deliverance, have been so long
Expectant that there is left only the posture.

A half century, without visitors, in the dark—
Poor preparation for the cracking lock
And creak of hinges. Magi, moonmen,
Powdery prisoners of the old regime,
Web-throated, stalked life triffids, racked by drought
And insomnia, only the ghost of a scream
At the flash-bulb firing squad we wake them with
Shows there is life yet in their feverish forms.
Grown beyond nature now, soft food for worms,
They lift frail heads in gravity and good faith.

They are begging us, you see, in their wordless way,
To do something, to speak on their behalf
Or at least not to close the door again.
Lost people of Treblinka and Pompeii!
'Save us, save us,' they seem to say,
'Let the god not abandon us
Who have come so far in darkness and in pain.
We too had our lives to live.
You with your light meter and relaxed itinerary,
Let not our naive labours have been in vain!'

Derek Mahon (b. 1941)

JAMES SIMMONS   210

4 January 1992

Dear Friends,
No one can have an absolute favourite poem but tonight mine would be
'A Toccata of Galuppi's' by Robert Browning. Shakespeare is my
favourite author but I presume you do not want an extract from his
plays. Poetry — language — with Shakespeare is used to illuminate
human predicaments and the oddities of the whole human enterprise.
So it is in Browning's poems, though he brings it off less often. In my
own work I have tried to follow their example and held a line against a
depressing sea of modern poetry that is either too oblique and 'clever'
or too personal and tedious. In this poem Browning takes a period in
history and feels his way into it until it reads like personal experience,
and thus it becomes his own history and our history, and anyone who
reads it attentively will be saddened and inspired.

Good luck with your work,
James Simmons

A Toccata of Galuppi's

I
Oh, Galuppi, Baldassaro, this is very sad to find!
I can hardly misconceive you; it would prove me deaf and blind;
But although I take your meaning, 'tis with such a heavy mind.

II
Here you come with your old music, and here's all the good it
    brings.
What, they lived once thus at Venice where the merchants were
    the kings,
Where Saint Mark's is, where the Doges used to wed the sea
    with rings?

III
Aye, because the sea's the street there; and 'tis arched by . . .
    what you call
. . . Shylock's bridge with houses on it, where they kept the
    carnival:
˙I was never out of England — it's as if I saw it all.

IV
Did young people take their pleasure when the sea was warm in
    May?
Balls and masks begun at midnight, burning ever to midday,
When they made up fresh adventures for the morrow, do you
    say?

V

Was a lady such a lady, cheeks so round and lips so red —
On her neck the small face buoyant, like a bellflower on its bed
O'er the breast's superb abundance where a man might base his
head?

VI

Well, and it was graceful of them — they'd break talk off and
afford
— She, to bite her mask's black velvet — he, to finger on his
sword,
While you sat and played toccatas, stately at the clavichord?

VII

What? Those lesser thirds so plaintive, sixths diminished, sigh
on sigh,
Told them something? Those suspensions, those solutions —
'Must we die?'
Those commiserating sevenths — 'Life might last! we can but
try!'

VIII

'Were you happy?' — 'Yes.' — 'And are you still as happy?' —
'Yes. And you?'
—'Then, more kisses!' — 'Did I stop them, when a million
seemed so few?'
Hark, the dominant's persistence till it must be answered to!

IX

So, an octave struck the answer. Oh, they praised you, I dare
say!
'Brave Galuppi! that was music; good alike at grave and gay!
I can always leave off talking when I hear a master play!'

X

Then they left you for their pleasure: till in due time, one by one,
Some with lives that came to nothing, some with deeds as well
undone,
Death stepped tacitly and took them where they never see the
sun.

XI

But when I sit down to reason, think to take my stand nor
swerve,
While I triumph o'er a secret wrung from nature's close reserve,
In you come with your cold music till I creep through every
nerve.

XII
Yes, you, like a ghostly cricket, creaking where a house was
    burned:
'Dust and ashes, dead and done with, Venice spent what Venice
    earned.
The soul, doubtless, is immortal — where a soul can be
    discerned.

XIII
'Yours for instance: you know physics, something of geology,
Mathematics are your pastime; souls shall rise in their degree;
Butterflies may dread extinction — you'll not die, it cannot be!

XIV
'As for Venice and her people, merely born to bloom and drop,
Here on earth they bore their fruitage, mirth and folly were the
    crop:
What of soul was left, I wonder, when the kissing had to stop?

XV
'Dust and ashes!' So you creak it, and I want the heart to scold.
Dear dead women, with such hair, too — what's become of all
    the gold
Used to hang and brush their bosoms? I feel chilly and grown
    old.

Robert Browning (1812–1889)

GALWAY KINNELL   211

20 January 1992

Dear Nicola Hughes, Paula Griffin, and Alice McEleney,
Thank you for your letter. One of my favorite poems is 'The Ferryer'
by Sharon Olds. I like it very much. I'm not sure I know why. One
aspect of it that I find affecting is its combination of harsh
truthfulness and loving forgiveness.

Yours truly,
Galway Kinnell

The Ferryer

Three years after my father's death
he goes back to work. Unemployed
for twenty-five years, he's very glad
to be taken on again, shows up

on time, tireless worker. He sits
in the prow of the boat, sweet cox, turned
with his back to the carried. He is dead, but able
to kneel upright, facing forward
toward the other shore. Someone has closed
his mouth, so he looks more comfortable, not
thirsty or calling out, and his eyes
are open, there under the iris the black
line that appeared there in death. He is calm,
he is happy to be hired, he's in business again,
his new job is a joke between us and he
loves to have a joke with me, he keeps
a straight face. He waits, naked,
ivory bow figurehead,
ribs, nipples, lips, a gaunt
tall man, and when I bring people
and set them in the boat and push them off
my father poles them across the river
to the far bank. We don't speak,
he knows that this is simply someone
I want to get rid of, who makes me feel
ugly and afraid. I do not say
the way you did. He knows the labor
and loves it. When I dump someone in
he does not look back, he takes them straight
to hell. He wants to work for me
until I die. Then, he knows, I will
come to him, get in his boat
and be taken across, then hold out my broad
hand to his, help him ashore, we will
embrace like two who were never born,
naked, not breathing, then up to our chins we will
pull the dark blanket of earth and
rest together at the end of the working day.

Sharon Olds (b. 1942)

LAURIS EDMOND   212

Dear Nicola, Paula and Alice,
Thank you for the invitation to take part in Lifelines. *I am delighted*
to be able to help Third World people in this way, all the more since I
have recently been in Zambia, one of these poor countries, and have
seen how desperately they need the help of those of us who live easier,
more comfortable lives.

The poem I have chosen is by C P Cavafy, a Twentieth Century Greek poet (he died in 1933), and one I find wonderfully illuminating. On the surface it is about a particular journey, one of the most famous in all literature, Odysseus's ten-year-long travels that took him home to Ithaca after the Trojan Wars. But as you read you become Odysseus yourself, the journey is yours. The poem is here in translation, so perhaps we have lost some of the quality, but even so it says with marvellous clarity and compassion how important it is to live your life fully; it is the journey itself that matters, wherever it takes you. How gently and with what simplicity he says at the end 'you must surely have understood by then what Ithacas mean'.

My greetings to you all and my best wishes for the success of your project.
Lauris Edmond

Ithaca

When you start on your journey to Ithaca,
then pray that the road is long,
full of adventure, full of knowledge.
Do not fear the Lestrygonians
and the Cyclopes and the angry Poseidon.
You will never meet such as these on your path,
if your thoughts remain lofty, if a fine
emotion touches your body and your spirit.
You will never meet the Lestrygonians,
the Cyclopes and the fierce Poseidon,
if you do not carry them within your soul,
if your soul does not raise them up before you.

Then pray that the road is long.
That the summer mornings are many,
that you will enter ports seen for the first time
with such pleasure, with such joy!
Stop at Phoenician markets,
and purchase fine merchandise,
mother-of-pearl and corals, amber and ebony,
and pleasurable perfumes of all kinds,
buy as many pleasurable perfumes as you can;
visit hosts of Egyptian cities,
to learn and learn from those who have knowledge.

Always keep Ithaca fixed in your mind.
To arrive there is your ultimate goal.
But do not hurry the voyage at all.
It is better to let it last for long years;
and even to anchor at the isle when you are old,
rich with all that you have gained on the way,
not expecting that Ithaca will offer you riches.

Ithaca has given you the beautiful voyage.
Without her you would never have taken the road.
But she has nothing more to give you.

And if you find her poor, Ithaca has not defrauded you.
With the great wisdom you have gained, with so much
   experience,
you must surely have understood by then what Ithacas mean.

Constantine P Cavafy (1863–1933)
Translated by Rae Davlen

JOSEPH O'NEILL   213

7 January 1992

Dear Nicola, Paula and Alice,
Thank you for your invitation to submit a poem for Lifelines IV. *I am very pleased to do so.*
It is impossible, of course, to choose a favourite poem, but there are two pieces which you might like.
The first is Frank O'Hara's 'A Step Away from Them', *which I have always enjoyed for its uninhibited celebration of aliveness and of our human variegation. I also admire the poem for its technical ease — they are difficult poems to write, the ones which seem as natural as breezes.*
The second poem is Raymond Carver's 'Through the Boughs', *which appears in his book* A New Path to the Waterfall. *This poem is also a celebration of aliveness, but a much sadder and more desperate one: the poem of someone who knew that he was very shortly to die.*
What links these poems, in my mind anyway, is that they alert us to the gift of existence — without wishing to sound pious, this is a gift which the children whom your book will benefit cannot, of course, take for granted as simply as we can.

Best wishes,
Joseph O'Neill

A Step Away from Them

It's my lunch hour, so I go
for a walk among the hum-colored
cabs. First, down the sidewalk

where laborers feed their dirty
glistening torsos sandwiches
and Coca-Cola, with yellow helmets
on. They protect them from falling
bricks, I guess. Then onto the
avenue where skirts are flipping
above heels and blow up over
grates. The sun is hot, but the
cabs stir up the air. I look
at bargains in wristwatches. There
are cats playing in sawdust.
                              On
to Times Square, where the sign
blows smoke over my head, and higher
the waterfall pours lightly. A
Negro stands in a doorway with a
toothpick, languorously agitating.
A blonde chorus girl clicks: he
smiles and rubs his chin. Everything
suddenly honks: it is 12:40 of
a Thursday.
                  Neon in daylight is a
great pleasure, as Edwin Denby would
write, as are light bulbs in daylight.
I stop for a cheeseburger at JULIET'S
CORNER. Giulietta Masina, wife of
Federico Fellini, *è bell' attrice.*
And chocolate malted. A lady in
foxes on such a day puts her poodle
in a cab.
                  There are several Puerto
Ricans on the avenue today, which
makes it beautiful and warm. First
Bunny died, then John Latouche,
then Jackson Pollock. But is the
earth as full as life was full, of them?
And one has eaten and one walks,
past the magazines with nudes
and the posters for BULLFIGHT and
the Manhattan Storage Warehouse,
which they'll soon tear down. I
used to think they had the Armory
Show there.
                  A glass of papaya juice
and back to work. My heart is in my
pocket, it is Poems by Pierre Reverdy.

Frank O'Hara (1926–1966)

Through the Boughs

Down below the window, on the deck, some ragged-looking
birds gather at the feeder. The same birds, I think, that come
every day to eat and quarrel. *Time was, time was,* they cry and
strike at each other. It's nearly time, yes. The sky stays dark all
day, the wind is from the west and won't stop blowing . . . .
Give me your hand for a time. Hold on to mine. That's right,
yes. Squeeze hard. Time was we thought we had time on our
side. *Time was, time was,* those ragged birds cry.

Raymond Carver (1930-1988)

DAVID LEAVITT   214

26 January 1992

Dear Nicola, Paula and Alice,
*Thanks very much for your letter. The poem I've decided to send you
is 'The Moose' by Elizabeth Bishop. It's rather a long poem as you
can see.*
*I think the reason I love this poem so much is because magically, it
articulates everything that seems to me to be important about
experiences — how the 'homely' can so easily glide into the
'otherworldly'; how a moose, caught in the twin beams of a Boston-
bound bus, can transcend its own earthliness to become something
both more and less than human, generating a 'sweet sensation of joy'.
There is a calmness to the language of this poem, an ease and
simplicity that belies the reality of its making. (It took Bishop years to
compose.) And it contains some of the most breathtaking descriptions
of nature that I've ever read. (In particular, I shall never forget 'the
sweet peas cling to their wet, white string'.)*

With very best wishes,
David Leavitt

('*The Moose*' was also Derek Mahon's choice. The poem appears in full on
pages 98–102.)

HUGO HAMILTON   215

8 January 1992

Dear Editors,
Many thanks for inviting me to submit my favourite poem.
I have selected a poem by Michael Davitt which has been translated

from the Irish by his fellow poet Paul Muldoon with the title 'The Mirror'. The poem and its translation both appear in Selected Poems 1968–84.

'The Mirror' *is the clearest description I've ever heard of the father and son relationship, the son taking up the job so unwisely taken on by the father. The grief for his father's death is declared by default, almost in a note of anger at his father taking down the mirror without the son's help. There is an image of the father as a stranger, a man recently retired from CIE, breathing life into his son through the mirror as they put it back up again together. It's how I felt about my own father.*

Yours sincerely,
Hugo Hamilton

An Scáthán
i gcuimhne m'athar

I
Níorbh é m'athair níos mó é
ach ba mise a mhacsan;
paradacsa fuar a d'fháisceas,
dealbh i gculaith Dhomhnaigh
a cuireadh an lá dár gcionn.

Dhein sé an-lá deora, seirí
fuiscí, ceapairí feola is tae.
Bhí seanchara leis ag eachtraí
faoi sciurd lae a thugadar
ar Eochaill sna tríochaidí
is gurbh é a chéad pháirtí é
i seirbhís Chorcaí / An Sciobairín
amach sna daicheadaí.
Bhí dornán cártaí Aifrinn
ar mhatal an tseomra suí
ina gcorrán thart ar vás gloine,
a bhronntanas scoir ó C.I.E.

II
Níorbh eol dom go ceann dhá lá
gurbh é an scáthán a mharaigh é . . .

An seanscáthán ollmhór Victeoiriach
leis an bhfráma ornáideach bréagórga
a bhí romhainn sa tigh trí stór
nuair a bhogamar isteach ón tuath.
Bhínn scanraithe roimhe: go sciorrfadh
anuas den bhfalla is go slogfadh mé
d'aon tromanáil i lár na hoíche . . .

Ag maisiú an tseomra chodlata dó
d'ardaigh sé an scáthán anuas
dan lámh chúnta a iarraidh;
ar ball d'iompaigh dath na cré air,
an oíche sin phléasc a chroí.

III
Mar a chuirfí de gheasa orm
thugas faoin jab a chríochnú:
an folús macallach a pháipéarú,
an fhuinneog ard a phéinteáil,
an doras marbhlainne
a scríobadh. Nuair a rugas ar an scáthán
sceimhlíos. Bhraitheas é ag análú tríd.
Chuala é ag rá i gcogar téiglí:
I'll give you a hand, here.

Is d'ardaíomar an scáthán thar n-ais in airde
os cionn an tinteáin,
m'athair á choinneáil
fad a dheineas-sa é a dhaingniú
le dhá thairne.

Michael Davitt (b. 1950)

The Mirror
in memory of my father

I
He was no longer my father
but I was still his son;
I would get to grips with that cold paradox,
the remote figure in his Sunday best
who was buried the next day.

A great day for tears, snifters of sherry,
whiskey, beef sandwiches, tea.
An old mate of his was recounting
their day excursion
to Youghal in the Thirties,
how he was his first partner
on the Cork/Skibbereen route
in the late Forties.
There was a splay of Mass cards
on the sitting-room mantelpiece
which formed a crescent round a glass vase,
his retirement present from C.I.E.

II
I didn't realise till two days later
it was the mirror took his breath away . . .

The monstrous old Victorian mirror
with the ornate gilt frame
we had found in the three-storey house
when we moved in from the country.
I was afraid that it would sneak
down from the wall and swallow me up
in one gulp in the middle of the night . . .

While he was decorating the bedroom
he had taken down the mirror
without asking for help;
soon he turned the colour of terracotta
and his heart broke that night.

III
There was nothing for it
but to set about finishing the job,
papering over the cracks,
painting the high window,
stripping the door, like the door of a crypt.
When I took hold of the mirror
I had a fright. I imagined him breathing through it.
I heard him say in a reassuring whisper:
I'll give you a hand, here.

And we lifted the mirror back in position
above the fireplace,
my father holding it steady
while I drove home
the two nails.

Michael Davitt (b. 1950)
(Translated by Paul Muldoon)

DECLAN KIBERD   216

English Dept, UCD
8 January 1992

Dear Wesley Students,
Thanks for your letter. My favourite poem is an Irish Bardic lyric
'M'Anam do Sgar Riomsa Araoir', to be found in Osborn Bergin's
Irish Bardic Poetry (ed. F Kelly) with English version.
It is the most moving elegy I have ever read, evoking the poet's dead
wife with a unique blend of tenderness and formality. The lines throb
with painful desire, and yet the whole utterance has been
dramatically disciplined, so that the reader feels overcome by the
energetic reticence of a speaker who is — for all his expressive power

— leaving the deepest things unsaid. Most of the Bardic poems of Gaelic Ireland were drearily formulaic in theme and in technique, and so I was rather bored when studying them in college; but I can still recall the explosion of feeling when first I heard this poem, read by Professor David Greene not long after the death of his own wife. Every time I re-read it, I feel that it is the work of a poet who knows that love is the only possible challenge to time. His wife, who was a joy to him in life, has become all the more mysterious in death. In saying that his soul separated from his body last night, he seems to suggest that the male and female will only become a single person again when they are reunited in heaven.

All good wishes for your project,
Declan Kiberd

M'anam do sgar riomsa a-raoir

M'anam do sgar riomsa a-raoir,
    calann ghlan dob ionnsa i n-uaigh;
rugadh bruinne maordha mín
    is aonbhla lín uime uainn.

Do tógbhadh sgath aobhdha fhionn
    a-mach ár an bhfaongha bhfann:
laogh mo chridhise do chrom,
    craobh throm an tighise thall.

M'aonar a-nocht damhsa, a Dhé,
    olc an saoghal camsa ad-chí;
dob álainn trom an taoibh naoi
    do bhaoi sonn a-raoir, a Rí.

Truagh leam an leabasa thiar,
    mo pheall seadasa dhá snámh;
tárramair corp seada saor
    is folt claon, a leaba, id lár.

Do bhí duine go ndreich moill
    ina luighe ar leigh mo phill;
gan bharamhail acht bláth cuill
    don sgáth duinn bhanamhail bhinn.

Maol Mheadha na malach ndonn
    mo dhabhach mheadha a-raon rom;
mo chridhe an sgáth do sgar riom
    bláth mhionn arna car do chrom.

Táinig an chlí as ar gcuing,
    agus dí ráinig mar roinn:
corp idir dá aisil inn
    ar dtocht don fhinn mhaisigh mhoill.

Leath mo throigheadh, leath mo thaobh,
    a dreach mar an droighean bán,
níor dhísle neach dhí ná dhún,
    leath mo shúl í, leath mo lámh.

Leath mo chuirp an choinneal naoi;
    's gúirt riom do roinneadh, a Rí;
agá labhra is meirtneach mé —
    dob é ceirtleath m'anma í.

Mo chéadghrádh a dearc mhall mhór,
    déadbhán agus cam a cliabh:
nochar bhean a colann caomh
    ná a taobh ré fear romham riamh.

Fiche bliadhna inne ar-aon,
    fá binne gach bliadhna ar nglór,
go rug éinleanabh déag dhún,
    an ghéag úr mhéirleabhar mhór.

Gé tú, nocha n-oilim ann,
    ó do thoirinn ar gcnú chorr;
ar sgaradh dár roghrádh rom,
    falamh lom an domhnán donn.

Ón ló do sáidheadh cleath corr
    im theach nochar raidheadh rum —
ní thug aoighe d'ortha ann
    dá barr naoidhe dhorcha dhunn.

A dhaoine, ná coisgidh damh;
    faoidhe ré cloistin ní col;
táinig luinnchreach lom 'nar dteagh —
    an bhruithneach gheal donn ar ndol.

Is é rug uan í 'na ghrúg,
    Rí na sluagh is Rí na ród;
beag an cion do chúl na ngéag
    a héag ó a fior go húr óg.

Ionmhain lámh bhog do bhí sonn,
    a Rí na gclog is na gceall:
ach! an lámh nachar logh mionn,
    crádh liom gan a cor fám cheann.

(Ascribed to Muireadhach Albanach)

The Dead Wife

My soul parted from me last night; a pure body that was dear
is in the grave; a gentle stately bosom has been taken from me
with one linen shroud about it.

A white comely blossom has been plucked from the feeble bending stalk; my own heart's darling has drooped, the fruitful branch of yonder house.

I am alone tonight, O God; evil is this crooked world that Thou seest; lovely was the weight of the young body that was here last night, O King.

Sad for me (to behold) yonder couch, my long pallet . . . ; we have seen a tall noble form with waving tresses upon thee, O couch.

A woman of gentle countenance lay upon one side of my pallet; there was naught save the hazel-blossom like to the dark shadow, womanly and sweet-voiced.

Maol Mheadha of the dark brows, my mead-vessel beside me; my heart the shadow that has parted from me, the flower of jewels after being planted has drooped.

My body has passed from my control, and has fallen to her share;

I am a body in two pieces since the lovely bright and gentle one is gone.

She was one of my two feet, one of my sides — her countenance like the white-thorn; none belonged to her more than to me, she was one of my eyes, one of my hands.

She was the half of my body, the fresh torch; harshly have I been treated, O King; I am faint as I tell it — she was the very half of my soul.

Her large gentle eye was my first love, her bosom was curved and white as ivory; her fair body belonged to no man before me.

Twenty years we spent together; sweeter was our converse each year; she bore to me eleven children, the tall fresh lithe-fingered branch.

Though I am alive, I am no more, since my smooth hazel-nut is fallen;

since my dear love parted from me, the dark world is empty and bare.

From the day that a smooth post was fixed in my house it has not been told me — no guest laid a spell therein upon her youthful dark brown hair.

O men, check me not; the sound of weeping is not forbidden; bare and cruel ruin has come into my house — the bright brown glowing one is gone.

It is the King of Hosts and the King of Roads who has taken her away in His displeasure; little was the fault of the branching tresses that she should die and leave her husband while fresh and young.

Dear the soft hand that was here, O King of bells and churchyards; alas! the hand that never swore (false) oath, 'tis torment to me that it is not placed under my head.

SUE LAWLEY   217

9 January 1992

Dear Nicola, Paula and Alice,
Thank you for asking me to make a contribution to Lifelines IV. *My*
choice of poem would be Matthew Arnold's 'The Forsaken
Merman'.
I don't think this is the most important poem that Arnold ever wrote
but it is one which I discovered aged about eleven and it has stayed
with me ever since. I recently introduced my daughter, also now
eleven years old, to it and she seems equally moved by this rather
pathetic tale of a merman who married a mortal but was ultimately
forsaken.
I think it is a perfect narrative poem which carries you along
rhythmically, holds your interest, enables you to identify with the
equivocations of the hero and, finally, leaves you with a feeling of
great sadness for his loss. Not a word is wasted (I could probably
quote most of them to you) and not an eye is dry.
Good luck with the book.

Best wishes,
Yours sincerely,
Sue Lawley

The Forsaken Merman

Come, dear children, let us away;
Down and away below!
Now my brothers call from the bay,
Now the great winds shoreward blow,
Now the salt tides seaward flow;
Now the wild white horses play,
Champ and chafe and toss in the spray.
Children dear, let us away!
This way, this way!

Call her once before you go —
Call once yet!
In a voice that she will know:
'Margaret! Margaret!'
Children's voices should be dear
(Call once more) to a mother's ear;
Children's voices, wild with pain —
Surely she will come again!
Call her once and come away;
This way, this way!
'Mother dear, we cannot stay!
The wild white horses foam and fret.'
Margaret! Margaret!

Come, dear children, come away down;
Call no more!
One last look at the white-walled town,
And the little grey church on the windy shore,
Then come down!
She will not come though you call all day;
Come away, come away!

Children dear, was it yesterday
We heard the sweet bells over the bay?
In the caverns where we lay,
Through the surf and through the swell,
The far-off sound of a silver bell?
Sand-strewn caverns, cool and deep,
Where the winds are all asleep;
Where the spent lights quiver and gleam,
Where the salt weed sways in the stream,
Where the sea beasts, ranged all round,
Feed in the ooze of their pasture ground;
Where the sea snakes coil and twine,
Dry their mail and bask in the brine;
Where great whales come sailing by,
Sail and sail, with unshut eye,
Round the world for ever and aye?
When did music come this way?
Children dear, was it yesterday?

Children dear, was it yesterday
(Call yet once) that she went away?
Once she sate with you and me,
On a red gold throne in the heart of the sea,
And the youngest sate on her knee.
She combed its bright hair, and she tended it well,
When down swung the sound of a far-off bell.
She sighed, she looked up through the clear green sea;
She said: 'I must go, for my kinsfolk pray
In the little grey church on the shore today.
'Twill be Easter time in the world — ah me!
And I lose my poor soul, Merman! here with thee.'
I said: 'Go up, dear heart, through the waves;
Say thy prayer, and come back to the kind sea caves!'
She smiled, she went up through the surf in the bay.
Children dear, was it yesterday?

Children dear, were we long alone?
'The sea grows stormy, the little ones moan;
Long prayers,' I said, 'in the world they say;
Come!' I said; and we rose through the surf in the bay.
We went up the beach, by the sandy down
Where the sea stocks bloom, to the white-walled town;
Through the narrow paved streets, where all was still,
To the little grey church on the windy hill.

From the church came a murmur of folk at their prayers,
But we stood without in the cold blowing airs.
We climbed on the graves, on the stones worn with rains,
And we gazed up the aisle through the small leaded panes.
She sate by the pillar; we saw her clear:
'Margaret, hist! come quick, we are here!
Dear heart,' I said, 'we are long alone;
The sea grows stormy, the little ones moan.'
But, ah, she gave me never a look,
For her eyes were sealed to the holy book!
Loud prays the priest; shut stands the door.
Come away, children, call no more!
Come away, come down, call no more!

　　　Down, down, down!
Down to the depths of the sea!
She sits at her wheel in the humming town,
Singing most joyfully.
Hark what she sings: 'O joy, o joy,
For the humming street, and the child with its toy!
For the priest, and the bell, and the holy well;
For the wheel where I spun,
And the blessed light of the sun!'
And so she sings her fill,
Singing most joyfully,
Till the spindle drops from her hand,
And the whizzing wheel stands still.
She steals to the window, and looks at the sand,
And over the sand at the sea;
And her eyes are set in a stare;
And anon there breaks a sigh,
And anon there drops a tear,
From a sorrow-clouded eye,
And a heart sorrow-laden,
A long, long sigh;
For the cold strange eyes of a little Mermaiden
And the gleam of her golden hair.

　　　Come away, away children;
Come children, come down!
The hoarse wind blows coldly;
Lights shine in the town.
She will start from her slumber
When gusts shake the door;
She will hear the winds howling,
Will hear the waves roar.
We shall see, while above us
The waves roar and whirl,
A ceiling of amber,
A pavement of pearl.

Singing: 'Here came a mortal,
But faithless was she!
And alone dwell forever
The kings of the sea.'

But, children, at midnight,
When soft the winds blow,
When clear falls the moonlight,
When spring tides are low;
When sweet airs come seaward
From heaths starred with broom,
And high rocks throw mildly
On the blanched sands a gloom;
Up the still, glistening beaches,
Up the creek we will hie,
Over the banks of bright seaweed
The ebb tide leaves dry.
We will gaze, from the sand hills,
At the white, sleeping town;
At the church on the hillside —
And then come back down.
Singing; 'There dwells a loved one,
But cruel is she!
She left lonely forever
The kings of the sea.'

Matthew Arnold (1822–1888)

MICHAEL BLUMENTHAL   218

Harvard University
Department of English and American Literature and Language
14 January 1992

Dear Nicola, Paula and Alice,
I'm, of course, happy to participate in your Lifelines *project, and flattered to have been asked. I'm a tad unhappier, I must admit, at being asked to identify my 'favourite' poem, as I have no such thing, really, only poems I love, as people, the intensity and depth of whose call to me on particular days and in particular moods varies, yet all of which I love dearly, and for different — albeit often intersecting — reasons. ALL of them are, equally my favourites.*
In any event, I appreciate and support what you're doing, and so herewith enclose today's choice for my 'favourite' poem — 'The Painter Dreaming in the Scholar's House', by our own late Poet Laureate and my good friend, Howard Nemerov.
I love this poem dearly for how beautifully it seeks to create a world

(the world of the poem) in which, to paraphrase the poet, 'spirit and sense are not at odds'. Its iambic pentameter is almost effortless seeming, and as light-handed and deft (I think) as Wordsworth's or Frost's. In this poem, clarity and mystery cohabit beautifully, neither at the expense of the other. And very delicately, never pompously or self-consciously it dares to take on the 'great' themes — the conflict of spirit and sense, the transience of life itself and of its small but meaningful exercises of virtue, the hoped-for redemptions of art as an act of faith, the need for an eye that is 'clarified towards charity'. When I first heard it read, some fifteen years ago at The Library of Congress, it made me weep. And it still makes me weep . . . . But 'it never breaks up its lines to weep', as a poem never should. And though, quite clearly, it is a poem that thinks, it is also a poem that thinks as Roethke said a poet should: by feeling.
I hope, and trust, that this will be helpful to you, and wish you all the best for continued success on your very worthwhile project.

Sincerely,
Michael Blumenthal

The Painter Dreaming in the Scholar's House
in memory of the painters Paul Klee and Paul Terence Feeley

I
The painter's eye follows relation out.
His work is not to paint the visible,
He says, it is to render visible.

Being a man, and not a god, he stands
Already in a world of sense, from which
He borrows, to begin with, mental things
Chiefly, the abstract elements of language:
The point, the line, the plane, the colors and
The geometric shapes. Of these he spins
Relation out, he weaves its fabric up
So that it speaks darkly, as music does
Singing the secret history of the mind.
And when in this the visible world appears,
As it does do, mountain, flower, cloud, and tree,
All haunted here and there with the human face,
It happens as by accident, although
The accident is of design. It is because
Language first rises from the speechless world
That the painterly intelligence
Can say correctly that he makes his world,
Not imitates the one before his eyes.
Hence the delightsome gardens, the dark shores,
The terrifying forests where nightfall
Enfolds a lost and tired traveler.

And hence the careless crowd deludes itself
By likening his hieroglyphic signs
And secret alphabets to the drawing of a child.
That likeness is significant the other side
Of what they see, for his simplicities
Are not the first ones, but the furthest ones,
Final refinements of his thought made visible.
He is the painter of the human mind
Finding and faithfully reflecting the mindfulness
That is in things, and not the things themselves.

For such a man, art is an act of faith:
Prayer the study of it, as Blake says,
And praise the practice; nor does he divide
Making from teaching, or from theory.
The three are one, and in his hours of art
There shines a happiness through darkest themes,
As though spirit and sense were not at odds.

II
The painter as an allegory of the mind
At genesis. He takes a burlap bag,
Tears it open and tacks it on a stretcher.
He paints it black because, as he has said,
Everything looks different on black.

Suppose the burlap bag to be the universe,
And black because its volume is the void
Before the stars were. At the painter's hand
Volume becomes one-sidedly a surface,
And all his depths are on the face of it.

Against this flat abyss, this groundless ground
Of zero thickness stretched against the cold
Dark silence of the Absolutely Not,
Material worlds arise, the colored earths
And oil of plants that imitate the light.

They imitate the light that is in thought,
For the mind relates to thinking as the eye
Relates to light. Only because the world
Already is a language can the painter speak
According to the grammar of the ground.

It is archaic speech, that has not yet
Divided out its cadences in words;
It is a language for the oldest spells
About how some thoughts rose into the mind
While others, stranger still, sleep in the world.

So grows the garden green, the sun vermilion.
He sees the rose flame up and fade and fall.
And be the same rose still, the radiant in red.
He paints his language, and his language is
The theory of what the painter thinks.

III
The painter's eye attends to death and birth
Together, seeing a single energy
Momently manifest in every form,
As in the tree the growing of the tree
Exploding from the seed not more nor less
Than from the void condensing down and in,
Summoning sun and rain. He views the tree,
The great tree standing in the garden, say,
As thrusting downward its vast spread and weight,
Growing its green height from dark watered earth,
And as suspended weightless in the sky,
Haled forth and held up by the hair of its head.
He follows through the flowing of the forms
From the divisions of the trunk out to
The veinings of the leaf, and the leaf's fall.
His pencil meditates the many in the one
After the method in the confluence of rivers,
The running of ravines on mountainsides,
And in the deltas of the nerves; he sees
How things must be continuous with themselves
As with whole worlds that they themselves are not,
In order that they may be so transformed.
He stands where the eternity of thought
Opens upon perspective time and space;
He watches mind become incarnate; then
   He paints the tree.

IV
These thoughts have chiefly been about the painter Klee,
About how he in our hard time might stand to us
Especially whose lives concern themselves with learning
As patron of the practical intelligence of art,
And thence as model, modest and humorous in sufferings,
For all research that follows spirit where it goes.

That there should be much goodness in the world,
Much kindness and intelligence, candor and charm,
And that it all goes down in the dust after a while,
This is a subject for the steadiest meditations
Of the heart and mind, as for the tears
That clarify the eye toward charity.

So may it be to all of us, that at some times
In this bad time when faith in study seems to fail,
And when impatience in the street and still despair at home
Divide the mind to rule it, there shall some comfort come
From the remembrance of so deep and clear a life as his
Whom I have thought of, for the wholeness of his mind,
As the painter dreaming in the scholar's house,
His dream an emblem to us of the life of thought,
The same dream that then flared before intelligence
When light first went forth looking for the eye.

Howard Nemerov (1920-1991)

CAHAL DALY   219

28 January 1992

Dear Miss Hughes,
On behalf of Cardinal Daly I wish to thank you for your recent
communication with regard to Lifelines.
Cardinal Daly's favourite poem is 'Poor Clare Christmas' by the
late Bishop William Philbin of Down and Connor. This poem is
particularly inspiring to His Eminence because of its ability to create
a deep sense of the inner peace, love and serenity of a contemplative
community in the heart of the violence and unrest of Belfast.
With all good wishes for your project,

Yours sincerely,
Eugene Sweeney (Rev)
Diocesan Secretary

Poor Clare Christmas
Belfast 1974

Their eyes are quiet waters; they move, speak
In interdeference, pressureless, unloud,
Unstirred by urgencies, soul-soldered, a crowd
Only by head-count; for contestation weak
Counter to engines, energies that wreak
A city's ruin might raised, raised too world's proud
Appurtenance might haunts with mushroom cloud:
Against force forceless, whisper combating shriek.

She said, *Our Christmas vigil is for adoring*
Christ in the Sacrament . . . . I saw outpouring
Resources from life's wellspring, power's being;
Levers undamming omnipotence, restoring
To mercy extravagance, need avidity, freeing
Divinity from trammels of our seeing.

William Philbin

GERALD BARRY 220

What is Love? I asked a lover —
    Liken it, he answered, weeping,
    To a flood unchained and sweeping
Over shell-strewn grottoes, over
        Beds of roses, lilies, tulips,
O'er all flowers that most enrich the
    Garden, in one headlong torrent,
Till they show a wreck from which the
    Eye and mind recoil abhorrent.
        Hearts may woo hearts, lips may woo lips,
And gay days be spent in gladness,
    Dancing, feasting, lilting, luting.
But the end of all is Sadness,
    Desolation, Devastation,
        Spoliation and uprooting!

James Clarence Mangan (1803–1849)

I like 'What is Love?' for its excess.

Gerald Barry

SHARON OLDS 221

New York

Dear Paula Griffin, Nicola Hughes and Alice McEleney,
Thank you kindly for your letter. I am honored to be asked and happy
to comply. What a fine project!
Here are two favorites of mine — 'Oatmeal' by Galway Kinnell, so
homey and beautiful, earthy and sublime and funny, singing in that
great unique Kinnell line of food for the body and the spirit (and
honoring poetry parents); and, if I might have two, Toi Derricotte's
'Before Making Love' (from 'Captivity'), which has for me a
Keatsian quality and a political/intimate ferocity and beauty I much
admire.

My respects and gratitude,
Sharon Olds

Oatmeal

I eat oatmeal for breakfast.
I make it on the hot plate and put skimmed milk on it.
I eat alone.
I am aware it is not good to eat oatmeal alone.
Its consistency is such that it is better for your mental health if
    somebody eats it with you.
That is why I often think up an imaginary companion to have
    breakfast with.
Possibly it is even worse to eat oatmeal with an imaginary
    companion.
Nevertheless, yesterday morning, I ate my oatmeal — porridge,
    as he called it — with John Keats.
Keats said I was absolutely right to invite him: due to its
    glutinous texture, gluey lumpishness, hint of slime, and
    unusual willingness to disintegrate, oatmeal should not be
    eaten alone.
He said that in his opinion, however, it is perfectly OK to eat it
    with an imaginary companion,
and that he himself had enjoyed memorable porridges with
    Edmund Spenser and John Milton.
Even if eating oatmeal with an imaginary companion is not as
    wholesome as Keats claims, still, you can learn something
    from it.
Yesterday morning, for instance, Keats told me about writing
    the 'Ode to a Nightingale.'
He had a heck of a time finishing it — those were his words —
    'Oi 'ad a 'eck of a toime,' he said, more or less, speaking
    through his porridge.
He wrote it quickly, on scraps of paper, which he then stuck in
    his pocket,
but when he got home he couldn't figure out the order of the
    stanzas, and he and a friend spread the papers on a table,
    and they made some sense of them, but he isn't sure to this
    day if they got it right.
An entire stanza may have slipped into the lining of his jacket
    through a hole in the pocket.
He still wonders about the occasional sense of drift between
    stanzas,
and the way here and there a line will go into the configuration
    of a Moslem at prayer, then raise itself up and peer about,
    and then lay itself down slightly off the mark, causing the
    poem to move forward with a reckless, shining wobble.
He said someone told him that later in life Wordsworth heard
    about the scraps of paper on the table, and tried shuffling
    some stanzas of his own, but only made matters worse.
I would not have known about any of this but for my reluctance
    to eat oatmeal alone.

When breakfast was over, John recited 'To Autumn.'
He recited it slowly, with much feeling, and he articulated the
    words lovingly, and his odd accent sounded sweet.
He didn't offer the story of writing 'To Autumn,' I doubt if there
    is much of one.
But he did say the sight of a just-harvested oat field got him
    started on it,
and two of the lines, 'For Summer has o'er-brimmed their
    clammy cells' and 'Thou watchest the last oozing hours by
    hours,' came to him while eating oatmeal alone.
I can see him — drawing a spoon through the stuff, gazing into
    the glimmering furrows, muttering.
Maybe there is no sublime; only the shining of the amnion's
    tatters.
For supper tonight I am going to have a baked potato left over
    from lunch.
I am aware that a leftover baked potato is damp, slippery, and
    simultaneously gummy and crumbly,
and therefore I'm going to invite Patrick Kavanagh to join me.

Galway Kinnell (b. 1927)

Before Making Love

I move my hands over your face,
closing my eyes, as if blind;
the cheek bones, broadly spaced,
the wide thick nostrils of the African,
the forehead whose bones push
at both sides as if the horns
of fallen angels lie just under,
the chin that juts forward with pride.
I think of the delicate skull of the Taung child —
earliest of human beings
emerged from darkness — whose geometry
brings word of a small town of dignity
that all the bloody kingdoms rest on.

Toi Derricotte (b.1941)

[The Taung child is a fossil, a juvenile *Australopithecus africanus,* from Taung,
South Africa, two million years old.]

PATRICIA DONLON   222

Leabharlann Náisiúnta na hÉireann
(National Library of Ireland)
Sr Chilldara
(Kildare Street)
Áth Cliath 2
(Dublin 2)
13 January 1992

Dear Nicola, Paula and Alice,
What a wonderful invitation issued on the first of January – and
what an impossible request! My favourite poem changes, with the
seasons, with time and above all, with the mood of the moment.
Right now, my favourite poem reflects the new year and the
aspirations and ambitions I cherish as I face into it. It is 'Invocation'
by Louis MacNeice:

Invocation

> Dolphin plunge, fountain play.
> Fetch me far and far away.

Fetch me far my nursery toys,
Fetch me far my mother's hand,
Fetch me far the painted joys.

And when the painted cock shall crow
Fetch me far my waking day
That I may dance before I go.

Fetch me far the breeze in the heat,
Fetch me far the curl of the wave,
Fetch me far the face in the street.
And when the other faces throng
Fetch me far a place in the mind
Where only truthful things belong.

Fetch me far a moon in a tree,
Fetch me far a phrase of the wind,
Fetch me far the verb To Be.

And when the last horn burns the hills
Fetch me far one draught of grace
To quench my thirst before it kills.

> Dolphin plunge, fountain play.
> Fetch me far and far away.

To me, this is everything a poem should be — full of mystery, magic and music. I am not at all sure that I understand what it means, but I love the beauty of sounds and the images — 'fetch me far the verb To Be' will be my catch cry in 1992 — provided it is to a 'place in the mind/Where only truthful things belong'.
Thank you for asking me and good luck with Lifelines IV.

Yours sincerely,
Pat Donlon
(Dr Patricia Donlon, Director)

MIROSLAV HOLUB   223

Praha
Československo
9 January 1992

Dear Nicola Hughes,
Dear Paula Griffin,
Dear Alice McEleney,

I am not sure that I read your letter correctly: should it be my *poem or any poem?*
I have chosen my own poem for the only reason that I must give my own poems more thought and that I must spend much more time with them. The poem 'Masterpiece' was published in the London Poetry Review *last Fall. And here is my comment.*
Among my own poems I like this one this year: it was written recently and therefore belongs to my actual self. It is childish enough to be a real poem and, which is most important, is not that gloomy as most poems written today anywhere.
Best wishes to your project,

Yours,
Miroslav Holub

Masterpiece

The only masterpiece
I ever created
was a picture of the moth Thysania agrippina
in pastel on grey paper.

Because I was never
much good at painting. The essence of art
is that we aren't very good at it.

The moth Thysania agrippina
rose from the stiff grey paper
with outstretched, comb-like antennae,

with a plush bottom resembling the buttocks
of the pigwidgeons of Hieronymus Bosch,
with thin legs on a shrunken chest
like those on Breughel's grotesque figures
in 'Dulle Griet', it turned into Dulle Griet
with a bundle of pots and pans in her bony hand,

it turned into Bodhiddharma
with long sleeves,

it was Ying or Shade
and Yang or Light, Chwei or Darkness
and Ming or Glow, it had
the black colour of water, the ochre colour of earth,
the blue colour of wood.

I was as proud of it as an Antwerp councillor,
or the Tenth Patriarch from the Yellow River,

I sprinkled it with shellac, which is
the oath that painters swear on Goethe's Science of Colours,

and then the art teacher took it to his study

and I forgot all about it
the way Granny used to forget
her dentures in a glass.

Miroslav Holub (b. 1923).
(Translated by Dana Hábová and David Young)

[When Miroslav Holub read *Lifelines IV* he felt that he had misunderstood the request and was uneasy about having submitted one of his own poems. He asked if the following letter and choice might also be included in this, the *Collected* Edition.]

Dear Paula, Nicola and Alice,
The term 'favourite poem' is very plastic, almost like the sea-god Proteus. The answer, for me, depends even on the nature of the person who asked.
For three beautiful girls, I would rather pick something very manly, like something from Ted Hughes or Galway Kinnell.
But, realising I have to answer as a Czech among Irish and English people, Vladimir Holan occurs to me, and this poem which was so close to our Poetry of Everyday that it reads like something deeply related, something I would wish to have written.

Miroslav Holub

Resurrection

Is it true that after this life of ours we shall one day be
  awakened
by a terrifying clamour of trumpets?
Forgive me, God, but I console myself
that the beginning and resurrection of all of us dead
will simply be announced by the crowing of the cock.

After that we'll remain lying down a while . . .
The first to get up
will be Mother . . . We'll hear her
quietly laying the fire,
quietly putting the kettle on the stove
and cosily taking the teapot out of the cupboard.
We'll be home once more.

Vladimir Holan (1905–1980)
(Translated by George Theiner)

Notes on the contributors *(in alphabetical order)*

Fleur Adcock (p 80)
Poet (*Selected Poems; The Incident Book; Time Zones*), translator, critic and anthologist.

Darina Allen (p 236)
Cookery expert and teacher. Author of the *Simply Delicious* series and presenter of the *Simply Delicious* cookery programmes on RTE television.

Sir Kingsley Amis (p 178)
Novelist (*Lucky Jim; The Old Devils*), poet (*Bright November*), anthologist and author of autobiographical and critical works.

Martin Amis (p 264)
Novelist (*Money; Time's Arrow*) and essayist (*The Moronic Inferno; Einstein's Monsters*).

Lord Jeffrey Archer (p 118)
Novelist (*Kane and Abel; As the Crow Flies*) and politician.

Simon Armitage (p 231)
Poet (*Zoom!; Kid*).

Margaret Atwood (p 157)
Canadian novelist (*The Handmaid's Tale; Cat's Eye*), short story writer and poet (*True Stories; Interlunar*).

Robert Ballagh (p 86)
Artist, designer and photographer.

Mary Banotti, MEP (p 174)
Politician. Member of European Parliament.

John Banville (p 31)
Novelist (*Kepler; The Book of Evidence*) and literary editor of *The Irish Times*.

Lynn Barber (p 223)
Journalist with *The Independent* and *The Independent on Sunday* (London) and author of *Mostly Men*.

Julian Barnes (p 242)
Novelist (*Flaubert's Parrot; A History of the World in 10½ Chapters; Talking It Over*).

Gerald Barry (p 302)
Composer (work includes opera: *The Intelligence Park*).

Sebastian Barry (p 221)
Poet (*The Rhetorical Town*), novelist (*The Engine of Owl-Light*), and playwright (*Boss Grady's Boys; Prayers of Sherkin*).

John Bayley (p 211)
Scholar, critic, author and Professor Emeritus at Oxford (*Tolstoy and the Novel; The Romantic Survival: A Study in Poetic Evolution*).

Mary Beckett (p 229)
Novelist (*Give Them Stones*) and short story writer (*A Literary Woman*).

Emmet Bergin (p 36)
Actor. Parts include Dick Moran in *Glenroe* on RTE television.

Sara Berkeley (p 81)
~~Poet (*Penn; Home Movie Nights*) and short story writer~~ (*The Swimmer in the Deep
Blue Dream*).

Pauline Bewick (p 14)
Artist, illustrator (*Irish Tales and Sagas*), designer and author (*An Artist's Year*).

Maeve Binchy (p 114)
Novelist (*Light a Penny Candle; Firefly Summer; The Copper Beech*), playwright,
journalist, critic and columnist with *The Irish Times*.

Kenneth Blackmore (p 147)
Headmaster, Wesley College, Dublin.

Michael Blumenthal (p 297)
American poet (*Days We Would Rather Know; Laps*) and Briggs-Copeland
Assistant Professor at Harvard University.

Eavan Boland (p 3)
Poet (*Night Feed; Outside History*) and critic.

Ken Bourke (p 158)
Playwright (*Wild Harvest*).

Clare Boylan (p 141)
Novelist (*Black Baby; Home Rule*) and journalist.

Alicia Boyle (p 159)
Artist.

Kenneth Branagh (p 243)
Actor and director. Played Henry V on stage at the RSC and on screen. A
director of The Renaissance Theatre Company.

Richard Branson (p 138)
Businessman. Chairperson of Virgin Group.

Séamus Brennan, TD (p 186)
Minister in Irish Government.

Noël Browne (p 225)
Former Minister of Health and author (*Against the Tide*).

Helen Lucy Burke (p 53)
Journalist, novelist (*Close Connections*) and short story writer (*A Season for
Mothers*).

Barbara Bush (p 204)
America's First Lady.

A S Byatt, CBE (p 167)
Novelist (*The Virgin in the Garden; Possession*), broadcaster and critic (*Unruly
Times: Wordsworth and Coleridge in Their Time*).

Gay Byrne (p 78)
Broadcaster. Presenter of *The Late, Late Show* on RTE television — the longest
running talk show in the history of television. Author of *The Time of My Life*.

Ollie Campbell (p 47)
Rugby player.

Noelle Campbell-Sharp (p 46)
Publisher.

Bunny Carr (p 16)
Chairman of Carr Communications Ltd.

Amy Clampitt (p 180)
American poet (*The Kingfisher; Westward*).

Anthony Clare (p 219)
Psychiatrist, broadcaster, author and presenter of *In the Psychiatrist's Chair* on BBC Radio 4.

Adam Clayton (p 172)
Musician. Member of U2.

Don Cockburn (p 63)
Newscaster on RTE television.

Shane Connaughton (p 224)
Novelist (*A Border Station*) and writer of screenplays.

Jilly Cooper (p 226)
Novelist (*Rivals* and *Polo*) and journalist.

Elizabeth Cope (p 166)
Artist.

Wendy Cope (p 260)
Poet (*Making Cocoa for Kingsley Amis; Serious Concerns*).

Anthony Cronin (p 248)
Poet (*The End of the Modern World*) and scholar (*No Laughing Matter: The Life and Times of Flann O'Brien*). Chairman and founder of Aosdána.

William Crozier (p 234)
Artist.

Dorothy Cross (p 219)
Artist, sculptor and photographer.

Cyril Cusack (p 56)
Actor, playwright, poet (*Between the Acts*) and author of autobiographical and critical works.

Niamh Cusack (p 210)
Actor. Has played Desdemona at the RSC and recent film work includes *The Playboys*.

Cardinal Cahal Daly (p 301)
Cardinal Archbishop of Armagh and church leader.

Ita Daly (p 94)
Novelist (*A Singular Attraction; Dangerous Fictions*), short story writer (*The Lady with Red Shoes*) and reviewer.

Derek Davis (p 59)
Journalist, broadcaster and presenter of *Live at Three* on RTE television.

Treasa Davison (p 4)
Broadcaster, producer and presenter of *Playback* on RTE Radio 1.

Seamus Deane (p 278)
Poet (*History Lessons*), novelist (*Reading in the Dark*), author (*A Short History of Irish Literature*) and Professor of Modern English and American literature at University College Dublin.

Greg Delanty (p 198)
Poet (*Cast in the Fire; Southward*).

Dame Judi Dench (p 140)
Actor. Acclaimed roles include Cleopatra in *Antony and Cleopatra* at the National Theatre, London, and Mistress Quickly in the film *Henry V*.

Thomas Docherty (p 247)
Academic, author (*John Donne, Undone*) and Professor of Modern English at Trinity College Dublin.

Patricia Donlon (p 305)
Director of the National Library of Ireland. Author.

Theo Dorgan (p 232)
Poet (*The Ordinary House of Love*), broadcaster and director of Poetry Ireland.

Anne Doyle (p 122)
Newscaster on RTE television.

Maria Doyle (p 91)
Singer and actor. Featured in the film *The Commitments*.

Margaret Drabble, CBE (p 49)
Novelist (*The Millstone; The Radiant Way*), biographer (*Arnold Bennett*), lecturer, critic and editor of *The Oxford Companion to English Literature*.

Alan Dukes, TD (p 45)
Politician and former leader of Fine Gael.

Myles Dungan (p 25)
Broadcaster, author and presenter of *Today at Five* on RTE Radio 1.

Eileen Dunne (p 8)
Newscaster on RTE radio and television.

Paul Durcan (p 92)
Poet (*The Berlin Wall Café; Daddy Daddy; Crazy About Women*).

Archbishop Robin Eames (p 222)
Archbishop of Armagh and Primate of All Ireland.

Lauris Edmond (p 283)
New Zealand poet (*Summer Near the Arctic Circle; New and Selected Poems*) and autobiographer (*Hot October; Bonfires in the Rain; The Quick Life*).

Felim Egan (p 270)
Artist.

Ben Elton (p 271)
Comedian, playwright, novelist (*Stark; Gridlock*).

Peter Fallon (p 215)
Poet (*The First Affair; Winter Work*), editor and founder of The Gallery Press.

Brian Farrell (p 70)
Broadcaster, academic, author and Professor of Politics at University College Dublin.

Desmond Fennell (p 90)
Author (*Beyond Nationalism; Bloomsway*), journalist, broadcaster and lecturer in communications at the College of Commerce, Rathmines, Dublin.

Anne Fine (p 236)
Novelist primarily for teenagers (*Bill's New Frock; The Granny Project*).

Mr Justice Thomas A Finlay (p 119)
The Chief Justice.

Garrett FitzGerald (p 3)
Author (*Towards a New Ireland; All in a Life — autobiography*), politician, lecturer and academic. Former Taoiseach and leader of Fine Gael.

Mary FitzGerald (p 154)
Broadcaster with RTE.

Theodora FitzGibbon (deceased) (p 43)
Cookery expert and author.

T P Flanagan (p 50)
Artist.

Bob Gallico (p 5)
Radio broadcaster.

Sir John Gielgud (p 121)
Actor. Has played most major roles and recently played Prospero in the film *Prospero's Books*.

Ellen Gilchrist (p 136)
American novelist (*The Anna Papers; Net of Jewels*), short story writer (*Drunk with Love; I Cannot Get You Close Enough*), poet (*The Land Surveyor's Daughter*).

Larry Gogan (p 155)
Broadcaster on RTE 2FM.

Patrick Graham (p 153)
Artist.

Victor Griffin (p 82)
Church leader and retired Dean of St Patrick's Cathedral.

Hugo Hamilton (p 287)
Novelist (*Surrogate City; The Last Shot*).

Eithne Hand (p 77)
Producer with RTE.

Mary Harney, TD (p 244)
Minister in Irish government.

Charles Haughey (p 187)
Politician. Former Taoiseach and leader of Fianna Fáil.

Isabel Healy (p 23)
Journalist, broadcaster and columnist.

Seamus Heaney (p 71)
Poet (*Death of a Naturalist; Seeing Things*), critic (*Preoccupations; The Government of the Tongue*) and professor at Harvard and Oxford.

Margaret Heckler (p 108)
American politician and former Ambassador to Ireland.

Chaim Herzog (p 142)
President of Israel.

Tom Hickey (p 34)
Actor.

Rita Ann Higgins (p 156)
Poet (*Goddess on the Mervue Bus; Philomena's Revenge*).

Desmond Hogan (p 164)
Novelist (*The Leaves on Grey; A Curious Street*) and short story writer (*The Diamonds at the Bottom of the Sea*).

Alan Hollinghurst (p 262)
Journalist and novelist (*The Swimming Pool Library*).

Michael Holroyd (p 79)
Biographer (*Lytton Strachey; Augustus John; G B Shaw*).

Miroslav Holub (p 306)
Czechoslovakian poet (*Go and Open the Door; Totally Unsystematic Zoology*) and scientist (*The Dimension of the Present Moment*).

Patricia Hurl (p 196)
Artist.

Jeremy Irons (p 163)
Actor. Played Charles in the television adaptation of *Brideshead Revisited*. Recent film work includes *Damage*.

Glenda Jackson, MP (p 239)
Actor (*Stevie; A Touch of Class*) and Member of Parliament (Labour Party) representing Hampstead and Highgate.

Jennifer Johnston (p 95)
Novelist (*How Many Miles to Babylon; The Invisible Worm*) and playwright.

Rónán Johnston (p 106)
Musician.

John Kavanagh (p 39)
Actor.

John B Keane (p 128)
Playwright (*Big Maggie; The Field*) and novelist (*The Bodhrán Makers; Durango*).

Richard Kearney (p 113)
Philosopher, author (*The Wake of Imagination; Modern Movement in European Philosophy*) and Associate Professor of Philosophy at University College Dublin.

Sr Stanislaus Kennedy (p 131)
Social Worker and director of Focus Point.

Brendan Kennelly (p 20)
Poet (*Cromwell; The Book of Judas*) and Professor of English at Trinity College Dublin.

Pat Kenny (p 139)
Broadcaster on RTE radio and television.

Declan Kiberd (p 290)
Author (*Men and Feminism in Modern Literature*), broadcaster, critic and lecturer in English at University College Dublin.

Benedict Kiely (p 29)
Author, lecturer, broadcaster, novelist (*Proxopera; Nothing Happens in Carmincross*), short story writer (*A Journey to the Seven Streams*) and journalist.

Galway Kinnell (p 282)
American poet (*Mortal Acts, Mortal Words; When One Has Lived a Long Time Alone*) and winner of the Pulitzer Prize.

Thomas Kinsella (p 187)
Poet (*Downstream; Fifteen Poems from Centre City*), lecturer, translator (*The Táin*), visiting professor at Temple University in Philadelphia and founder of The Peppercanister Press.

Mick Lally (p 64)
Actor. Roles include Miley in *Glenroe* on RTE television.

Barry Lang (p 20)
Broadcaster/presenter on RTE 2FM.

Mary Lavin (p 130)
Short story writer (*Tales from Bective Bridge; A Family Likeness*) and novelist (*The House in Clewe Street*).

Sue Lawley (p 294)
Broadcaster and presenter of *Desert Island Discs* on BBC Radio 4.

David Leavitt (p 287)
American novelist (*Equal Affections*) and short story writer (*A Place I've Never Been*).

Louis Le Brocquy (p 230)
Artist.

Laurie Lee (p 88)
Writer (*Cider with Rosie; As I Walked Out One Midsummer Morning*) and poet (*The Bloom of Candles*).

Mary Leland (p 103)
Novelist (*The Killeen; Approaching Priests*) and journalist.

Brian Lenihan TD (p 212)
Fianna Fáil politician.

Hugh Leonard (p 15)
Playwright (*Da; A Life; Moving*), novelist (*Parnell and the Englishwoman*) and
journalist.

Doris Lessing (p 225)
Novelist (*The Grass is Singing; The Golden Notebook*) and short story writer.

Rosaleen Linehan (p 160)
Actor

David Lodge (p 184)
Novelist (*Nice Work; Paradise News*), critic (*The Novelist at the Crossroads*) and
Professor of English at the University of Birmingham.

Michael Longley (p 249)
Poet (*Man Lying on a Wall; Gorse Fires*).

Seán Lucy (p 60)
Poet (*Unfinished Sequence*), critic and retired Professor of English at University
College Cork.

Joe Lynch (p 149)
Actor. Parts include Dinny in RTE's *Glenroe*.

Ferdia MacAnna (p 230)
Broadcaster, writer (*Bald Head*), television producer and novelist (*The Last of the
High Kings*).

Joan McBreen (p 261)
Poet (*The Wind Beyond the Wall*).

Nell McCafferty (p 72)
Journalist, broadcaster and author (*The Best of Nell*).

Mr Justice Niall McCarthy (p 127)
Supreme Court Judge.

Thomas McCarthy (p 162)
Poet (*The Sorrow Garden; The Non-Aligned Storyteller*) and novelist (*Beyond
Power*).

Tom McCaughren (p 161)
Author (*Run with the Wind; Rainbows of the Moon*) and Security Correspondent
with RTE radio and television.

Margaret MacCurtain (Sr Benvenuta) (p 19)
Lecturer in Modern Irish History at University College Dublin and author
(*Tudor and Stuart Ireland*).

Mary McEvoy (p 37)
Actor. Parts include Biddy in RTE's *Glenroe*.

Michael McGlynn (p 272)
Composer (works include *The O'Malley Mass*) and director of An Uaithne.

Medbh McGuckian (p 162)
Poet (*The Flower Master; Marconi's Cottage*).

Frank McGuinness (p 77)
Playwright (*Observe the Sons of Ulster Marching towards the Somme; Someone Who'll Watch Over Me*).

Sir Ian McKellen (p 176)
Actor. Roles include Romeo and Macbeth at the RSC and Coriolanus at the National Theatre, London. Has performed his one man show *Acting Shakespeare* worldwide.

Bernard MacLaverty (p 24)
Novelist (*Cal; Lamb*) and short story writer (*The Great Profundo*).

Bryan MacMahon (p 194)
Educator and writer of plays, novels (*Children of the Rainbow*) and short stories (*The Lion Tamer; The Red Petticoat*).

Sean McMahon (p 245)
Author, reviewer and anthologist. Novels for teenagers include *The Three Seals*.

Flo McSweeney (p 17)
Singer and actor.

Jimmy Magee (p 10)
Broadcaster with the Sports Department, RTE.

Alice Maher (p 182)
Artist.

Derek Mahon (p 98)
Poet (*The Hunt by Night; Antarctica*), translator and anthologist.

Thelma Mansfield (p 116)
Broadcaster and presenter of *Live at Three* on RTE television.

Augustine Martin (p 11)
Scholar, critic and Professor of Anglo-Irish Literature at University College Dublin.

Maxi (p 105)
Broadcaster on RTE radio.

Paula Meehan (p 265)
Poet (*Return and No Blame; The Man who was Marked by Winter*).

Máire Mhac an tSaoi (p 117)
Poet (*Codladh an Ghaiscígh; An Cian go Dtí Seo*).

Sue Miller (p 137)
American novelist (*The Good Mother; Family Pictures*) and short story writer (*Inventing the Abbotts*).

John Montague (p 87)
Poet (*A Chosen Light; The Rough Field*), short story writer (*Death of a Chieftain*), visiting professor in America.

Mary Mooney (p 114)
Politician.

Christy Moore (p 239)
~~Singer and songwriter.~~

Brian Moore (p 167)
Novelist (*The Lonely Passion of Judith Hearne; Lies of Silence*).

Andrew Motion (p 12)
Poet (*The Pleasure Steamers; Love in a Life*), novelist (*Pale Companions*), critic and biographer.

Dame Iris Murdoch (p 32)
Novelist (*The Sea, The Sea; The Book and the Brotherhood*), playwright (*The Servants and the Snow*) and philosopher (*The Sovereignty of Good; Metaphysics as a Guide to Morals*).

Mike Murphy (p 143)
Broadcaster on RTE radio and television. Presenter of *The Arts Show* on Radio 1.

Richard Murphy (p 252)
Poet (*High Island; The Price of Stone*) and visiting professor in America.

Tom Murphy (p 123)
Playwright (*Conversations on a Homecoming; The Gigli Concert*).

Kevin Myers (p 125)
Journalist with *The Irish Times*.

Doireann Ní Bhriain (p 132)
Broadcaster and producer with RTE.

Eiléan Ní Chuilleanáin (p 124)
Poet (*Acts and Monuments; The Magdalene Sermon*) and lecturer in English at Trinity College Dublin.

Nuala Ní Dhomhnaill (p 144)
Poet (*An Dealg Droighin; Selected Poems/Rogha Dánta*).

David Norris (p 84)
Senator, Joycean scholar and lecturer in English at Trinity College Dublin.

Conor Cruise O'Brien (p 254)
Politician, academic, lecturer, journalist and author (*States of Ireland; God Land: Reflections on Religion and Nationalism*).

Julie O'Callaghan (p 6)
Poet (*Edible Anecdotes; What's What*).

Eilís O'Connell (p 197)
Artist and sculptor.

Joseph O'Connor (p 233)
Novelist (*Cowboys and Indians*) and short story writer (*True Believers*).

Ulick O'Connor (p 7)
Writer and critic (*Celtic Dawn: A Portrait of Irish Literary Renaissance; A Terrible Beauty is Born: the Irish Troubles 1912–1922*)

Mary O'Donnell (p 273)
Poet (*Reading the Sunflowers in September*), short story writer (*Strong Pagans*) and novelist (*The Lightmakers*).

Dennis O'Driscoll (p 89)
Poet (*Kist; Hidden Extras*).

Cardinal Tomás Ó Fiaich (deceased) (p 51)
Cardinal Archbishop of Armagh and church leader.

Emer O'Kelly (p 28)
Newscaster with RTE radio and television, journalist and short story writer.

Sharon Olds (p 302)
American poet (*The Gold Cell; The Father*) and teacher of poetry workshops at New York University, Columbia University and Goldwater Hospital on Roosevelt Island in New York.

Michael O'Loughlin (p 208)
Poet (*Atlantic Blues; The Diary of a Silence*), short story writer (*The Inside Story*) and translator.

Andy O'Mahony (p 183)
Broadcaster on RTE Radio 1. Presenter of *Dialogue* and *The Sunday Show*.

Tony O'Malley (p 68)
Artist.

Liam Ó Murchú (p 49)
Broadcaster on RTE radio and television.

Joseph O'Neill (p 285)
Novelist (*This is the Life*).

Hilary Orpen (p 21)
Producer with RTE.

Micheal O'Siadhail (p 221)
Poet (*Springnight; The Image Wheel; The Chosen Garden*).

Fintan O'Toole (p 109)
Journalist, critic, broadcaster and author (*No More Heroes: A Radical Guide to Shakespeare; A Mass for Jesse James*).

Lord David Owen (p 169)
Politician. Founder of the SDP.

Geraldine Plunkett (p 13)
Actor. Parts include Mary in RTE's *Glenroe*.

James Plunkett (p 170)
Novelist (*Strumpet City; Farewell Companions*) and short story writer (*The Trusting and the Maimed*).

Maureen Potter (p 36)
Comédienne, actor and author (*Theatre Cat*).

Kathy Prendergast (p 85)
Artist and sculptor.

Sir V S Pritchett (p 228)
Novelist (*Clare Drummer*), critic, short story writer (*When My Girl Comes Home; The Camberwell Beauty*).

Deirdre Purcell (p 191)
Novelist (*A Place of Stones; That Childhood Country*) and journalist.

Marian Richardson (p 112)
Broadcaster and reporter with RTE.

Christopher Ricks (p 240)
Scholar and author (*Milton's Grand Style*) and Professor of English at Boston University.

Vivienne Roche (p 277)
Sculptor and artist.

Neil Rudenstine (p 275)
Scholar, academic and President of Harvard University, Cambridge, Massachusetts.

Patricia Scanlan (p 238)
Novelist (*Apartment 3B; Finishing Touches*).

Anna Scher (p 220)
Founder and director of The Anna Scher Theatre and author (— with Charles Verrall — *100 + Ideas for Drama*).

Fiona Shaw (p 172)
Actor. Stage roles include Katharine in *The Taming of the Shrew* and Hedda Gabler. Film work includes *My Left Foot*.

Antony Sher (p 153)
Actor, author (*The Year of the King*) and novelist (*Middlepost; The Indoor Boy*).

James Simmons (p 280)
Poet (*The Long Summer Still to Come; Poems 1956–1986*).

Archbishop George Otto Simms (deceased) (p 8)
Church leader and scholar.

Maria Simonds-Gooding (p 135)
Artist.

Ailbhe Smyth (p 227)
Director of WERRC, Women's Education Research and Resource Centre, University College Dublin; academic and broadcaster.

Camille Souter (p 181)
Artist.

Michele Souter (p 269)
Artist.

Alan Stanford (p 96)
Actor. Parts include George in RTE's *Glenroe*. Appears regularly at the Gate Theatre, Dublin.

Amelia Stein (p 250)
Photographer

Francis Stuart (p 192)
Novelist (*Black List, Section H; Memorial*) and poet (*We Have Kept the Faith*).

Alice Taylor (p 165)
Author (*To School Through the Fields; Quench the Lamp; The Village*).

Mother Teresa (p 214)
Missionary nun dedicated to serving the poor, the sick and the lonely. Founder of the Missionaries of Charity in Calcutta.

Sue Townsend (p 213)
Playwright, novelist and creator of Adrian Mole.

William Trevor (p 200)
Short story writer (*The Ballroom of Romance*) and novelist (*Fools of Fortune*).

Gerrit van Gelderen (p 40)
Film-maker and artist.

Helen Vendler (p 206)
Scholar, critic, Harvard University professor, writer (*Part of Nature, Part of Us; The Music of What Happens*) and editor of *The Harvard Book of Contemporary American Poetry*.

Michael Viney (p 198)
Naturalist, artist, author and columnist with *The Irish Times*.

Martin Waddell (p 268)
Writer for young people (*Tales from the Shop that Never Shuts*). Also writes under the name Catherine Sefton (*In a Blue Velvet Dress; The Ghost Girl*).

Kathleen Watkins (p 102)
Broadcaster. Presenter of *Faces and Places* on RTE television.

Padraic White (p 133)
Businessman.

Macdara Woods (p 193)
Poet (*Stopping the Lights in Ranelagh; The Hanged Man was not Surrendering*).

Index of poets and their works

Anonymous   *page*
'Appolinaire said....'   164
Desiderata   9
Hail Mary   216
Pallid the Sun   182
Psalm 121   223
The Book of Ecclesiastes (an excerpt)   4
The Lover Compareth Himself To The Painful Falconer   116
The Monk and His Pet Cat   52

Muireadhach Albanach
M'anam Do Sgar Riomsa A-raoir (translation p 292)   291

Matthew Arnold (1822–1888)
Dover Beach   274
The Forsaken Merman   294

John Ashbery (b. 1927)
Crazy Weather   247

W H Auden (1907–1973)
A Summer Night   32
Petition   136
The More Loving One   232

Leland Bardwell (b. 1928)
Without Touching   196

George Barker (1913–1991)
Summer Song I   237

Samuel Beckett (1906–1989)
Gnome   153
'my way is in the sand flowing....'   225

Hilaire Belloc (1870–1953)
Tarantella   191
The Death and Last Confession of Wandering Peter   120

John Betjeman (1906–1984)
A Subaltern's Love-Song   37
Business Girls   140

Elizabeth Bishop (1911–1979)
The Moose   98

William Blake (1757–1827)
Epilogue from For the Sexes the Gates of Paradise   192
Never Seek to Tell Thy Love   50
Songs of Experience (Introduction) — an excerpt   264
Songs of Innocence (Introduction)   166
The Garden of Love   21
The Mental Traveller   53

N M Bodecker
Snowman Sniffles   154

Eavan Boland (b. 1944)
Child of Our Time 19
The Journey 266

Bertolt Brecht (1898–1956)
Coal for Mike 156

Emily Brontë (1818–1848)
No Coward Soul is Mine 163

Rupert Brooke (1887–1915)
The Old Vicarage, Grantchester — an excerpt 15

Robert Browning (1812–1889)
A Toccata of Galuppi's 280

Charles Bukowski (b. 1920)
Rock 172

Bunny Carr
'I carved my name upon the Instant tree....' 17

Lewis Carroll (1832–1898)
Jabberwocky 180

Raymond Carver (1938–1988)
Happiness 233
Through the Boughs 287

C P Cavafy (1863–1933)
Candles (translated by Rae Dalven) 170
Ithaca (translated by Rae Dalven) 284

Paul Celan (1920–1970)
Psalm (translation p32 by Michael Hamburger) 31

G K Chesterton (1874–1936)
The Ballad of the White Horse 117

Austin Clarke (1896–1974)
The Envy of Poor Lovers 261
The Planter's Daughter 38

Arthur Hugh Clough (1819–1861)
Amours de Voyage — an excerpt 228
Say Not the Struggle Naught Availeth 83

Samuel Taylor Coleridge (1772–1834)
The Ancient Mariner — an excerpt 226

Padraic Colum (1881–1972)
A Drover 23

Evelyn Conlon (b. 1952)
Hens 72

John Cooper Clarke (b. 1948)
valley of the lost women 18

William (Johnson) Cory (1823–1892)
'They told me, Heraclitus, they told me you were dead....'   8

George Crabbe (1754–1832)
The Parish Register — an excerpt   60

Hart Crane (1899–1932)
Voyages (II)   249

e e cummings (1894–1962)
maggie and milly and molly and may   86

Cyril Cusack (b. 1910)
Confiteor   59

Michael Davitt (b. 1950)
An Scáthán (translation p289 by Paul Muldoon)   288

Walter de la Mare (1873–1956)
The Listeners   149

Toi Derricotte (b. 1941)
Before Making Love   304

Emily Dickinson (1830–1886)
How Happy is the Little Stone   22
'I stepped from Plank to Plank....'   160
'The Bustle in a House....'   142

John Donne (1572–1631)
Death Be Not Proud   81

Paul Durcan (b. 1944)
Martha's Wall   176
The Man with Five Penises   251

T S Eliot (1888–1965)
Ash Wednesday — an excerpt   229
The Love Song of J Alfred Prufrock   187

Paul Eluard (1895–1952)
Liberté — an excerpt (translation p235)   234

D J Enright (b. 1920)
Biography   80

Sergei Essenin
My Teper' Ukhodom Ponemnogu   164

Padraic Fallon (1905–1974)
Book of Job   69

James Farrar (d. 1944)
After Night Offensive   181

Carolyn Forché (b. 1950)
The Colonel   199

Percy French (1854–1920)
The End of the Holiday   20

Robert Frost (1874–1963)
Stopping By Woods On A Snowy Evening 88
The Road Not Taken 78

Patrick Galvin (b. 1927)
Prisoners of the Tower 61

Ellen Gilchrist (b. 1935)
Shut Up, I'm Going To Sing You A Love Song 93

Oliver Goldsmith (?1730–1774)
The Deserted Village — an excerpt 10

Robert Graves (1895–1985)
A Slice of Wedding Cake 238

W S Graham (1918–1986)
The Alligator Girls 6

Thomas Gray (1716–1771)
Elegy Written in a Country Churchyard — an excerpt 144

Thom Gunn (b. 1929)
Night Taxi 262

Anne Haverty
Whenever I Think of Francis 248

Seamus Heaney (b. 1939)
Bogland 50
Follower 39
From the Republic of Conscience 175
Mother of the Groom 28
Poem 197
Sonnet 3 from 'Clearances' 103
Sonnet 8 from 'Clearances' 271
The Forge 133
The Otter 14

Robert Herrick (1591–1674)
Upon Julia's Clothes 3

F R Higgins (1896–1941)
Pádraic O Conaire, Gaelic Storyteller 195

Ralph Hodgson
Stupidity Street 161

Vladimir Holan (1905–1980)
Resurrection (translation by George Theiner) 308

Miroslav Holub (b. 1923)
Fairy Tale 96
Masterpiece 306

Gerard Manley Hopkins (1844–1889)
Felix Randal 58
Pied Beauty 220
The Leaden Echo and The Golden Echo 177

A E Housman (1859–1936)
Additional Poems IV   261
Bredon Hill   121
Tell Me Not Here, It Needs Not Saying   179
XII   242

Ted Hughes (b. 1930)
An Otter   138
Lineage   277

Pat Ingoldsby
For Rita With Love   105
Up and Down the Strip   106

Patrick Kavanagh (1904–1967)
A Christmas Childhood   57
Epic   123
Free Soul   165
In Memory of My Mother   171
On Raglan Road   159
Stony Grey Soil   245
Street Corner Christ   132
from Tarry Flynn   268

John Keats (1795–1821)
To Autumn   276

Brendan Kennelly (b. 1936)
A Man I Knew   134
Mary — an excerpt   84
Water   129

Galway Kinnell (b.1927)
Oatmeal   303

Rudyard Kipling (1865–1936)
The Gods of the Copybook Headings   126
The Thousandth Man   118

Philip Larkin (1922–1985)
An Arundel Tomb   104
The Old Fools   137

Mary Lavin (b. 1912)
Christ If You Wanted My Shining Soul   131

Seán Lysaght (b. 1957)
Cuckoo   239

Patrick MacDonogh (1902–1961)
Be Still as You are Beautiful   49

Liam MacGabhann
Connolly   155

Roger McGough (b. 1937)
Motorway   27
Sad Aunt Madge   27

Tom MacIntyre
The Yellow Bittern   35

Louis MacNeice (1907–1963)
Entirely   22
Invocation   305
June Thunder   46
Les Sylphides   160
Snow   183
The Introduction   25

Derek Mahon (b. 1941)
A Disused Shed in Co. Wexford   278
Antarctica   147

Osip Mandelstam (1891–1938)
'What shall I do with the body that has been given me....' 233

James Clarence Mangan (1803–1849)
'What is Love? I asked a lover....'   302

Andrew Marvell (1621–1678)
The Garden   169
To His Coy Mistress   94

Máire Mhac an tSaoi (b. 1922)
Finit   90

Paula Meehan (b. 1955)
Buying Winkles   231

John Milton (1608–1674)
On the Morning of Christ's Nativity   254

Adrian Mitchell (b. 1932)
Back in the Playground Blues   115

Thomas Moore (1779–1852)
As Slow Our Ship   47

Paul Muldoon (b. 1951)
Immram — an excerpt   86

Howard Nemerov (1920–1991)
The Painter Dreaming in the Scholar's House   298

Pablo Neruda (1904–1973)
I'm Explaining a Few Things   110

Nuala Ní Dhomhnaill (b. 1952)
Fáilte Bhéal na Sionna Don Iasc (translation p113)   112

Pastor Niemoeller
'First they came for the Jews ....'   213

Frank O'Connor (1903–1966)
The Drowning of Conaing   11

Frank O'Hara (1926–1966)
A Step Away from Them   285

Sharon Olds (b. 1942)
The Ferryer   282

Seán Ó Ríordáin (1916–1977)
Saoirse (translation p66)   65

P K (Patricia Kathleen) Page (b. 1916)
The Snowman   157

Boris Pasternak (1890–1960)
Bread (a translation by Michael Harari)   252

William Philbin
Poor Clare Christmas   301

Sylvia Plath (1932–1963)
Contusion   220
Edge   13
The Arrival of the Bee Box   145

Jacques Prévert (1900–1977)
Barbara — an excerpt   42
Paris at Night   9

Aleksandr Pushkin (1799–1837)
Ruslan and Lyudmila (prologue)   211

Kenneth Rexroth (1905–1982)
Blues   199

Arthur Rimbaud (1854–1891)
Aube (translation p273)   272

Edwin Arlington Robinson (1869–1935)
Mr Flood's Party   29

Amanda Ros (1860–1939)
Jamie Jarr   79

Saint Francis of Assisi
Prayer for Peace   214

William Shakespeare (1564–1616)
Fear No More The Heat O' The Sun   243
'How sweet the moonlight sleeps upon this bank!....'   36
Sonnet 29   153
Sonnet 109   77
Sonnet 94   221

Percy Bysshe Shelley (1792–1822)
Ozymandias   224

James Shirley (1596–1666)
Dirge   83

Stevie Smith (1902–1971)
Not Waving But Drowning   82

Stephen Spender (b. 1909)
'I think continually of those who were truly great...' 130

Wallace Stevens (1879–1955)
The Auroras of Autumn — an excerpt 207

Eithne Strong
Identity 227

Algernon Charles Swinburne (1837–1909)
'As one that ere a June day rise....' 64

John Millington Synge (1871–1909)
Patch-Shaneen 4

Bert Leston Taylor
Treasure Island 5

Alfred, Lord Tennyson (1809–1892)
The Lady of Shalott 200
To E FitzGerald 240

Dylan Thomas (1914–1953)
Fern Hill 97
Poem in October 44
Schoolmaster 148

Edward Thomas (1878–1917)
Adlestrop 141

E Jarvis Thribb
'So Farewell....' 26

Chidioch Tichborne (1558–1586)
Tichborne's Elegy 89

César Vallejo (1892–1938)
XII Masa (translation p209 by Ed Dorn) 209

Helen Waddell (1889–1965)
I Shall Not Go To Heaven 246

Oscar Wilde (1854–1900)
The Ballad of Reading Gaol — an excerpt 270
The Harlot's House 91

Macdara Woods (b. 1942)
Houserules 125

William Wordsworth (1770–1850)
I wandered lonely as a cloud 48
Ode — Intimations of Immortality (an excerpt) 205
The Prelude — an excerpt 136

James Wright (1927–1980)
Saint Judas 222

Thomas Wyatt (1503–1542)
They Flee from Me 12

W B Yeats (1865–1939)
Among School Children   184
Cuchulain Comforted   71
Down by the Salley Gardens   124
In Memory of Eva Gore-Booth and Con Markiewicz   128
Leda and the Swan   7
Memory   225
Sailing to Byzantium   87
The Lake Isle of Innisfree   143
The Second Coming   174
The Song of Wandering Aengus   173
The Stolen Child   40
When You Are Old   219

Index of first lines

	page
A man that had six mortal wounds, a man	71
— And yet this great wink of eternity	249
A sudden blow: the great wings beating still	7
Al fin de la batalla	209
All I know is a door into the dark	133
All things have their season, and in their times	4
Ancient nomadic snowman has rolled round	157
And then the dark fell and 'there has never'	266
Appolinaire said	164
Are you to tell me where my soul is cast	6
As I pass through my incarnations in every age and race	126
As one that ere a June day rise	64
As slow our ship her foamy track	47
As the cold winter evenings drew near	27
At the end of the battle	209
At winter's end	154
Be still as you are beautiful	49
Before the gods that made the gods	117
Beside yon straggling fence that skirts the way	10
Beyond the shadow of the ship	226
By the shores of a bay there is a green oak-tree	212
Christ if you wanted my shining soul	131
Chuckling in gutters	129
Colour floods to the spot, dull purple	220
Come, dear children, let us away	294
Comes little lady, a book in hand	5
Dear Eustatio, I write that you may write me an answer	228
Death be not proud, though some have called thee	81
Do you remember an Inn	191
Dolphin plunge, fountain play	305
Down below the window, on the deck, some ragged-looking	287
Down by the salley gardens my love and I did meet	124
Even now there are places where a thought might grow —	278
Farewell to an idea . . . A cabin stands	207
Fear no more the heat o' the sun	243
Felix Randal the farrier, O he is dead then? my duty all ended	58
First they came for the Jews	213
Fold up the box, the wind is chill	20
From narrow provinces	98

From the geyser ventilators   140
Glory be to God for dappled things   220
Glowed through the violet petal of the sky   181
Go placidly amid the noise and haste   9
God! I will pack, and take a train   15
Had we but World enough, and Time   94
Hail Mary, full of grace   216
He built himself a house   96
He was no longer my father   289
Hear the voice of the Bard   264
Her pleasure — what gave her pleasure — was to be walked   176
Here lies a blooming rascal   79
Here were all these males tuning their guitars   172
Hoop-la said my working wife   125
How happy is the little Stone   22
How she lay with her true love in bed without touching   196
How sweet the moonlight sleeps upon this bank   36
How to kéep — is there ány any, is there none such, nowhere   177
How vainly men themselves amaze   168
'I am just going outside and may be some time'   147
I and my white Pangur   52
I can see them now   61
I carved my name upon the Instant tree   17
I do not think of you lying in the wet clay   171
I dream to save you   93
I dreamed I was back in the playground   115
I eat oatmeal for breakfast   303
I have heard that in Ohio   156
I have held the summer dawn in my arms   273
I have lived in important places, times   123
I know not whether Laws be right   270
I looked into my heart to write   237
I met a traveller from an antique land   224
I move my hands over your face   304
I ordered this, this clean wood box   145
I saw Christ today   132
I saw with open eyes   161
I shall not go to Heaven when I die   246
I stepped from Plank to Plank   160
I think continually of those who were truly great   130
I thought of walking round and round a space   271
I traveld thro' a Land of Men   53

I walk through the long schoolroom questioning 184
I wandered lonely as a cloud 48
I went out to the hazel wood 173
I went to the Garden of Love 21
I will arise and go now, and go to Innisfree 143
I will go down amongst the people 66
I will lift up mine eyes unto the hills 223
I'm a hen 73
If we could get the hang of it entirely 22
In summertime on Bredon 121
In the beginning was Scream 277
Is it true that after this life of ours we shall one day be awakened 308
'Is there anybody there?' said the Traveller 149
It is no gift I tender 261
It was my thirtieth year to heaven 44
It's my lunch hour, so I go 285
It's the tingle between your legs 106
It's this crazy weather we've been having 247
'I want no easy grave' he said to me 134
Lady, three white leopards sat under a juniper-tree 229
Le seans a chuala uathu scéala an chleamhnais 90
Léim an bhradáin 112
Let us go then, you and I 187
Life in a day: he took his girl to the ballet 160
Looking up at the stars, I know quite well 232
Lord, make me a channel of Thy peace 214
Love, I shall perfect for you the child 197
M'anam do sgar riomsa a-raoir 291
maggie and milly and molly and may 86
Miss J Hunter Dunn, Miss J Hunter Dunn 37
My father was a man with five penises 251
My father worked with a horse-plough 39
My mother had just been fed by force 86
My mother would spare me sixpence and say 231
My prime of youth is but a frost of cares 89
My soul parted from me last night; a pure body that was dear 292
my way is in the sand flowing 225
Never seek to tell thy love 50
Next died the Widow Goe, an active dame 60
Niemand knetet uns wieder aus Erde und Lehm 31
Níorbh é m'athair níos mó é 288
No coward soul is mine 163

No one moulds us again out of earth and clay   32
Nobody heard him, the dead man   82
Now as I was young and easy under the apple boughs   97
O dear my Lord, but what a tricky   59
O stony grey soil of Monaghan   245
O, never say that I was false of heart   77
Oh yes, yes, I remember him well   148
Oh, Galuppi, Baldassaro, this is very sad to find   280
Old Eben Flood, climbing alone one night   29
Old Fitz, who from your suburb grange   240
On an apple-ripe September morning   268
On either side the river lie   200
On Raglan Road on an autumn day I met her first and knew   159
On the threshold of my door   235
One by one we gradually are leaving   164
One had a lovely face   71
One man in a thousand, Solomon says   118
One side of the potato-pits was white with frost   57
One-eyed Spring gone wrong and a rather   227
Open city   262
Out on the lawn I lie in bed   32
Pallid the Sun   182
Piping down the valleys wild   166
Pity poor lovers who may not do what they please   261
Raghaidh mé síos i measc na ndaoine   65
Rappelle-toi Barbara   42
Rest in one piece, old fellow   80
Say not, the struggle naught availeth   83
Scarcer now   239
Season of mist and mellow fruitfulness   276
Shaneen and Maurya Prendergast   4
Sickens my gut. Yellow Bittern   35
Side by side, their faces blurred   104
Sir, no man's enemy, forgiving all   136
So early it's still almost dark out   233
So Farewell   26
Spend the years of learning squandering   153
Sur le tremplin de ma porte   234
Tell me not here, it needs not saying   179
That is no country for old men.   87
The Bustle in a House   142
The curfew tolls the knell of parting day   144

The days of our future stand before us 170
The glories of our blood and state 83
The Junes were free and full, driving through tiny 46
The laws of God, the laws of man 242
The leap of the salmon 113
The light of evening, Lissadell 128
The man was all shot through that came today 155
The only masterpiece 306
The painter's eye follows relation out 298
The politicians 27
The room was suddenly rich and the great bay-window was 183
The sea is calm tonight 274
The shining waters rise and swell 11
The simple thing is to die 69
The soaring hawk from fist that flies 116
The three Marys took three husbands 84
The tops of the higher peaks 199
The woman is perfected 13
the windows are frigidaire icebergs 18
Their eyes are quiet waters; they move, speak 301
There was a time when meadow, grove, and stream 205
They flee from me, that sometime did me seke 12
They that have power to hurt and will do none 221
They told me, Heraclitus, they told me you were dead 8
They were introduced in a grave glade 25
They've paid the last respects in sad tobacco 195
This is the Month, and this the happy morn 254
Three years after my father's death 282
To Meath of the pastures 23
Trois allumettes une à une allumées dans la nuit 9
Truly my Satan thou art but a Dunce 192
Turning and turning in the widening gyre 174
'Twas brillig, and the slithy toves 180
Two roads diverged in a yellow wood 78
Underwater eyes, an eel's 138
We caught the tread of dancing feet 91
We have no praries 50
What you have heard is true. I was in his house. 199
What do they think has happened, the old fools 137
What is Love? I asked a lover — 302
What shall I do with the body that has been given me 233
What she remembers 28

When all the others were away at Mass   103
When I landed in the republic of conscience   175
When I went out to kill myself, I caught   222
When night stirred at sea   38
When Peter Wanderwide was young   120
When you are old and grey and full of sleep   219
When you plunged   14
When you start on your journey to Ithaca   284
When, in disgrace with fortune and men's eyes   153
Wheneas in silks my Julia goes   3
Whenever I think of Francis   248
Where dips the rocky highland   40
Whose woods these are I think I know   88
Why have such scores of lovely, gifted girls   238
With half a century to pile   252
Yes. I remember Adlestrop   141
Yesterday I knew no lullaby   19
Yesterday I saw the Earth beautiful   165
You are going to ask: and where are the lilacs   110
You came home from school   105

Acknowledgements

A note from the editor and compilers

The *Lifelines* project was seven years in the making and we are very grateful to the following who helped bring it to completion: Christopher Adam, Philip Armitage, Kate Bateman, Kenneth Blackmore, Sarah Boles, Susan Brennan, Gillian Brownell, Eda Byrne, Caleb Clarke, Helen Clayton, Mary Clayton, Emma Coburn, Paul Coffey, Desmond Corbett, Frank Cinnamond, Susan Ellis, Craig Fox, Ewan Gibson, John Gillespie, Trevor Gillis, Richard Goodbody, Nicholas Graham, Gillian Hayden, Josephine Hughes, Peter Jennings, Carol Johnson, Mavis Johnson, Karen Henderson, Susan Henderson, Marybeth Joyce, Stanford Kingston, Stephen Kirk, Angela Logue, David Logue, Helen Lovell, Mervyn McCullagh, Ingrid McKenna, Rachel Macmanus, John MacMonagle, Sean MacMonagle, Craig McMurrough, Hazel Marshall, Linda Miller, Elizabeth O'Donnell, Michael O'Donnell, Cliona O'Dwyer, Christopher Pillow, Rachel Pope, Jeanne Prendergast, Rosemary Roe, Elizabeth Sibley, Thelma Smyth, Leigh Standing, Julie Sutton, Clare Thorp, Christopher Van Der Lee, Emma Walls and David Warren.

And a very special word of thanks to Treasa Coady, Elaine Campion and Bernie Daly of Town House and Country House.

For permission to reprint copyright material, the editor and publishers are grateful to the following:

Carcanet Press Ltd for 'Crazy Weather' from *Selected Poems* by John Ashbery; Faber and Faber Ltd for 'A Summer Night', 'Petition' and 'The More Loving One' from *W H Auden: Collected Poems* edited by Edward Mendelson; Leland Bardwell for 'Without Touching'; Faber and Faber Ltd for 'Summer Song, I' from *Collected Poems* by George Barker; The Beckett Estate and The Calder Educational Trust, London, for 'Gnome' and 'my way is in the sand flowing' from *Collected Poems 1930–1978* by Samuel Beckett, copyright © Samuel Beckett 1934, 1948, 1986; Peters Fraser & Dunlop Group Ltd for 'Tarantella' and 'The Death and Last Confession of Wandering Peter' by Hilaire Belloc; John Murray (Publishers) Ltd, London, for 'A Subaltern's Love-Song' and 'Business Girls' by John Betjeman; Farrar, Straus & Giroux, Inc. for 'The Moose' from *The Complete Poems 1927–1979* by Elizabeth Bishop, © 1979, 1983 by Alice Helen Methfessel; Carcanet Press Ltd for 'Child of Our Time' and 'The Journey' from *Selected Poems* by Eavan Boland; Methuen, London, for 'Coal for Mike' from *Poems 1913–1956 by Bertolt Brecht*, translated by Edith Anderson; Black Sparrow Press, California, for 'Rock', © 1981 by Charles Bukowski, reprinted from *Dangling in the Tournefortia*; Harper Collins Publishers for 'Happiness' and 'Through the Boughs' by Raymond Carver; John Johnson Ltd for M Hamburger's translation of 'Psalm' by Paul Celan; R Dardis Clarke, 21 Pleasants Street, Dublin 8 for 'The Envy of Poor Lovers' and 'The Planter's Daughter' by Austin Clarke; The Estate of Padraic Colum for 'A Drover'; Evelyn Conlon for 'Hens'; EMI Songs Ltd/Dinsong Ltd, London WC2H OEA, for 'valley of the lost women' by John Cooper Clarke, © 1978; Liveright Publishing Corporation for 'Voyages II', reprinted from *The Collected Poems and Selected Letters and Prose of Hart Crane*, copyright © 1933, 1958, 1966 by Liveright Publishing Corporation; MacGibbon & Kee, an imprint of HarperCollins Publishers Ltd for 'maggie and milly and molly and may' from *The Collected Poems 1913–1962* by e e cummings; Colin Smythe Ltd, Bucks, for 'Confiteor' by Cyril Cusack; Raven Arts Press for 'An Scáthán' by Michael Davitt; The Literary Trustees of Walter de la Mare and The Society of Authors as their representative for 'The Listeners'; The University of Pittsburgh Press for 'Before Making Love' from *Captivity* by Toi Derricotte, © 1989 by Toi Derricotte; The Blackstaff Press, Belfast, for 'Martha's Wall' and 'The Man with Five Penises' from *The Berlin Wall Café* by Paul Durcan; Faber and Faber Ltd for 'The Love Song of J Alfred Prufrock' and for excerpt from 'Ash Wednesday' from *Collected Poems 1909–1962* by T S Eliot; Watson, Little Ltd for 'Biography' by D J Enright from *Paradise Illustrated*; Macmillan Ltd for Gordon McVay's translation of 'My Teper' Ukhodom Ponemnogu' by Sergei Essenin from *Isadora and Esenin* (1980); The Estate of Padraic Fallon for 'The Book of Job'; The